UNDERSTANDING
DEVELOPMENT

second edition

UNDERSTANDING DEVELOPMENT

Theory and Practice in the Third World

John Rapley

LYNNE
RIENNER
PUBLISHERS

BOULDER
LONDON

Published in the United States of America in 2002 by
Lynne Rienner Publishers, Inc.
1800 30th Street, Boulder, Colorado 80301
www.rienner.com

and in the United Kingdom by
Lynne Rienner Publishers, Inc.
3 Henrietta Street, Covent Garden, London WC2E 8LU

Library of Congress Cataloging-in-Publication Data
Rapley, John, 1963–
   Understanding development : theory and practice in the Third World /
John Rapley.—2nd ed.
      p.   cm.
   Includes bibliographical references and index.
   ISBN 1-58826-099-2 (pbk. : alk. paper)
   1. Developing countries—Economic policy. 2. Structural adjustment
(Economic policy)—Developing countries. 3. Economic development.
I. Title.
HC59.7 .R272 2002
338.9'009172'6—dc21   2002017812

British Cataloguing in Publication Data
A Cataloguing in Publication record for this book
is available from the British Library.

Printed and bound in the United States of America

   The paper used in this publication meets the requirements
∞   of the American National Standard for Permanence of
   Paper for Printed Library Materials Z39.48-1984.

   5 4 3 2

CONTENTS

ACKNOWLEDGMENTS

MANY PEOPLE HAVE HAD A HAND IN THE CREATION OF THIS BOOK, FROM THE genesis of its first edition when I was a postdoctoral fellow at Queen Elizabeth House, Oxford University, to the completion of this new edition, now that I am a senior lecturer in the Department of Government at the University of the West Indies, Mona. Generous support from the Social Sciences and Humanities Research Council of Canada made it possible for me to devote two years of my life to research, during which time I began the first edition. For the second edition, I benefited from the generosity of Georgetown University's Woodstock Center, which offered me a visiting fellowship for what became one of the most fruitful and stimulating years of my life. I owe much to my hosts in Washington, D.C., Joanne and Terence Cooney, whose generosity and wisdom played no small part in the completion of this volume. Equally, I am grateful to the Institut d'Etudes Politiques in Aix-en-Provence, France, which provides me with a "spring home" at which to do much of my writing. Yet, the completion of both editions would have been difficult were it not for the support I received here at the university from the Mona Campus Research and Publications Fund.

Frances Stewart, Barbara Harriss-White, Jacques Barbier, Mark Figueroa, Ashu Handa, Roger Tangri, Colin Leys, Gavin Williams, and Bob Rapley all assisted me with their useful insights and comments along the way, as did three anonymous reviewers at Lynne Rienner Publishers. Suggestions for the second edition also came from Marsha Pripstein-Posusney and Judith Hellman. The librarians at Queen Elizabeth House have been a constant source of support. Tom Forrest helped me with his characteristically deep insights, offered to me over our breakfasts at the St. Giles Cafe. Lynne Rienner Publishers, as usual, has proved to be a steadfast supporter, and I have in particular to thank Lynne Rienner, Lesli Athanasoulis, and Scott Vickers. Of course, at the end of the day, none of these people bear responsibility for the contents of this book.

As always, I thank my wife and parents. In the end, none of this would have been possible were it not for their inexhaustible support.

—J. R.

INTRODUCTION

THE LEFT IS DEAD; LONG LIVE THE LEFT.

In some respects, this phrase, which opened the first edition of this book, still captures the present state of the development debate. The terms "left" and "right" distinguish competing sides of the debate in terms of their attitude to the state's role in the development process. In the twentieth century, the left—which included not only socialists and communists but also modern liberals—generally, if not always, favored using the state as an agent of social transformation. The state, it was held, could both develop economies and alter societies in such a way as to make them suit human needs. Underlying this was a belief that the state could embody collective will more effectively than the market, which favored privileged interests. Although the old right, from conservatives through to fascists, also favored strong states and held an equal suspicion of the market, as a political force it declined throughout the post–World War II period. In its place emerged a new right based on resurgent classical liberalism that regarded the state as a potential tyrant and venerated the freedom and productive potential of the market.

In the early postwar period, development thought, like conventional economic wisdom, was really neither left nor right. There existed a broad consensus that economies needed more state intervention than they had been given in the past (in fact, in Latin America it was right-wing authoritarian regimes that began employing statist development strategies). Meanwhile, the horrors of the Depression and postwar political developments had given Keynesian economics pride of place in both academic and policy circles in the first world. This influenced third-world academics, whose confidence in the state was further reinforced by the emergence of structuralist economics. Aware of the imperfections in the market and global capitalism, and confident that the state could overcome them, development theorists proposed models that assigned the state a leading role in the economy. Pretty soon, the left came to espouse these models. Many third-world governments, some of which had just won their independence, eagerly adopted the models, for they seemed to promise a rapid journey into the industrial age.

At first, the models seemed to deliver just that. With the postwar world economy booming, demand for third-world products rose. This provided third-world governments with the capital they needed to develop their industry and infrastructure. However, as time went by, problems in these strategies came to light. It became increasingly clear that many third-world economies were growing more slowly than required to continue improving the standards of living of the world's poorest citizens. The industrial development that took place consumed more resources than it generated, a waste exacerbated by inefficient states. When the postwar boom came to an end in the 1970s, the shortcomings of state-led development became plain.

It was around this time that the right began to resurface. Dissident voices belonging to an old-school, neoclassical theory, had for decades been firing occasional volleys from the sidelines of development studies. They claimed that the main problem in the third world was the state itself, and that rapid development could only come about if the state was rolled back. At the same time, as earlier development models became compromised, new left-wing schools of thought emerged to claim that the market itself was the problem, and that if anything was needed, it was a greater role for the state. The development debate polarized. By the late 1970s the left had become politically weak, its theorists engaged either in internecine squabbles or in strident defenses of orthodoxy. The time was ripe for neoclassical theory to start a revolution. First-world electorates and governments, anxious for solutions to the worsening economic situation in their countries, looked to the new ideas and turned to the new right. This initiated a long attack on the state and the other institutions, such as unions, that were seen to be hindering the operation of the market. First-world donor agencies began pressuring third-world governments to make similar changes in their policies. Many third-world governments acceded reluctantly, because the debt crisis had weakened their bargaining power with their creditors. Others rolled back the state more eagerly because local constituencies had already started pushing for reform.

Less state, more market: this was the essential thrust of the strategy known as structural adjustment, which was soon applied in much of the third world. The idea seemed sound, but as time would tell, structural adjustment contained its own problems. Its shortcomings, which grew more evident with the passage of time, shed a new and damaging light on neoclassical theory. Structural adjustment yielded some positive gains in the more advanced third-world countries. However, in the poorer countries, those most in need of rapid change, it was less effective and may even have done more harm than good. While out of power, neoclassical writers, like any opposition, could proclaim their theory's perfect virtue and point to the imperfections of the governing party. Once in power, though, neoclassical theorists had to defend policies that were not working in quite the way the public had been led to expect. Meanwhile, its journey through the political wilderness had liberated the left. No longer required to defend sacred truths and orthodoxies, it was free to begin a new debate. Whereas neoclassical theory remains dominant in practice, in the academic realm the pendulum has begun to swing back toward the left—though perhaps not as far as it went in the postwar period, and not even toward the same corner. For if the old left is dead, a new left has arisen to take its place.

And yet in many parts of the third world the pendulum may swing neither to the left nor the right; it may not be swinging at all. As we begin the twenty-first century, the troubling questions are not those posed by the left or the right, but those raised by the experiences of people in much, perhaps most, of the third world who have benefited little from the development debate, and who are unlikely to do so soon. One thing seems clear in much of the third world today: what works on paper may not work in practice. Neither neoclassical theory nor the new statist models may offer much to the world's poorest countries. We are left to wonder if an entirely new development debate is about to begin.

In this book, I chart the rise of statist development theory in the early postwar period (Chapter 1) and its failures in practice (Chapter 2). Chapter 3 looks at the neoclassical prescription for remedying the third world's underdevelopment; Chapter 4 considers the uneven results the neoclassical recipe produced. Chapter 5 examines the contemporary development debate, focusing on the rise of the new statist development model—the developmental state—that has won so much admiration among the left. Chapter 6 discusses the feasibility of this new statism, which appears in doubt. This leads us to consider a new development debate (Chapter 7) and the elements that current research tells us will have to be brought into future development theories.

If the theme of this second edition departs in any way from that of the first, it is in recognizing that the cries heard in the world's streets, whether in third-world austerity protests or demonstrations at first-world financial gatherings, have now entered the academic and policy debates. If these voices have not yet coalesced around what they seek, they are more certain about what they reject. And the urgency they bring is invigorating the development debate, possibly helping to point a way forward.

I

Development Theory in the Postwar Period

EARLY IN THE SUMMER OF 1944, ALLIED TROOP COLUMNS ROLLED EASTWARD through France. Berlin lay on the horizon. World War II had entered its final phase and Allied victory was just a matter of time.

Having begun to ponder the possible shape of the postwar world, the Allied leaders held a conference to discuss the structure they would give to the world economy. This meeting took place at a hotel in Bretton Woods, New Hampshire. It began within a month of D-Day and lasted three weeks. The absence of the USSR signaled the imminent split of the world economy into two blocs, the Western capitalist one, and the Eastern state-socialist one. The Bretton Woods conference would provide the blueprint for the postwar capitalist economy.

The intellectual shadow of the leading economic thinker of the age, John Maynard Keynes, loomed large over the conference, and Keynes made important contributions to its proceedings. Chief among the concerns of the participants was the desire to create a favorable international trading environment. They wanted to put behind them the conditions that had worsened the Depression. Monetary instability and lack of credit had inhibited trade among nations and led governments to adopt protectionist policies when they could not pay for their imports. To this end the Bretton Woods conference gave rise to the International Monetary Fund (IMF) and the International Bank for Reconstruction and Development, which became known as the World Bank. In 1947 the Bretton Woods system, as it came to be known, was rounded out by the General Agreement on Tariffs and Trade (GATT). All were designed to create as stable and freely flowing an international trading environment as possible.

GATT was a treaty organization that aimed over time to reduce tariffs, or taxes on imports, thereby lowering the barriers to trade among member states. The IMF was set up to provide short-term loans to governments facing balance-of-payments difficulties, the problem a government encounters when more money leaves its economy through imports, capital flows, and spending abroad than enters it. In the past, governments had dealt with this problem by taking measures to reduce their imports, but this brought retaliation from the countries whose exports they were blocking. The IMF was to lend governments the money they needed to cover their balance-of-payments deficits, so that governments would no longer resort to the sort of tactics that set off protectionist spirals, reducing trade. Member governments would pay into the IMF and then draw on its deposits when necessary. The IMF later extended credit beyond its members' resources. However, in cases in which governments repeatedly ran balance-of-payments deficits, the IMF was allowed to demand, as the price for further loans, government reforms to rectify structural problems in the economy—in effect, the IMF was to be the world economy's conservative and parsimonious banker, slapping the wrists of governments that had been careless with their checkbooks. The World Bank was created to invest money in the reconstruction of war-ravaged Europe. When it had completed this task, it turned its attention to the development of the third world.

Finally, to ensure that goods flowed freely across borders, the world needed a universal medium of exchange, a currency all participants in the economy would accept. Because the World Bank did not have the power to issue currency, the U.S. dollar filled the role by default. By U.S. law, every thirty-five dollars any individual or government accumulated could be exchanged for one ounce of gold, from U.S. gold reserves held at Fort Knox. In effect, this made the dollar as good as gold, and virtually all governments, including those in the Soviet bloc, were willing to accept U.S. dollars for payment.

The Bretton Woods conference failed to take Keynes's advice to create an international trade organization, which would have enjoyed more power than did GATT to enforce the compliance of member states, and would also have been able to stabilize commodity prices. No institution could discipline any government into improving its trade practices. As a treaty organization, GATT could only rule when member governments were entitled to retaliate against other governments; it could not end protectionism, though it could discourage it and give it some order. Importantly, GATT did not deal with nontariff barriers such as quotas. As tariff barriers fell, governments began using nontariff barriers to block trade, which undermined GATT. Keynes had also recommended that the IMF be able to pressure balance-of-payments surplus countries into opening up to trade. Instead, the IMF could only pressure those countries to which it made loans, namely, deficit countries. Pressure on surplus countries would have benefited the world economy by expanding trade, whereas pressure on deficit countries to curtail their spending slows the world economy.[1]

I The Impact of Keynes in the First World

The Bretton Woods conference was concerned primarily with establishing a favorable international environment for economic growth, but Keynes's influence was evident in another way: his thinking had come to exercise a profound impact on a generation of political leaders. Keynes's recipe for economic development was accepted not only for the international system but for domestic economies as well. His vision of a smoothly running capitalist economy involved a much greater role for the state than had been tolerated in classical and neoclassical models of development, which had been more concerned with the free market.

Classical political economy, whose key contributors included Thomas Malthus, David Ricardo, and J. B. Say, and whose most lasting expression is found in Adam Smith's *Wealth of Nations,* stressed the role of the free market and individual liberty in economic success. Individuals, unfettered by state interference, would use their ingenuity to the greatest extent. Division and specialization of labor would allow resources to be used in the most efficient and productive manner possible. If all individuals pursued their narrow self-interests, all of society would benefit inadvertently. State interventions to relieve poverty would inhibit initiative, and would stifle investment because they would rely on increased taxes. Therefore, the prescribed role for the state in the economy was a minimal one. Smith identified only three functions for the state to perform: defense of national sovereignty, the protection of citizens' rights against violation by one another, and the provision of public or collective goods. Public or collective goods are those that society needs but the market will not normally provide because the gains are so widely dispersed. An example is traffic signals: almost everyone depends on them, but no individual will bear their cost. The state fills the gap by exacting a small payment from everyone in order to cover the cost of installing traffic signals wherever they are deemed necessary.

The other important feature of classical political economy was its conception of citizens' rights, which it was the state's task to defend. Classical political economy, along with classical and neoclassical liberalism, conceived of individual rights in negative terms. Citizens enjoyed certain liberties from coercion, such as freedom to practice religion, trade, and economic enterprise, and these could not be violated by either the state or other individuals. Citizens did not, however, possess positive rights, that is, rights *to* something, whether it be employment, housing, education, or the like. This conception of rights emerged only with the development of modern liberalism, and has always been rejected by neoclassical thinkers. To the latter, freedom has always meant simply freedom from physical restrictions imposed by another person or by the state. The price of this negative freedom is inequality: because people have different aptitudes, endowments, and inheritances, some will prosper and others will not. Neoclassical thinkers, along with their classical forebears, have always insisted that it is not the state's task to redistribute resources to equalize society. They contend that, in fact, the least well-off in society benefit more from this inequality—because it speeds up economic progress, which in turn benefits them—than they do from an egalitarian society that inhibits economic progress.

At any rate, classical political economy saw the capitalist system as a complex and delicate mechanism that could easily break down once the state started meddling with it. Left to itself, the free market was seen to be self-regulating: even when it appeared to have broken down, it was still functioning and would repair itself naturally. Hence the term "laissez-faire capitalism," which means precisely a capitalism that is left alone. For example, in an economic depression there is a slowdown of economic activity and widespread unemployment. The economy appears to have stopped functioning. But classical political economy, and the neoclassical economics this tradition spawned in the late nineteenth century, sees a silver lining to the gray cloud. With so many people unemployed, there are more people competing for fewer jobs; they must offer to work for less than their competitors. Thus, labor prices drop, and employers respond by hiring more workers. More workers with more money to spend translates into increased demand for goods and services, which in turn causes producers to expand their activity, which compels them to hire more workers, and so forth.

Keynes had no problem with the market economy. He liked the machine, but judged it to be in need of improvement if it was to operate well. In particular, Keynes took issue with the conventional economic assumption that during a downturn, labor prices drop, causing employers to hire more workers and thereby mop up unemployment. The Depression led Keynes to believe that high unemployment could persist indefinitely. He advocated the use of fiscal policy—government spending—to deal with recession. This was an instrument that virtually all governments were then loath to use. (Even Roosevelt's New Deal eschewed deficit spending, which Keynes favored.) By building roads and dams, for example, a government could create jobs, which in turn would create more demand for goods and services, which would cause factories to increase their output and then to take on more workers, and so on in an upward spiral. Once good times returned, the government could prevent the economy from overheating by taking money back out of it. In short, Keynes's prescription for improving the capitalist economy was for governments to save in good times, spend in bad.

Keynes was not the first to advise governments to spend their way out of recessions. However, his innovation was to call on governments to *borrow,* if necessary, to pump money into the economy.[2] The loans would be repaid later from the earnings generated by a newly robust economy. Neoclassical theorists worried that such public spending would worsen inflation, as more money would chase fewer goods. But Keynes argued that this expansionary fiscal shock would not cause inflation because increased investment would occur along with increased demand. It all heralded the advent of managed capitalism; this revolution in economic policymaking overthrew the doctrine of laissez-faire capitalism that the Depression had discredited.

In the late 1940s, governments in Western Europe and North America started taking Keynes's advice. By then, the USSR had begun to consolidate its hold on Eastern Europe by establishing puppet regimes in the six countries it had liberated from Nazi rule (East Germany, Poland, Romania, Bulgaria, Hungary, and Czechoslovakia). This solidified the iron curtain that Winston Churchill said had fallen across Europe, dividing it in two. It was becoming obvious that the new Soviet bloc was not going to join the economic order prescribed at Bretton Woods. The dust was slowly settling in Western Europe, though, even if the future looked uncertain immediately after the war, especially with communist parties threatening to take power in Italy, France, and Greece. Capitalism only firmly reestablished its hold on Western Europe when the United States instituted the Marshall Plan, whereby it injected billions of dollars into the reconstruction of Western Europe's ravaged infrastructure. At the same time, liberal democratic parties committed to a more equitable social order came to power in Western Europe.

What emerged in the politics of Western Europe, and indeed in virtually all the developed capitalist countries, has come to be known as the postwar Keynesian consensus. Not only did this innovation safeguard capitalism, it also won the support of the Western world's working classes. Western governments made full employment a top priority, along with improved social benefits such as public education, housing, and health care. Postwar capitalism was to be both redistributive and managed. Western governments, through nationalization of declining or important private companies, regulation of the economy, public spending, and other means, involved themselves far more deeply in the management of their economies than ever before. In its new version, capitalism was to be not only more efficient, but indeed more humane. It was a recipe for social peace like none seen before: investors would grow richer—Keynes himself had grown rich on the stock market—but so too would workers, and poverty would become a thing of the past. Scholars proclaimed that correct economic management would prevent there ever being another Depression, and that the high growth rates that followed in the 1950s were a permanent feature.[3] All of this was possible because the ingredient missing from earlier capitalism—an appropriate interventionist role by the state—was now in place.

1   The Emergence of the Third World

This was the political and intellectual climate into which the third world was born at the end of World War II. The industrial world had polarized between capitalism and Soviet communism, while a new form of statist liberalism had taken hold in the capitalist West.

The term "third world" originally denoted those countries that were neither advanced capitalist (the first world) nor communist (the second world). In practice, "third world" came to refer to all developing countries, including those that called themselves communist.

A number of features characterize third-world countries. First, by comparison with the advanced capitalist economies of Western Europe and North America, their per capita incomes are low. This poverty translates into shorter life expectancies, higher rates of infant mortality, and lower levels of educational attainment. Typically, a high proportion of the population is engaged in agriculture. The secondary, or manufacturing, sector occupies a relatively less important place in the economy than it does in the first world, and exports come mainly from the primary sector (the cultivation or extraction of natural resources, as in farming or mining). Such a characterization, of course, fails to capture the great variety within the world. Some rich countries, such as Canada, are relatively underindustrialized, relying on primary exports for their wealth. Some poor countries have made remarkable strides in improving health and education. Yet as a rule, there is a correlation between national income and a country's ability to improve the social indicators of its citizenry. With the exception of the few countries endowed by nature with an abundance of natural resources, there is also a correlation between industrialization and growing national income. There are factors other than economic that are common to third-world countries, including a tendency to high population-growth rates. However, perhaps the most important common thread is the political one: virtually every third-world country began its modern history as a colony of one of the former imperial powers of Europe or Asia (Britain, France, Belgium, Germany, Spain, Portugal, the Netherlands, and the Ottoman Empire).[4]

Most of Latin America threw off Spanish or Portuguese rule in the early nineteenth century. However, it was not until the twentieth century that the bulk of the third world in Asia, Africa, and the Caribbean would win its independence. As the Ottoman Empire crumbled in the late nineteenth and early twentieth centuries, giving way at its core to modern Turkey, some subject peoples constituted themselves as states, although the Arab territories in the Middle East were rapidly recolonized by Britain and France. The bold venture of Mustafa Kemal, who took on the name Atatürk (father of Turkey) in leading the creation of the independent republic of Turkey, inspired nationalist thinkers in the colonies of Africa and Asia.

The two world wars further altered the relationship between colonizer and colonized. Japanese conquests of European colonies early in World War II punctured any myths about white superiority, while soldiers recruited in the colonies to assist the Allied war effort felt they had earned their peoples the status of equals. Drained of military and police resources by the war, colonial regimes found it difficult to maintain or reimpose control over peoples who had grown tired of colonial rule. A number of colonies effectively obtained their independence during World War II when they were vacated by the Axis powers (Italy or Japan; Germany, the third Axis power, had already lost its overseas colonies in World War I). Occasionally, as in Indochina and Indonesia, former colonial masters tried to reverse this situation, but failed.

When in 1947 the British government granted the Indian subcontinent its independence, giving birth to modern India and Pakistan, the floodgates opened. Independence followed in short order for most of the other colonial territories of South and Southeast Asia. Africa came next. North of the Sahara, bloody struggles brought independence to Morocco and Tunisia; south of the Sahara, Ghana ushered in the postcolonial era peacefully in 1957. The Portuguese held out for two more decades, and it was not until 1990 that South Africa gave up its hold on Namibia. But apart from these holdouts, and a few small colonies scattered around the globe, the curtain had been drawn on colonial rule within twenty years of India's declaration of independence.[5]

Thus, very much of the world had, in the early postwar period, shaken off the bonds of colonialism. Most of this new world was poor. The rulers of the newly independent countries therefore had two overriding priorities: development and independence.

In practice, the two were often seen to go together. The generation that had led the third world to independence usually equated development with industrialization. Although some nationalist leaders glorified rural utopias, as did India's Mahatma Gandhi, many more took the opposite view. Most of Africa and Asia was rural and poor, and blame for this state of affairs was placed squarely on imperialism. Third-world nationalists argued that by using the colonies as sources of raw materials and markets for finished goods, and by establishing intra-imperial free-trade blocs that prevented colonial administrations from using protective barriers to nurture industrial development, the imperial countries had actually impoverished the third world in order to enrich the first. Where shoots of industrialization had begun to sprout, as in precolonial India, the imperialists rolled it back by swamping the colonial markets with the cheap manufactures of their factories. Thus, claimed third-world nationalists, the first world's entry into the industrial age had been made possible by its appropriation of the third world's resources; independence would be illusory if the colonial economic structure was not overthrown along with the colonial masters. Looking to the first world, third-world leaders saw that industry was the key to modernity and wealth. The ability to produce finished goods, and not rely on the imports of their old masters, would signify the complete rupture of the ties that had bound third-world economies for so long.

Latin America seemed to point the way forward. Even though Latin American countries had become independent in the nineteenth century, the structure of the continent's economies remained largely colonial for much of the century despite bursts of prosperity. South American agriculture had by and large become dominated by big, typically inefficient plantations, and virtual serfdom continued in several countries. The colonial pattern of exporting primary goods in return for finished products deepened throughout the nineteenth century. British merchant houses took the place of those of the Spanish and Portuguese. What emerged to replace colonialism was an agrarian economy closely tied to Europe, and a political order dominated by authoritarian *caudillos,* or strongmen, who ruled in alliance with the agrarian elites.

The ground slowly started to shift as, late in the century, small numbers of private industrialists began to appear, often calling upon governments to change policy direction and nurture their development.[6] They made little political impact over the following four decades, but their importance emerged. When change came, and governments enacted ambitious industrial-development policies, there were capitalists at hand ready and eager to take advantage of these new policies.

And change came. During the 1930s Depression, the fall in first-world demand caused world prices on Latin America's exports to collapse. This was followed by the wartime loss of European markets and supplies. Revenue from exports of primary goods plummeted. The resulting lack of foreign exchange restricted opportunities for importing manufactured goods. If local demand was to be satisfied, it would have to be done internally. Latin America found itself confronted with the necessity of industrialization.

The Depression and wartime experiences prompted a sort of "trade pessimism" among Latin America's economic analysts. The world market suddenly appeared volatile, certainly not the type of horse to which one would want to hitch the cart of a national economy. Greater independence from the first world seemed now a distinct virtue. To secure this goal, Latin American governments decided to build up their industrial bases and trade more among themselves. By creating large state firms and encouraging private firms to produce substitutes for goods previously imported, governments sought to shelter themselves from the vicissitudes of the global economy. This strategy came to be known as import substitution.

Latin America's first wave of import substitution, during the Depression, had been a reaction to the sudden changes in the world economy. The second wave sought to anticipate further shocks, and began in 1939 when Chile created the Corporación de Fomento de la Producción to foster industrial development. By this time, Mexico had nationalized its foreign-owned railways and oil companies. Such actions provided the blueprint for an industrial strategy that would be applied throughout Latin America after World War II.

I Development Theory After Keynes

During the 1940s, Keynesianism began finding its way into the work of development theorists. Economists in the third world read the *General Theory* with great interest. Many obtained their training in first-world universities, where Keynesianism had become prominent by the late 1940s. Meanwhile, the apparent successes of Soviet central planning in the 1930s, when Soviet industry had surged ahead at a time when Western capitalism seemed in decay, as well as the prestige the Soviet system earned with its victorious effort in World War II, led many Western academics to develop an interest in statism. Under such influences, new currents of thought emerged from third-world academies that lent further support to the principle of an expanded state role in the economy.

Shortly after the war, two economists, Raul Prebisch and Hans Singer, published separately the results of their studies of first world–third world trade. Though working independently of one another, they reached similar conclusions. Their recommendations, which would dominate development thinking for years to come, became known as the Prebisch-Singer thesis. In a nutshell, the thesis was that over time, third-world countries would have to export more of their primary commodities just to maintain their levels of imports from the first world. If they wanted to increase their imports, they would have to increase their exports even more. They called this syndrome the declining terms of trade.[7]

As an economy industrializes, capital tends to concentrate. Small firms either expand or fall by the wayside. With fewer firms competing for customers, possibilities for either open or implied collusion emerge. Firms feel less competitive pressure to lower prices, and profit margins rise. Traditional producers of primary products, on the other hand, usually operate in very competitive markets, and must keep their prices and profit margins low.

Put simply, Prebisch and Singer argued that prices in more technically advanced economies rose more quickly than those in more backward ones. Differences in income elasticities of demand strengthened this effect. Demand for finished goods rises with income: as people get richer they buy more televisions, stereos, and childrens' toys. Demand for primary goods varies less with income: no matter how rich they get, people will buy only so much coffee. Ragnar Nurkse added to this by arguing that the search for substitutes among industrial producers could actually reduce demand for third-world primary exports.[8] He used the example of chicle, an ingredient in chewing gum that was imported from Latin America. The discovery of a synthetic substitute meant that chewing gum producers would need less chicle. In the long run the prices of first-world goods were expected to rise relative to those for third-world goods. First-world populations would grow wealthy, with unions securing a share of the growing pie for their members. The third-world countries, while possibly still moving forward, would nevertheless fall further behind the front-runners.

The implications were obvious. If things continued the way they had been going, third-world countries would sink deeper into poverty. To import even a fixed amount of finished goods, they would need to export more and more primary goods. They would end up running to stand still. The requirements of increased primary production would in turn gobble up a growing share of the nation's resources, reducing what was left for development. There was only one way to break free of this syndrome: alter the structure of the economy's production. Third-world economies had to rely more on industry for their wealth, and less on the primary sector.

However, many economists believed that this would never happen if things were left to the free market. For instance, P. N. Rosenstein-Rodan said a "big push" in infrastructure investment and planning was needed to stimulate industrialization, but that the resources for this lay beyond the reach of the private sector.[9] Nurkse also believed that markets in the third world were too small to attract private investment. He proposed a balanced pattern of public investment in several different industries as a way to kickstart an economy by creating the demand that would draw in private investors.[10]

Because these economists spoke of the structural obstacles blocking the third world's path to development, they became known as the structuralists. Structuralism, which came to dominate development economics for the next couple of decades, found its intellectual center in Chile. Raul Prebisch went to Chile in 1950 to direct the UN's newly created Economic Commission for Latin America (ECLA). He then recruited Celso Furtado, Aníbal Pinto, Osvaldo Sunkel, and Dudley Seers, all of whom went on to publish important contributions to structuralist theory. The structuralists judged that the only way third-world countries could remove the obstacles from their path was through concerted state action. States had to push industrialization along, and third-world countries had to reduce their dependence on trade with the first world and increase trade among themselves. Support for structuralist theory came from outside its camp when in 1954 W. A. Lewis published a paper on labor and development.[11] Lewis argued that in a third-world economy, the wage rate was set at a constant level as determined by minimum levels of existence in traditional family farming.

This ensured a virtually unlimited supply of cheap labor, which was an advantageous factor in industrial development. With state support, this cheap labor supply could be harnessed to build up a nation's industry.

In the course of the 1950s Latin American governments began to implement the advice of ECLA. The belief that industrialization would remedy underdevelopment spread throughout not only Latin America but most of the third world.[12] This optimism was mirrored in the emergence of the American modernization school, which looked forward to the third world's entry into the modern, and Western, world.

| Modernization Theory

Modernization theory sprang from what has been called the behavioral revolution, a shift in U.S. social scientific thought that began in the late 1940s and continued through the 1960s. Before World War II, for example, U.S. political scientists had devoted themselves to the study of constitutions and institutions. However, the rise of totalitarianism in Hitler's Germany and Stalin's USSR battered their faith in constitutions (both countries having started out with model constitutions). Whereas political philosophy had always concerned itself with questions of human behavior and how best to organize society, the behavioralists inaugurated a revolution by trying to replace philosophy with science. They were interested not in society as it should be, but simply as it was. They set out to observe, compare, and classify human behavior in the hope of making general inferences about it.

Modernization theory sought to identify the conditions that had given rise to development in the first world, and specify where and why these were lacking in the third world. Modernization theorists, depending on their focus, reached varying conclusions. To some, the problem of the third world was a mere shortage of capital; development required a rise in the savings rate.[13] To others, it was a question of value systems: third-world peoples lacked the cultural values, such as the profit motive, that would make them entrepreneurial. In this case development required Westernizing elites, or some kind of education in capitalist values.[14] Yet whether from a sociological, political, or economic standpoint, modernization theorists generally concurred on one important point: underdevelopment was an initial state. The West had progressed beyond it, but other countries lagged behind. However, the West could help speed up the process of development in the third world, for instance by sharing its capital and know-how, to bring these countries into the modern age of capitalism and liberal democracy.[15]

Reflecting the optimism and idealism of their time, behavioralism in general and modernization theory in particular eventually ran into problems. Chief among these was that the scientific method they tried to apply to the study of human behavior and society was not of the highest quality, being closer to nineteenth-century positivism than to contemporary scientific theory. Whereas philosophers of science were then writing about the extent to which opinions, biases, and judgments influenced scientific research, the behavioralists, in their quest for value-free science, were not always sufficiently sensitive to the biases they carried. Modernization theory was a prime example. It reflected not only the age's optimism and idealism, but also its anticommunism. W. W. Rostow called his book *The Stages of Economic Growth* a noncommunist manifesto. Because they assumed that all societies progressed in linear fashion along the same path toward development, from which fascism and communism were aberrations, modernization theorists could not easily accept that the third world might differ fundamentally from the first.

Modernization theory resembled structuralism in its emphasis on physical-capital formation, but differed somewhat in its more benign view of first-world capitalism and imperialism and the role they played in third-world development. Modernization theorists looked to Westernizing elites, trained in the secular, bureaucratic, and entrepreneurial values of the first world, to lead their countries into the modern age. At first the differences between structuralism and modernization theory were not so great—after all, both Prebisch and Lewis favored foreign investment. But as time went by, a more radical second generation of structuralism emerged that reacted angrily against modernization theory. This was dependency theory.

Modernization theory grew out of a time in which many academics spoke about the end of ideology. The idea was that the postwar period had given rise to a grand consensus. It was supposed that everyone agreed that market economies, harnessed to an interventionist state, were the wave of the future, that left and right had met up and become one. By the 1960s, however, whatever consensus did exist had begun to fray in academic circles. The radical left had resurfaced, and argued that market economies created certain injustices that no amount of state tinkering could rectify. Whereas modernization theory espoused the market, radical theorists repudiated it. The left-right divide was back. In development studies, it was dependency theory that carried the torch.

Dependency Theory

Although it had roots in Indian nationalist thought from the turn of the century, dependency theory first came to light in *The Political Economy of Growth,* written by Paul Baran in the 1950s.[16] However, a decade would pass before dependency literature would begin to proliferate. Whereas modernization theorists saw the first world as guiding third-world development through aid, investment, and example, Baran argued that the first world actually hindered the emergence from poverty of the third world. The Westernizing elites in whom modernization theorists placed their faith would not lead their countries out of backwardness. Rather, argued Baran, they were fifth columnists who conspired to keep their homelands poor. Though it appeared illogical, this strategy was shrewd: it impoverished most of the population, but enriched the few who applied it.

Baran suggested that third-world bourgeoisies ruled in alliance with traditional landed elites, spending their profits on ostentation rather than on the investment that would accelerate growth. Imperialism had not exported capitalism to the third world; rather, it had drained the colonies of the resources that could have been used for investment, and had killed off local capitalism through competition. Imperialism had, in effect, cut short the natural process of capitalist development that Marx had identified. André Gunder Frank later sharpened Baran's analysis,[17] stressing that development and underdevelopment were, in effect, two sides of the same coin. By siphoning surplus away from the third world, the first world had enriched itself. By keeping the third world underdeveloped, the ruling bourgeoisies of the first world ensured a ready market for their finished goods and a cheap supply of raw materials for their factories.

Dependency theory took as axiomatic the view that the dominant class in any developed capitalist society was the bourgeoisie, or capitalist class, and thus that the foreign policies of first-world countries would be concerned primarily with the promotion and protection of capitalist interests. The capitalist states of the first world were able to thwart the development of the third world by striking alliances with the dominant classes of the third world, the dependent bourgeoisies. This latter class was essentially a rural oligarchy, though it often had interests in the modern sector in trade and services. It benefited from its dependence by earning its revenue on the export market and spending its profits on imported luxury goods. A national industrialization strategy would threaten the well-being of the members of the dependent bourgeoisie, because it would entail heavy taxes on their income to fuel savings, and protective barriers that would block their access to cherished luxury goods. Keeping its country backward thus preserved the wealth and privileged position of a third-world ruling class. At the same time that Frank was developing his theory, Samir Amin, working thousands of miles away, was reaching similar conclusions in his study of the economy of Côte d'Ivoire.[18] There he discovered a "planter bourgeoisie" that evinced little interest in development and was content to be a parasite living off the avails of foreign capital. Côte d'Ivoire was too small to contain Amin, who quickly generalized his theory into an explanation for the underdevelopment of West Africa[19] and eventually the entire third world.[20]

Early versions of dependency theory were inclined to claim that third-world countries would remain locked into "classical dependence," producing primary goods and importing finished goods. They did not foresee the change in the structure of production called for by the structuralists, namely industrial development. However, time belied this pessimism. Industrial development did take place in many third-world countries that had been labeled dependent. Some, such as Brazil and Argentina, developed sizable industrial bases.

Nevertheless, the later generation of dependency theorists maintained that this development would not free third-world countries from their dependence. They argued that industrialization in the third world, which in any event reached only a handful of countries, did not emerge from the development of these countries but from that of the first world. First-world companies seeking access to protected third-world markets, or to their cheap labor, would export capital-intensive assembly plants, but none of their research and development capacity. Thus, third-world industry would be based on second-generation production technology and would be owned by foreigners who processed imported inputs and created few jobs or linkages to other producers in the economy. Capitalism would not spread far beyond these firms, and the need for imported inputs would drive up the country's import bill. The drain of foreign-currency reserves would be worsened as foreign companies sent their profits back home. This would compel the host country to export more primary goods to earn foreign currency. The health of the economy would thus continue to rest on exports of primary goods to first-world countries, while the lack of job creation would leave most of a dependent country's population seeing few of the fruits of growth. In sum, whatever economic development took place would bring little social development, and would still be determined by the development of another economy.

Over time, many writers contributed to the dependency debate,[21] adding nuances and variations, but the broad thrust of all dependency theorists remained the same: as long as third-world economies were linked to the first world, they could never break free of their dependence and poverty. What they needed were autonomous national-development strategies. They had to sever their ties to the world economy and become more self-sufficient. Dependency theorists did not expect any third-world bourgeoisie to launch such a strategy. It was more likely that a dependent bourgeoisie would resist national development on the grounds that its well-being depended on foreign capital, whose firms it serviced or in which it owned minority shares. This assumption, as well as the belief that walls would have to be erected to insulate a national economy from the world economy, led dependency theorists to place their faith in the state as the motor for development. The state alone could crush the domination of the parasitic local bourgeoisie and stand up to the might of foreign capital, so as to engineer a development strategy that was in the national interest rather than in the interest of a single class.

In the end, dependency theory proved to be of less practical import than structuralism. Its recipe for development was applied briefly in Chile under Salvador Allende and in Jamaica under Michael Manley. Structuralism, on the other hand, influenced policymakers all over the third world. However, it is of great significance that dependency theory became popular on the left at the same time that neoclassical theory reappeared on the right. Chapter 3 will show that when changes in the world economy seemed to demand new approaches, neoclassical theorists would appear to offer them. The left, on the other hand, would end up calling for more statism.

1 Statism in the Third World

With statist theories such as Keynesianism and structuralism ascendant, the quarter century that followed World War II witnessed a degree of state intervention in economies all over the world on a scale hitherto unseen. In the first world, intervention took the form of generous welfare legislation, nationalization of private industries, and immense public programs. In the third world it took the form of legislation to nurture emerging industries and to create public ones where the private sector had failed to do so.

In addition to the weight of theoretical opinion there were practical factors that made statist development strategies appealing to third-world governments. Colonialism left behind immature capitalist classes. Where capitalists existed, their numbers were usually limited, and they most often confined their activities to trade and services, in no small part because colonial administrations had hindered their involvement in large-scale activities in the productive sector.[22] Even if a new regime favored its bourgeoisie—which many did not, having linked capitalism with imperialism—it could not rely solely on the private sector to rapidly push the economy into the industrial age. When countries sought to industrialize rapidly, but lacked bourgeoisies upon whom to devolve the task, the obvious agent for this transformation was the state. In Africa there was an added imperative to statism in development strategies. Arguably, most of Africa's independence movements had been led by modern petty bourgeoisies, made up of teachers and civil servants, who had vested interests in the state and few if any in the private sector. To these people, the state seemed a natural instrument for social change.

Furthermore, in South Asia and Africa policymakers confronted limited industrial bases. Early industrializers such as Britain had developed their industrial firms gradually from small ateliers and cottage industries to the immense factories of the modern day. Over a period of more than a century, entrepreneurs had been able to gradually amass the capital necessary for the creation of larger and larger production units. By the time countries in Africa became independent, the costs of establishing a new industrial venture were estimated, in relative terms, to be 250 times what they had been for an entrepreneur in the early days of the Industrial Revolution.[23] Faced with such circumstances, development planners had various options. One was to cut the national economy off from the world economy and try to take it through its own process of indigenous development, a model known as autarky. A second option was to attract those with the necessary capital, namely foreign companies, to build up the industrial sector. A third was to use the state to accumulate the necessary resources. Through taxation, borrowing, or control of the marketing of primary products, the state in many third-world countries could mobilize capital far beyond the reach of even the wealthiest of its citizens.

The first option, autarky, has historically been more popular in theory than in practice, and in practice has seldom proved feasible. In this century the chief experiments in autarky have been in Albania in the later years of the Hoxha regime (1945–1985), and in Cambodia under the Khmer Rouge (1975–1979). Neither made autarky attractive, with Cambodia's bold attempt degenerating into a tragedy from which the country took years to emerge. Autarky seems to offer the most promise when practiced on a small scale. For example, Anabaptist (Hutterite, Mennonite, Amish) farm communities in North America succeed in building self-reliance and fostering strong networks of social support. However, even these communities depend for their economic well-being on the sale of their farm produce and other commodities to the outside world. In today's world, in which steamships and airplanes crisscross the globe laden with cargo, autarky is a rare species. When Bhutan opened its border and built a road to India in 1959, the world's last truly autarkic national economy entered the history books.

Today the logic of comparative advantage makes foreign trade an essential component in rapid economic growth. In economic theory, a country enjoys a comparative advantage over another in the production of a good if it can produce it at a lower opportunity cost, that is, if it has to forgo less of other goods to produce it. For example, a given country could invest heavily to develop its own rubber industry, but for a fraction of the investment could produce enough cocoa to buy the rubber from a country that can produce it more inexpensively. It will then have resources left over for investment elsewhere in the economy. Thus, rather than try to satisfy all its own needs, an economy will prosper more if it specializes in the production of a few goods in which it enjoys a comparative advantage, and relies on imports to satisfy the remainder of its needs. This can even apply to food production. Alarm bells often sound when it is said that a given country cannot feed itself, but if food can be imported more cheaply than it can be produced locally, and if the imports are coming from a friendly country unlikely to cut food supplies for strategic reasons, then food self-sufficiency may be a costly goal.

Instead of autarky, most third-world governments opted for development strategies that blended the other two approaches and exploited comparative advantages. They sought to build up industry by mobilizing foreign and state investment, finding the revenue they needed for state investment through the sale of traditional exports. The strategy they adopted is known as import substitution industrialization (ISI).

| Import Substitution Industrialization

The logic underlying ISI is simple. Let us assume that a given country is exporting primary goods in order to import finished goods. It wants to begin producing those finished goods itself. It can do this by restricting imports of the goods in question by way of tariffs—taxes on imported goods—or of nontariff barriers such as quotas, content regulations, and quality controls. Quotas limit how much of a given good can be brought into the country. Content regulations and quality controls impose qualitative restrictions on the goods being imported. For example, a content regulation might demand that 50 percent of the given product be locally produced; a quality control can create a list of requirements that local producers are able to meet but that importers have a more difficult time satisfying. Such restrictions raise the prices of imported goods to local consumers, either by adding a surcharge to the world price, as tariffs do, or by reducing supply and thereby causing buyers to bid up the price, as nontariff barriers do. Either way, local investors who could not normally compete with foreign suppliers find the market suddenly benign. Provided they can get hold of the start-up capital, they can import the production machinery and begin to produce the good locally.

Because the domestic market is relatively small, producers will operate at lower volumes than does the foreign competition. This means they will not be able to take advantage of economies of scale, which is the basic economic principle that as volume of output increases, unit production costs decrease. For example, it will take one person more time to build a car in a garage than it will take a thousand people to build a thousand cars in a factory, because of the time involved in switching tasks, not to mention the time needed to build up all the specializations involved. In a factory, each individual performs one simple task repetitively, so that efficiency is maximized. This production technique was masterminded by Henry Ford; the ability to produce large volumes of goods cheaply underlay the U.S. industrial triumph of the twentieth century.[24] Because third-world producers operating in an ISI regime cannot exploit economies of scale, the prices on their goods will be higher than those on the world market. Nevertheless, provided these prices remain below the administratively inflated prices of imports, any venture can turn a profit.

Governments can go further to guarantee profits. They can establish licensing schemes that limit the number of firms allowed to produce a given product or import a needed input. Some governments even allowed only one firm to produce a given product, in effect giving it a legal monopoly that, in combination with import restrictions, provides an almost watertight guarantee of profits. Many third-world governments went further still to encourage investment, offering firms access to foreign exchange at concessionary rates by overvaluing their currencies, thus allowing local firms to import inputs at artificially reduced prices.

A simple example illustrates how currency overvaluation keeps foreign imports artificially cheap. Assume the market rate for a given currency to be two to one—that is, for every two units of local currency one could buy one unit of hard currency, which is a currency, most often the U.S. dollar, that can be used for international transactions. A government could overvalue its currency by offering to exchange it at its central bank at a rate of one to one. As a result, local buyers can obtain twice the amount of hard currency for the same price. In local terms, this halves the cost of imports. Given that currency overvaluation aims to benefit local industry, will the reduced cost of imports mean that, even taking trade barriers into account, imported consumer goods will now be cheaper than local ones and will drive local producers out of business? The answer is, usually, no. Unlike local currency, which can be printed, foreign exchange is a scarce commodity; it must be obtained through sales. When its price is set so low, local demand will go up, so much so that not enough is available to go around. The government then has to ration foreign exchange, and will tend to favor local industries rather than local importers of finished goods. Of course, the government can also choose to favor its friends in the allocation of foreign exchange, and herein lies one of the abuses of currency overvaluation, as neoclassical critics were soon to discover.

With prices kept high, and costs low, the attractions to invest are enough to persuade even the most conservative of investors. If a local entrepreneur cannot find the money to set up a venture, a foreign firm probably will. Import barriers may have closed off an export market to a foreign firm, but by setting up a branch plant it can sneak in under the wire and realize even greater profits than it had been earning when it was selling goods shipped from its home plant. When a foreign firm creates a branch plant under this arrangement, or when it licenses a local firm to use its technology to produce its product, it will typically allow the branch plant/licensee to produce only for the domestic market, and not for export. This prevents the branch plant/licensee from ever competing with the parent company in export markets and thereby eroding any of its sales.

Governments can further accelerate the industrialization process by offering firms subsidies and cheap credit. In a developing country, the way a government obtains the capital for subsidies or cheap loans is often by skimming off the revenue from the sale of its primary exports. By taxing primary exporters, and by establishing marketing boards that pay local producers less than the world price for their goods, and then pocketing the difference once they sell the product on the world market, governments have been able to realize far greater savings than the private sector might have. Several countries have used this strategy of rural-urban transfer to build up their savings pool.

I Conclusion

The appeal of ISI spread rapidly throughout the third world. The strategy went on to become one of the twentieth century's boldest and most widespread economic experiments. Holes eventually appeared in the fabric of ISI, but in the early days this development strategy promised many gains. The third world, it seemed, was about to come of age.

I Notes

1. H. W. Singer and Sumit Roy, *Economic Progress and Prospects in the Third World* (Aldershot, England: Edward Elgar, 1993).

2. Mark Blaug, *Economic Theory in Retrospect,* 3d ed. (Cambridge: Cambridge University Press, 1978), pp. 684–686.

3. See, for example, Andrew Shonfield, *Modern Capitalism* (London: Oxford University Press, 1965), especially chapter 4. The optimism of Keynesian economists is captured in a quotation from Michael Stewart, who once wrote, "The days of uncontrollable mass unemployment in advanced industrial countries are over." See Michael Stewart, quoted in Derek W. Urwin, *Western Europe Since 1945,* 4th ed. (London: Longman, 1989), p. 152.

4. Not all former colonies are third-world countries, however, nor are all former imperial countries necessarily in the first world. These subtle but important distinctions are often overlooked.

5. A few of these, especially in the Caribbean, remain colonies or overseas territories to this day.

6. On this subject see Markos J. Mamalakis, *The Growth and Structure of the Chilean Economy* (New Haven and London: Yale University Press, 1976), chapter 8; Henry W. Kirsch, *Industrial Development in a Traditional Society* (Gainesville: University Presses of Florida, 1977), chapter 7; Werner Baer, *Industrialization and Economic Development in Peru* (Homewood, Ill.: Richard D. Irwin, 1965); Rosemary

Thorp and Geoffrey Bertram, *Peru 1890–1977: Growth and Policy in an Open Economy* (New York: Columbia University Press, 1978).

7. See R. Prebisch, *The Economic Development of Latin America and Its Principal Problems* (New York: United Nations, 1950), and H. W. Singer, "The Distribution of Gains Between Investing and Borrowing Countries," *American Economic Review* 2 (1950).

8. See Ragnar Nurkse, "Balanced and Unbalanced Growth," in *Equilibrium and Growth in the World Economy,* edited by Gottfried Haberler and Robert M. Stern (Cambridge, Mass.: Harvard University Press, 1961). Nurkse actually developed his theory in the 1950s.

9. P. N. Rosenstein-Rodan, "Problems of Industrialization of Eastern and South-Eastern Europe," *Economic Journal* 53 (June-September 1943).

10. Nurkse, "Balanced and Unbalanced Growth," p. 247.

11. W. A. Lewis, "Economic Development with Unlimited Supply of Labour," *Manchester School of Social and Economic Studies* 22, no. 2 (1954).

12. Magnus Blomström and Björn Hettne, *Development Theory in Transition* (London: Zed Books, 1984), p. 42.

13. W. W. Rostow, *The Stages of Economic Growth* (Cambridge: Cambridge University Press, 1966).

14. David E. Apter, *The Politics of Modernization* (Chicago: University of Chicago Press, 1965); Myron Weiner, ed., *Modernization: The Dynamics of Growth* (New York: Basic Books, 1966).

15. See Apter, *Politics of Modernization*, and G. A. Almond and G. B. Powell, *Comparative Politics: A Developmental Approach* (Boston: Little Brown, 1965).

16. Paul Baran, *The Political Economy of Growth* (New York: Monthly Review Press, 1957).

17. See André Gunder Frank, *Capitalism and Underdevelopment* (New York: Monthly Review Press, 1967).

18. Samir Amin, *Le développement du capitalisme en Côte d'Ivoire* (Paris: Editions de Minuit, 1967).

19. Samir Amin, *Neo-Colonialism in West Africa* (Harmondsworth, England: Penguin, 1973).

20. Samir Amin, *Unequal Development* (New York: Monthly Review Press, 1976).

21. A good survey of the dependency debate, along with criticisms, can be found in Blomström and Hettne, *Development Theory in Transition.*

22. E. A. Brett, "State Power and Economic Inefficiency: Explaining Political Failure in Africa," paper presented to the Political Science Association Conference, Manchester, England, 1985.

23. Paul Bairoch, *Révolution industrielle et sous-développement* (Paris: SEDES, 1964), p. 198.

24. In the late twentieth century, however, this production technology was challenged by the Japanese concept of total quality management. Invented by an American, the process seeks to reincorporate the worker in the decisionmaking process, with workers verifying the quality of products each step of the way. Although this slows down production, it lowers prices by eliminating waste.

2

State-Led Development in Practice

THE POPULARITY OF IMPORT SUBSTITUTION INDUSTRIALIZATION BEGAN TO SPREAD throughout the third world after World War I, gaining speed after World War II. Although not all countries implemented the strategy, most at least experimented with some version of it. Early results were generally positive as countries benefited from the booming world economy. However, by the late 1960s and the 1970s, as the world economy slowed, the failings of ISI started coming to light. Radical theorists then blamed the persistent poverty of the third world on its dependent relationship to the world economy, and called for third-world countries to sever these ties. However, where such breaks were made and countries experimented with socialist development strategies, the results were scarcely any better. Statist development theories, it seemed, were not all they had been held out to be.

I ISI: The Early Decades

Events, rather than theory, drove the early experiments with ISI, with nationalism playing a strong supporting role. Economic changes forced governments to find ways to reduce their import bills, while the desire to roll back the influence of former colonial masters, or the threatening weight of the great powers, led governments to seek greater economic independence.

Some of the first moves into ISI took place in the Middle East. World War I interrupted these countries' imports and highlighted their dependence on foreign manufactured goods. However, serious action to remedy this situation was hampered by the limited autonomy allowed colonial regimes. (At the end of World War I, Britain and France had stepped in to fill the void left in the Middle East by the collapse of the Ottoman Empire.) During the 1920s, however, while maintaining their tight grip on most of North Africa, Britain and France allowed their Middle Eastern possessions greater leeway in determining policy. When in the 1930s prices on raw materials fell, leading to balance-of-payments problems, these governments instituted high tariff protection. Persia (Iran) and Iraq set up development banks, while the Egyptian government advanced funds through Bank Misr, which had been set up by Egyptians in 1920. Modest industrialization thus proceeded in the 1930s; it received a fillip when World War II cut off the region's access to European goods, and the enormous Allied expenditure created new demand for local industry.[1]

It was in Turkey that one of the boldest early moves into state-led development took place. Modern Turkey, cobbled together painfully from the remains of the Ottoman Empire, enjoyed one big advantage over its neighbors—independence, which allowed it more latitude to draft policies to build up its industry. This was a top priority for the nationalists who, led by Kemal Atatürk, created the country in 1923. In 1929 the Lausanne treaty, which imposed a free-trade regime on the new republic, expired. Shortly afterward the lira began falling, and to save the currency the government decided to reduce imports. Beginning in 1930 it erected barriers to trade; in the 1930s, impressed by Soviet economic successes, the government added more protectionist measures and Atatürk introduced his country to the economic philosophy of statism. Its cornerstone was a wide range of state enterprises, some of which were wholly state-owned and others of which were public-private partnerships. To feed these enterprises, the government used trading monopolies to take surplus revenues out of the agricultural sector. Five-year plans, introduced in 1934, rounded out state planning.[2]

It was at about this time that Latin American governments, faced with the effects of the Depression, began implementing similar policies, though they stopped short of central planning. Mexico was among the first. President Lázaro Cárdenas came to power in the 1930s on a wave of nationalist rhetoric that at times verged on socialism, but the policies he put in place did more to build up capitalism than a workers' paradise. He began with an ambitious land-reform program (which, however, lost much of its steam under his successors) and also nationalized the oil sector and railways. By the 1940s a fairly comprehensive ISI structure was in place, with high tariffs—and, in the 1950s, import licensing—protecting industrialists operating in Mexico. In addition, starting in 1941 new enterprises were given tax holidays of up to ten years, duties on imported inputs were often rebated to manufacturers, and subsidized credit was provided through a government bank established in 1933, Nacional Financiera. These measures conspired to keep Mexican profit rates among the highest in the world. As a result, both domestic and foreign investment boomed. To facilitate the operation of new industries, the Mexican government invested heavily in infrastructure.

Some other Latin American countries shied away from this strategy or, like Peru, employed it less wholeheartedly; but Chile, Argentina, and Brazil followed suit. Chile's experiment was perhaps the boldest. Its government created 140 public firms between 1940 and 1970, most of them assuming leading roles in their sectors. In all of Latin America, only communist Cuba surpassed Chile in the share of economic output accounted for by the state.[3] As in Mexico, nationalism, and especially the desire to resist encroaching U.S. influence, occupied a central position in the Latin American development approach.

As a rule, the first wave of Latin American ISI came during the Depression and World War II as a short-term response to the problems caused by the sudden loss of overseas markets and supplies. In the 1950s, propelled by the new intellectual contributions made by development theorists, ISI was systematized into a long-term development strategy. Import licensing and tariffs, which in some cases exceeded 100 percent, sheltered the local market from foreign competition. In Chile and Brazil the government established development banks or corporations, while in Argentina Juan Perón (president from 1946 to 1955) created a marketing board that siphoned resources from the primary sector and channeled them into industrial development. Governments invested heavily in nationalization, industry, and infrastructure.

The Middle East showed some similarities to this pattern. The Turkish experiment with statism in the 1930s stood mostly alone. However, after World War II, ironically at a time when Turkey was retreating temporarily from statism, Middle Eastern governments began adapting the Turkish model. Egypt led this second wave after the Free Officers coup in 1952, and aggressive nationalization, planning, and rising supicion of both foreign investment and the private sector became widespread in the region.[4]

By the time the Congress Party led India to independence in 1947, statist development policies enjoyed not only a generation of experimentation, but also the aura of intellectual sanction. State industry, protectionism, and planning became the hallmarks of the Indian development model. In fact, although it did not originate ISI, India is often considered to have been the paradigmatic case of this development strategy.

In opposition the Congress Party had been quite socialistic, calling for public ownership of land and minerals, but once in office it toned down its approach. The government instituted a modest program of land reform (which, like the Mexican one, soon lost vigor) but in the end, the world's second most populous country chose to steer a middle course between the first and second worlds. It adopted Soviet-style planning with a focus on heavy industry, but allowed the development of a private, if tightly controlled, economy. Five-year plans set investment and growth targets in the public sector. The state concentrated its resources in heavy industry, leaving the consumer-goods sector to local capitalists whose operations were favored by protective tariffs and, in some cases, complete prohibitions on imports. The state also assumed sole responsibility for the distribution of essential commodities such as cotton, cement, and steel.

The private sector prospered, but not in a free-market environment. India broke with the relatively laissez-faire industrial policies of its colonial past and began implementing a series of regulations to direct the development of the private sector. In time a complex web of regulations emerged: companies often had to obtain licenses before they could begin operations, factories seeking foreign technology or investment had to get permission from several different government agencies, and any transactions involving foreign currency had to be made through the Reserve Bank.

This combination of planned industrial development and a mixed economy became, in effect, the South Asian model for development. Virtually all of India's neighbors adopted similar strategies, with variations in the effectiveness of plans and the degree of state involvement in the economy. Sri Lanka, for example, used central planning in name only from its independence in 1948 until the 1956 election, when a more radical nationalist government came to power.[5] The government proceeded to nationalize road transport and created a number of state industries as the first steps in an ISI strategy. Then, with an eye fixed firmly on the apparent planning successes of its powerful neighbor to the north, Sri Lanka began to implement central planning. Some states were more ambitious than India in their intervention. Burma (Myanmar) set itself on a socialist path when it won its independence in 1948; the process accelerated in 1962 when a coup d'etat brought to power a doctrinaire faction that created a state-socialist economy, albeit with an essentially private peasant economy. And when East Pakistan seceded from Pakistan in 1971, constituting itself as Bangladesh, most of the Pakistani business class fled. This left the state to take over the ownership and direction of almost all large-scale industry.[6]

ISI also moved into some Southeast Asian countries, although their experiments with planning and ISI were not always so ambitious.[7] Malaysia put more emphasis on rural development than did most developing countries, and although it began using ISI in the 1950s, the country still followed a relatively liberal course. Perhaps the biggest exception to the rule lay in Singapore. Like Taiwan and South Korea, which will be discussed at greater length in Chapter 5, Singapore eschewed ISI following a brief flirtation, and moved into export industrialization.

The economies of Brazil, Mexico, Turkey, and India were relatively large. India, especially, had the domestic market to support just about any factory's or industry's existence without having to look for export markets. When African countries entered the independence era in the 1960s, they faced a different situation. These countries entered the postcolonial age with small and poor markets. Yet that seldom dampened their enthusiasm for ISI.

Ghana paved the way to independence for sub-Saharan Africa when its charismatic leader Kwame Nkrumah ushered in the country's independence in 1957. Most observers expected Ghana to be Africa's success story, perhaps the first developed country of postcolonial Africa. It had come to independence with healthy foreign reserves, a wealth of natural resources, and an impressive transportation infrastructure. As chief minister in the final years of British colonialism, Nkrumah and his Convention People's Party (CPP) had for all intents and purposes begun governing by the mid-1950s. In its first decade in power, the CPP practiced a form of moderate nationalism. The strategy yielded little fruit, however, and in 1961 Nkrumah began steering the country onto a new path, that of African socialism.

Early in his career, Nkrumah had come under the influence of U.S. and Caribbean black nationalist thought, but in the 1960s he started toying with the new and exciting philosophy of African socialism. Other seminal African socialist thinkers were Léopold Sédar Senghor, who became Senegal's first president, and Julius Nyerere, Tanzania's first president. Despite their differences, African socialists tended to agree on a common goal: Africa needed to invent its own development strategy, one that eschewed both capitalism and communism, which were seen as essentially European political-economic systems. African socialism typically sought to build a collectivist African economy while steering clear of Soviet-style socialism. It stressed human dignity and the traditional collectivism in African society and the village economy. But whereas Nyerere extolled the virtues of the peasant, Nkrumah frowned upon agriculture, seeing it as little more than bondage and, in the case of the lucrative cocoa sector, a bastion of capitalism.[8] In his view, agriculture was to be the handmaiden to industry, its revenues used to fuel urban investment, and it had to be transformed and modernized. Ghana instituted an ambitious program of large, mechanized state farms that would supplant the small peasant farms that then dominated the rural economy. At the height of the program, 105 farms covered 1 million acres.[9]

Nkrumah's view of the agricultural export sector as little more than a cash cow to be used to feed industrial development was not unusual. Not only was this official attitude commonplace in Africa, but it did not really diverge from conventional development theory of the day. Ghana's focus on rapid industrialization and physical-capital formation was quite respectable at the time.[10] Yet in few places was agriculture treated in so cavalier a manner as in Ghana, and in time this would have detrimental consequences. Farmers saw much of their revenue siphoned off by the marketing board to fuel urban investments; the prices they were paid slid while inflation worsened in the 1960s; and they had to make "special development contributions" and contribute to "forced savings."

Other African countries implemented less ambitious development strategies than Ghana's, yet still stuck to ISI. Both Côte d'Ivoire and Kenya, for instance, established protective barriers and incentive programs to attract foreign investment in industry. Their chief difference from Ghana was that both governments encouraged the development of a local business class.[11] State firms certainly played an important part in the Kenyan and Ivoirien development strategies, but they were more a means to channel resources to the private sector (e.g., development banks), or to build up industrial capital that could later be divested to local businesspeople, than a replacement for the private sector. Although agriculture would be used to fuel urban industrial development, both countries were more successful than Ghana in stimulating increases in primary exports, thereby gaining the revenue needed for their strategy. Rather than trying to leap into the creation of large mechanized farms, Kenya and Côte d'Ivoire relied on peasant farming. Finally, Côte d'Ivoire added a nuance to its development strategy that made it almost unique in Africa: once ISI had advanced some way, in the mid-1970s the country shifted to an export-oriented industrialization strategy that added value to local production rather than replacing imported production.

Although nationalism often played a strong role in ISI policies, the irony is that these strategies frequently relied on foreign capital to succeed. Latin American governments always drew significant foreign investment, especially from the United States, and by the 1960s Mexico was borrowing heavily on foreign markets to sustain its infrastructure investment. And even while African socialists sought to build a noncapitalist society, they often, like Ghana, looked to foreign capitalists to help them in this process. Yet at the same time that they attracted foreign capital, governments in Ghana and, later, in Angola and Zimbabwe made life difficult for their own entrepreneurs. There was a logic to this apparent paradox of nationalist regimes intensifying the very foreign dependence they claimed they would break. Foreign investment was seen as a necessary evil in the early years of development, simply because it could provide large sums of money that would be difficult to obtain locally. However, foreign capital could be controlled in enclaves and made to serve a socialist strategy. By contrast, the rise of a local bourgeoisie would lead to bourgeois politics, undermine the regime, and lead to a capitalist country. Only a handful of African countries, Côte d'Ivoire and Botswana among them, actively encouraged the development of a local capitalist class.

In the early years, the achievements of state-led development policies spoke for themselves. During the 1930s, at a time when the world economy was stagnating, Turkey's economic growth rate reached an annual average of 7 percent.[12] Although the economy declined during World War II, it rebounded during the 1950s and 1960s, a period of rising prosperity across much of the Middle East.[13] Latin America's move into ISI ushered in healthy growth rates in the 1940s and 1950s, with industry outpacing overall economic growth.[14] Right through to 1970 the Mexican economy grew at annual average rates of 6.5 percent,[15] in league with the world's fastest-growing economies. During the course of India's first five-year plan, from 1951 to 1956, national income grew by 18 percent and, aided by inflows of foreign aid, the government succeeded in building up the economy's physical capital. Sheltered from foreign competition, several Indian industrial companies reaped heavy profits that allowed them to become strong. Buoyed by the success of the first plan, the next two were even more ambitious, with the second (1956–1961) carrying further the development of heavy industry, and the third (1961–1966) shifting its attention to the infrastructure needed to service the booming industrial sector. India's move further into the industrial age pleased nationalists, who had always faulted colonialism for keeping India backward and agricultural. The fruits of this strategy were undeniable: over the course of the first three plans, for example, steel production increased sixfold.[16] It was at about this time that Ghana's industrialization strategy began to pay its dividends. The investment made possible by agricultural surpluses went to build state-industrial ventures. Public investment in new undertakings boomed, and by 1965 there were fifty-three state corporations in several subsectors of the industrial economy.[17] The most significant of these, actually predating the turn to socialism, was the Volta Dam. Financed by foreign capital, the dam was to provide cheap energy for the emerging Ghanaian industrial economy. In return for their participation the foreign investors, a syndicate of Kaiser and Reynolds, were sold electricity at cost—then the cheapest rate in the world—for the aluminum plant they would build. On this plant they were given a five-year tax holiday and a thirty-year import-duty exemption on their inputs. The dam was completed ahead of schedule and below cost, and exceeded forecasts of power sales and profitability.[18]

At the same time these countries were developing their industrial bases, great strides were being made in global agriculture. For while ISI paid little regard to agricultural development, this neglect was initially made up for by the successes of the Green Revolution. During the 1960s, with funding from the Rockefeller Foundation, laboratories in Mexico, the United States, the Philippines, and Taiwan had conducted research on improving agricultural techniques. The results of this research were some dramatic technological developments that would revolutionize third-world agriculture. Most important of these innovations were new high-yield varieties (HYVs) of seeds, and improved chemical fertilizers. The Green Revolution did much to alleviate the widespread fear that the planet, and especially its poor countries, would soon be unable to feed its growing population. For example, Mexico's wheat yields per hectare more than doubled between the mid-1960s and the mid-1970s.[19] India also boosted its crop yields when, after a series of severe droughts in the mid-1960s, the new technologies were imported from Mexico and spread throughout the countryside. The chief innovation adopted in India was the new HYVs, though use of chemical fertilizers and mechanization, especially tractors, also increased. By the 1970s output was surging. India changed from a famine-prone country into one that was essentially self-sufficient in food output. This was one of the third world's most remarkable accomplishments in the postwar period.

The Green Revolution also drew criticism, though. Because the new technologies were expensive and required high and regular water inputs, they were frequently accessible only to richer farmers, and thereby worsened rural inequalities. Moreover, as crop yields expanded, prices dropped, and many farmers were driven off the land. To varying degrees this scenario was played out in several countries, including Mexico and India. It is difficult to determine whether the Green Revolution worsened income inequality; the weight of opinion leans toward the view that the new technologies did concentrate incomes, but the evidence is mixed.[20] However, it does seem safe to say that the most effective Green Revolution strategy is one that maximizes the access of less prosperous farmers to the new technology rather than allowing only the rich to get their hands on it. At any rate, the successes of postwar development strategies could not be denied: cities were growing, industry was developing, and countries had augmented their food output.

I The Postwar World Economy

Such successes could not be credited only to the right policies. From the late 1940s international conditions favored growth, and it would have taken some doing for a government to implement a development strategy that did *not* produce healthy growth rates. The successes of the time actually obscured what were, in most cases, insufficient performances. However, this would not become obvious until the world economy slowed down in the 1970s.

Toward the end of the 1940s, once the political and economic chaos that plagued Europe after the war had settled, the world economy had begun to boom. The Marshall Plan, whereby the U.S. government pumped reconstruction money into Western Europe, had inaugurated this growth phase.[21] Following hot on its heels, the Korean War brought a further leap in demand. The United States emerged from World War II more robust than when it entered it. The rise in demand brought on by the war, coupled with the fall in European output, produced such an imbalance that in 1945 the United States accounted for a third of the world's economic output and more than half of its production of manufactured goods.[22] U.S. military power stretched around the globe, and the United States was able to impose a degree of order on the world economy that had been sorely lacking in the prewar period (a lack largely to blame for the Depression). To begin with, the U.S. use of the gold standard helped provide a stable international trading environment. The United States went on to subsidize recovery in the world economy by allowing liberal access to its own market and tolerating the outflow of U.S. investment capital and official aid. Although the resultant capital outflow produced persistent balance-of-payments deficits, this was not a problem, at least not yet. Because virtually all governments were willing to take payments in dollars, the U.S. government could pay its bills simply by printing more money.

Western Europe and North America were poised for an economic boom. In Western Europe the supply of investment and human capital faced a situation of slack capacity because so much of Europe's industry and infrastructure had been destroyed in the war. On top of this, the Western world experienced a baby boom that created all sorts of new demands on the economy. Demand and investment rose throughout most of the world. In the postwar period the world economy grew at average annual rates of between 5 percent and 6 percent, and there did not appear to be any end in sight to this growth. Such high expectations led to greatly expanded welfare states, and fueled pay settlements in North America and Western Europe that outpaced improvements in productivity.

Given such rising demand, it was not surprising that, initially, things went well for many third-world countries. Although by the mid-1950s a downturn had set in in some Latin American countries,[23] in Africa the opposite occurred. With regional variations, the decade after 1948 had been a good one for Africa's economies. Official and private foreign investment grew; in many colonies trade boomed; even Kenya, riven by the Mau Mau insurgency, saw positive growth. On such a resource-rich continent, faced with continuing increases in demands for its chief exports, the logic of taxing agriculture or other primary industries to build industry seemed inescapable. The cash cow, agriculture or mining, could not be expected to run dry.

However, the golden age could not last. The slack capacity would eventually be used up, the baby boom would run its course, and the declining productivity and rising incomes would feed inflation, a hydra that began to rear its head in the late 1960s. Moreover, by the early 1970s the United States was suffering from a "gold overhang." The government had been printing money not only to cover deficits, but also to fund its war in Vietnam. Eventually far more dollars were in global circulation than there was gold in Fort Knox. Printing money to cover balance-of-payments deficits would not be an option for much longer. In 1971 the United States ran its first trade deficit of the century.[24] That same year, partly in response to this crisis, President Richard Nixon abandoned the gold standard. Currency instability followed, and the United States made clear that it would no longer allow the generous access to its economy that it had formerly given its allies, unless they agreed to widen their doors in return.

Soon thereafter, the world economy was shaken by one of the greatest tremors yet: the first of the oil shocks. In 1973 the Organization of Petroleum Exporting Countries (OPEC) announced an embargo on oil supplies to the United States, Europe, and Japan to protest their support for Israel in the Yom Kippur War. This sudden cut in supply led to a fourfold increase in the world price of oil over the next two years. The crisis plunged the economies of the developed world into recession, heralding the end of the golden age. Growth phases, if more modest, would return to the world economy; but then so too would recessions. The era of steady, high growth was now at an end. What emerged to take its place was a new phenomenon that bedeviled policymakers in their search for a cure: economic stagnation, coupled with high inflation, or as it came to be known, stagflation.

At the onset of the OPEC crisis, some observers concluded hopefully that the era of first-world dominance of the world economy was also being brought to an end. They construed the OPEC crisis in North-South terms: the success of the oil-producing countries in raising a commodity price was seen as an attempt by commodity-producing countries to increase their share of the world's wealth at the expense of the rich consuming countries. There was a flurry of optimism that maybe the same could be tried by producers of other primary commodities. The third world, it was believed, would finally get its fair share of the wealth generated by world trade.

Although there is a grain of truth in this interpretation, the oil crisis in fact boded ill for most of the third world. The handful of oil-exporting countries got much richer, but the remainder, who imported oil, faced the same jump in energy costs as did first-world countries. In the meantime, the recession in the world economy had reduced demand for their products. The first world had sneezed; much of the third world caught pneumonia. Worse was yet to come. The oil shock unleashed a virus that crept into the body of the third world at once, but would only become apparent much later on when it manifested itself in a terrible, seemingly incurable illness. This was the debt crisis.

With oil prices skyrocketing, OPEC countries found themselves awash in hard currency. Try as they might, the rulers of these countries could not spend all that was flowing into their coffers, so they deposited these monies in their accounts with Western banks. The banks, which had to pay their depositors interest on this money, had to find someone to whom they could lend at a higher rate of interest in order to avoid losing money. So flooded were they with money that many banks threw caution to the wind in their hunt for borrowers and offered low-interest loans for questionable projects.

The offer was too good for many third-world governments to resist. They borrowed heavily in order to invest in development projects and sustain overvalued currencies.[25] In doing so they were acting no more unreasonably than would someone borrowing money to expand a business, counting on the future revenues that would result to pay off the debt. The problem was that many of the projects they invested in were ill thought out, and in some cases monies even disappeared at once into current accounts. As for the anticipated revenues, these presumed a continued growth in the world economy that was not to materialize.

Although the 1973 oil shock had plunged the first world into recession, in the third world things did not always look so bad. With investment capital available in abundance, sometimes at real interest rates close to zero, the governments of many third-world countries could be forgiven for paying scant heed to the problems of the first world. However, when in 1979 a second oil shock brought on a second bout of stagflation in the first world, the crisis came home to most developing countries: most commodity prices plummeted.

Meanwhile, first-world governments began fighting inflation through tight monetary policies, raising interest rates to heights unknown in the postwar period. This had a doubly detrimental effect on developing countries. First of all, the higher interest rates raised the repayment cost on debts, many of which were short-term and thus subject to variable rates of interest. Second, with money flowing into the high-interest havens in the first world in order to take advantage of the high returns on deposits, the demand for U.S. dollars in particular rose. The value of the dollar thus increased, and because most third-world debt was denoted in dollars, the value of the debts of developing countries was effectively hiked. With less money available to pay off debts, but payments rising quickly, third-world governments found themselves in a crippling squeeze. When in 1982, Mexico, Brazil, and Argentina all announced they could not meet their current debt obligations, the debt crisis erupted. Donor agencies such as the World Bank relegated development projects to a secondary status, and devoted their energy to trying to recover old debts and improve the solvency of their debtors.

The revenue from the sales of primary commodities was increasingly used not to fuel industrial development, but to pay off old debts. Governments had to squeeze money from their budgets to meet debt obligations, and were forced to cut their investment and social expenditure. They had little space to maneuver: when, for example, President Alan Garcia tried to set an upper limit on Peru's debt repayment to avoid causing too much hardship for his people, creditor agencies reacted with a credit boycott that was too much for the country to bear. The cost of debt repayment thus fell on ordinary people. Whatever development was supposed to mean, they were not seeing its fruit. There were even cases in which projects built with borrowed money lay idle, the anticipated economic growth that would have brought them into operation having never materialized. By now, high inflation had become a serious problem in many developing countries, particularly in Latin America. It was eating away the gains of growth and reversing, sometimes rapidly, per capita incomes. Many governments found they had no choice but to turn to the World Bank and the IMF for assistance. This would be forthcoming, but with strings attached.

I   The Fruits of Postwar Development Strategies

Meanwhile, the many shortcomings of the ISI model were becoming obvious. The approach had been directed, intentionally, at physical-capital formation,[26] and neglected to foster competitiveness, innovation, technological capability, and other features of development. With its focus on savings and investment, ISI proved very effective at building factories and infrastructure. In other regards, though, it was failing.

I   *Poor Export Performance*

The first problem of ISI is that while it altered the structure of an economy's output, it did less than hoped to alter the structure of its exports. Whereas many third-world countries increased the profile of manufactured goods in their exports, change came slowly. Between 1960 and the end of the 1970s, for example, India increased the share of its exports accounted for by manufactured goods by a third, and Mexico more than doubled its share. However, in the same period, South Korea—which was not using a conventional ISI model—increased that proportion more than sixfold.[27] Moreover, increased exports of manufactured goods often arose from trading agreements with neighboring countries and did not represent increased exports of manufactured goods to first-world countries.[28] In other words, third-world countries were selling more manufactured goods to each other, but not to their traditional trading partners in the first world. In the end, third-world countries continued to rely on primary exports to the first world for their foreign-currency earnings. This problem was most acute in Africa, whose share of the world's manufactured exports actually declined throughout the 1960s and 1970s,[29] and whose dependence on primary exports actually increased between 1965 and 1980.[30]

Given that ISI was designed to alter the trade patterns between the first and third worlds and end the tendency for third-world governments to export primary goods and import finished ones, it was not meeting its goal. Although third-world countries were importing fewer consumer goods from the first world, they were not necessarily importing fewer finished goods.

Local producers had replaced imports, but the technology and often the inputs used to produce those goods were usually imported. Aimed in part at improving a country's balance of payments by reducing its imports, in a few cases ISI actually worsened the balance, with the cost of imported inputs actually outweighing the savings generated by local production of consumer goods.[31] Moreover, ISI often precluded the sale of finished goods abroad. In many cases, being sheltered from competition by protective barriers, local industries simply could not produce goods of a price or quality that could find a market abroad. Moreover, branch plants were often set up exclusively to produce for local markets, with licensing arrangements precluding the possibility of exporting. Kenya, for example, which leaned heavily on such protectionism to attract foreign investment in industry, was able to increase its manufactured exports mainly by virtue of its membership in the East African Community. Because Uganda and Tanzania have even less-developed industrial sectors than does Kenya, that country led the competition. Elsewhere, however, Kenya's achievements in market penetration were more modest.[32]

Some countries sought to get around this problem by developing their own heavy industry in order to supply the inputs and capital goods (such as machinery) for their factories. Big countries could support their own capital-goods sectors, but smaller countries, such as Argentina or Tanzania, could hardly hope to recoup the cost of their investment through domestic sales. Export sales to other third-world countries presented one possible outlet, which Argentina used to greater effect than Tanzania, but even then the costs usually outweighed benefits. In such cases the construction of a capital-goods base ate up much of a country's scarce resources. It would have been cheaper for countries to import capital goods than to produce them themselves.[33] Although the Indian government could make back its investment through domestic sales, the fact that the country produced capital goods inferior to those available from abroad not only limited the export markets for its goods, but also kept the quality of the consumer goods produced with these capital inputs too low to compete well on foreign markets.[34]

Inefficiency

ISI frequently allocated resources inefficiently. Because trade barriers raised consumer prices, people could not buy and save as much as they would in a free-trade regime. In effect, this restricted the size of both the local market and the savings pool. The large profits being made by protected companies could be channeled into savings, but where the companies were owned by foreigners, the profits were more likely to be shipped back home than to be reinvested locally. This became an acute problem in Latin America during the 1970s. Some governments responded to capital flight by imposing currency controls—limiting the amount of money anyone could take out of the country—and taxing profits. The former was partly counterproductive in that it frightened away future foreign investment. The latter was easily avoided by means of transfer pricing: by overbilling for licensing fees or supplies to branch plants, parent companies could find ways to sneak their money out of host countries and show meager profits or even losses at the end of every year.[35]

The lack of competition fostered by protection created its usual set of problems. Firms became lazy, product quality was poor, and productivity remained low.[36] Not only did local consumers lose out, but the possibility of expanding into export markets dwindled. Firms ate up money that could have been invested elsewhere in the economy. In some countries, India being a case in point, firm managers devoted much of their time to securing favorable arrangements with government officials rather than to improving the operation of their firms or the quality of their products.

Protection also led to an inefficient allocation of resources in the way production technology was chosen. With profits assured, firms had few incentives to look for the most efficient technology or adapt it to local needs. Most often, they bought production technology that had been developed in the first world, where the markets were comparatively huge and the demand was for highly differentiated, packaged, and promoted products. Not only did this produce unnecessarily expensive goods, but it also built factories with immense production capacities and, in the worst cases, a heavy reliance on imported inputs and even imported managers. Given that such factories were producing for small domestic markets, their unused capacity led to high unit costs, which were passed on to the consumer in the form of higher prices. When inputs had to be imported—because, for instance, the technology could not process local supplies—this further worsened the country's balance of payments. Among the best-known examples of this syndrome remains Ghana's aluminum plant, built by the Kaiser-Reynolds Syndicate alongside the Volta Dam. Although the project itself was successful, it used not only imported capital technology but even imported bauxite, rather than local supplies, and thereby created few spinoff benefits for the Ghanaian economy.[37]

| Underemployment

All the while, such capital-intensive modern technology created few local jobs, further limiting the growth of the domestic market and concentrating the gains of development in a few hands (the owners of capital and the small industrial working class). So serious was this problem in India that by the 1960s growth slowed. The unequal gains of development had hindered the emergence of a mass market for consumer goods, which in turn inhibited the further development of the capital-goods sectors.[38] In a similar vein, much of Africa witnessed the emergence of "economic islands," small industrial enclaves that purchased foreign inputs and whose beneficiaries earned incomes high enough to spend on imported goods. Few linkages connected these islands to the rest of the economy. Where W. A. Lewis had expected a growing urban economy to draw the rural sector behind it, in fact the urban economy boomed while the rural sector, in which most of the population lived, fell behind. The third world witnessed the tragic paradox of fabulous wealth living side by side with subhuman squalor.

This situation undermined the Lewis thesis, which had provided some of the theoretical underpinning for state-led development. Lewis had anticipated that the wage rate would remain at the level of the agricultural-subsistence rate, providing industry with cheap supplies of labor, but while rural wages often remained low, urban wages outstripped them considerably. Several explanations have been put forth for this. Employers using sophisticated technology require skilled labor, which is in short supply and thus more costly. They also want to minimize turnover rates to control the expense of training new employees in the use of their technology. To a point, higher wages can also induce higher productivity, due to increased morale and better nutrition; it can therefore be in employers' interests to raise wages. Finally, if workers are unionized, or even if unorganized they are a potent political force, employers may feel the need to treat them better than agricultural employers do their workers.[39]

Whatever the reasons in any given case, there arose what are called segmented labor markets. Urban labor markets were not governed by the rules that obtained in the rural sector. Not only did this worsen the rural-urban discrepancy and contribute to the emergence of a "labor aristocracy," but the resulting high wages attracted many more job seekers than could find work. By the 1980s in Côte d'Ivoire, for instance, urban populations were growing by up to 10 percent per year, while in the rural hinterland in the north of the country the population remained unchanged.[40] Cities teemed with unemployed migrants who tried to find work in the informal sector, in petty trade, menial labor, and inevitably, prostitution and crime. Many third-world cities grew rapidly, consuming a disproportionate share of the government's resources, yet authorities simply could not keep pace in the provision of security and infrastructure. Squatter townships soon engulfed many third-world cities. Urban poverty and overcrowding in cities that lacked the resources to build new housing, roads, and sewers created public-health and crime problems. These include such horrific responses as the private gangs that prowl the streets of some Latin American cities, "cleansing" them of street children.

| *Poor Agricultural Performance*

The worsening of the urban-rural gap (sometimes referred to as dualism) reflected one of ISI's most serious omissions: primary development. Not only did ISI neglect agriculture in its race to build urban industry, it frequently penalized it. Very often, investment in the primary sector was greatly outweighed by the money taken out in the form of taxes and marketing-board surpluses. In squeezing agriculture to fuel urban development, third-world states often kept agricultural producer prices so low that farming became less and less attractive, fueling the rural-urban exodus. Meanwhile, primary exports grew sluggishly or, in the worst cases, plummeted. In Ghana, the cocoa marketing board presided over declines in exports; in Nigeria, exports of groundnuts and palm oil, of which Nigeria was the world's largest producer in the early 1960s, fell to zero in the 1970s.[41] This restricted the income available for investment and worsened balance-of-payments problems. It also tended to produce narrowly based income growth, which led to a demand for nonfood and capital-intensive products imported from abroad; those countries that continued to encourage agricultural development saw more broad-based income growth, which created more demand for local goods.[42] The irony in this was that ISI strategies sometimes did less to encourage industrialization than did strategies focused on developing agriculture.

| *Corruption*

The mechanisms of ISI gave considerable scope for abuse. License administration enabled ministers and officials to reward favorites or demand kickbacks; directorships of marketing boards and public firms could be used to skim off resources for personal use; discretionary government budgets could be plumbed to further individual interests. In India such abuse translated into lost time as managers spent much of their time in queues at government offices, and into expensive management practices: many companies established virtual embassies in Delhi in order to promote and protect their interests.[43] In some African countries, marketing boards were treated almost like tax concessions, with government officials squeezing more and more revenue from peasant farmers even at times when world commodity prices were falling. Some governments maintained highly discretionary tax regimes, and embezzlement of public funds was common. Cynics suggested that third-world dictators such as Ferdinand Marcos of the Philippines and Mobutu Sese Seko of Zaire (today the Democratic Republic of Congo) kept alive the Swiss banking industry, with its confidential accounts. Civil-service promotions often went not to the best-qualified people but to political clients, who kept their jobs not by doing them well but by maintaining their loyalty. In the worst cases, such as Zaire, Uganda, and the Philippines during the Marcos administration, official corruption seriously drained the economy of resources and put a crimp in investment. For example, it has been estimated that from the mid-1970s to the mid-1990s, the economy of the Philippines lost $48 billion to corruption.[44] Dismantling the structure that made possible such theft became an appealing option to many.

Extreme Statist Experiments: Soviet Central Planning in the Third World

When the failings of ISI first became apparent, dependency theorists blamed the world economy. They argued that structuralist experiments failed to break the link with the first world, which they claimed lay at the heart of the third world's condition. However, those countries that did attempt such a break with world capitalism and applied socialist central planning in the Soviet mold could boast little more for it.

The principle underlying socialist central planning was that the economy should be organized to serve people, and not people the economy. The state, as the representative of the people, was the agent that should perform this task. The Soviet interpretation was that to abolish exploitation, one had to abolish the market economy. The people as a whole should own the property, and the state should manage it on their behalf. Beyond that, there was a not unreasonable conviction that in underdeveloped societies a rapid and extensive mobilization of resources could only be achieved if the state took full control of the economy and compelled all available resources to be put to productive use. Along the lines of the Soviet model, states nationalized the economy, taking full ownership of its resources and in effect turning all citizens into state employees. The economy was then directed from a central-planning office, which planned investment, set wages and prices, decided on which resources would be allocated for what purposes, and set production targets. Such socialist central planning was tried in Cuba, Ethiopia, Mozambique, Vietnam, Laos, Cambodia, Burma (Myanmar), North Korea, and China. Less ambitious experiments were made in a handful of other countries.

Overall, the record of socialist central planning in the third world was not very good, at least not with regard to economic matters. Although in some countries external factors such as civil wars drained socialist governments of resources, these alone could not account for all the shortcomings of socialist central planning. In the least-developed countries, namely Ethiopia and Mozambique, these experiments ran up against a dearth of administrative capacity. The states were simply too poor and resource-starved to be able to exert effective central planning. Control over the economy was therefore far less than in the Soviet or Chinese models. A skilled bureaucracy to design and supervise central planning was lacking. So too was the communications infrastructure that was necessary if effective central control was to be maintained. Any development strategy in which the production of thousands and even millions of items is planned and coordinated by a central agency depends on complete access to reliable data from all over the economy, not to mention some skillful management. Given that a state machinery as large as the USSR's could not always meet such requirements, poor countries with a shortage of skilled bureaucrats and an inadequately developed communications infrastructure were not likely to do better. In Burma, for example, the construction of new plants was often not properly coordinated with the production and transportation of raw materials; shortages that slowed the operation of plants and raised inefficiency costs became commonplace.[45]

Certain other problems bedeviled central planning everywhere. The Soviet experiment proved that when it comes to expanding output, building new plants, or bringing new resources into production, central planning can be more effective and rapid than a market economy. Central commands, forced saving, price distortion in order to mobilize savings, and other such tools can rapidly build up the size of an economy. However, though it can greatly increase the quantity of output, central planning is not always up to the task of improving quality. Nor does it tend to encourage the efficient use of resources. Soviet oil fields, for example, were notorious for the amount of oil lost or wasted in the production process because firm managers were concerned with increasing output and not with making extraction less costly. Quantity could be monitored by bureaucrats; quality was much more problematic. A consumer market seems a more effective means of identifying and rewarding improvements in product quality. After all, the average consumer does not care how many shoes the economy has produced, but only whether the pair he or she bought is comfortable, durable, attractive, and reasonably priced. Soviet firm managers, however, were typically reluctant to develop new products or technologies for fear that production might temporarily lag and thus disrupt the economic plan.[46]

In the third world this tendency to inefficiency was most evident in the farming sector. State farms run by managers were unproductive, consuming resources that would have been more effectively used on small peasant farms. It is now well established that in third-world settings, where labor is abundant, small household farms will be more cost-effective than large, mechanized ones, which rely on expensive capital inputs and displace labor through their use of machinery. Ghana's state farms, despite the resources pumped into them, were between four and five times less productive than peasant farms.[47] In Cuba, workers on sugar plantations sometimes cost more than the value of what they produced;[48] in Ethiopia and Mozambique the heavy concentration of resources in a few state farms meant that communal villages and peasant agriculture were virtually ignored.[49] In Tanzania, which was not a centrally planned economy like these, the government did try to collectivize agriculture but found the peasantry far more independent-minded than it had suspected: peasant resistance undermined the government's "villagization" policy.[50]

Nevertheless, in criticizing socialist central planning one risks throwing the baby out with the bathwater. Although economically inefficient, socialism in the third world sometimes made important social and political gains. Committed as they were to egalitarianism, such regimes often implemented progressive social policies that increased the people's access to health care or basic education, or made significant strides toward granting women greater rights. In the same vein, communist Havana remains a safer, cleaner city than capitalist Kingston, Jamaica, because so much more money has been invested in public amenities, parks, and services, than in building private mansions amid widespread squalor. As a rule, socialist regimes also avoided the worst excesses of corruption into which some neighboring governments were plunged; this was especially so in Africa. Finally, third-world socialism even made some economic gains. In China, for example, it built up the rudiments of an industrial base that could later be exploited when the country opened up to capitalist influences. Some suggest that China's current economic boom would not have happened so soon were it not for this phase of extensive industrial development. Perhaps it is safest to say that socialist central planning outlives its usefulness when the phase of heavy industrialization reaches its maturity, at which point an economy needs to move into consumer industry and export markets.

Why the Failures? Theoretical Perspectives on Statist Development Theories

Statist development theories, especially in their radical leftist versions, presumed a certain rationality on the part of the state that may not have been present. Neoclassical theorists would subsequently argue that there was no reason to assume people would behave any differently in the public sector than they did in the private sector. In other words, the same selfish behavior that prevailed in the marketplace would continue in the state, except that its effects there would be more damaging. The existence of official corruption seemed to confirm this argument. Moreover, although the ready assumption that the state encapsulates the public interest and thus should spearhead development on the nation's behalf suits common sense, it lacks empirical support. Elite theorists have long pointed out that significant political participation is restricted to a minority of the population, while political power is the preserve of small elites (which, not surprisingly, are often market elites).[51] The state, argued critics of statist development models, was not necessarily more representative of the public will than was the market.

In its more radical versions, in particular dependency theory, statist theory ran into even more problems. It seemed insufficiently attentive to microeconomic theory, and in particular failed to deal with the issue of incentives. For instance, it seldom explained why the state officials who would engineer development would run their firms efficiently and maximize their outputs and profits. After all, they often had to wrestle among competing priorities, including calls for a rapid improvement in the conditions of their workers. The market incentives that imposed discipline on firm managers and encouraged producers to increase output were not always provided by the state.

Interestingly, some of the strongest criticisms of dependency theory came not from the right but from the left. Marxists took such theorists as A. G. Frank to task for suggesting that capitalist imperialism had choked off the indigenous processes of capitalist development in the colonies. In fact, these critics alleged, capitalist development did *not* occur, at least not in the Americas or Africa, until the advent of imperialism.[52] Furthermore, imperialism in Latin America took place during the period of Iberian feudalism, not capitalism, so it could not have been first-world capitalism that underdeveloped this part of the world.[53] Placing the blame for third-world underdevelopment on the drain of resources to the imperial countries probably overstates the role the colonies played in Europe's development. Seldom did colonial trade account for more than a small share of the colonizing country's economy, and most of the first world's enrichment grew from trade within the developed world, as it does to this day. If anything, the problem was not that capitalism had exploited the third world, but that it had underexploited it.[54] Where waves of settlers flowed to the colonies, investing and importing new technologies while also constituting effective lobbies for infrastructure development and against protectionist groups back home,[55] development was more likely to result. It is worth remembering that the United States began its life as a collection of colonies. However, where the imperial powers did not exploit colonies very much but used them mainly as sources of raw materials and markets for finished goods, as was the case in most of Africa, underdevelopment often resulted. In such colonies and regions, the imperial powers did little to encourage industrialization, and the arrival of their manufactures drove local producers out of business. Other colonies, such as the inland territories of West Africa, fared even worse. Turned into labor reserves for neighboring colonies that were being developed, they were drained of the most important resource to development: labor. Today such countries number among the world's poorest.

Finally, dependency theory's conception of the domestic bourgeoisie as parasitic and dependent on foreign capital was simplistic. It assumed that the bourgeoisies of different countries would behave differently, even as enemies. In fact, capitalists everywhere tend to follow the laws of the market and frequently find more in common with each other than with compatriots from different classes.[56] In any event, time would show that many third-world capitalists were anything but parasitic, sluggish, or dependent.

ISI itself rested on some assumptions that later research drew into question. Designed to build up modern industry, it encouraged large-scale units of production and concentrated them in urban areas. To fuel this development, the state in effect taxed rural dwellers by such means as marketing-board surpluses. Aside from moral concerns—namely the possibility that ISI left peasants little better off than they had been under colonialism, while enriching a small minority—the economic problems in this approach soon came to light. Research found that, given the comparative advantages prevalent in most developing countries, rural investment yielded higher returns than did urban investment. Among other things, urban development required expensive housing and infrastructure, and the rate of return on these was comparatively low.[57] Even if governments were eager to break out of their dependence on agriculture and industrialize, it was not obvious that an "urban-biased" strategy offered the best means of doing so. Specialists on appropriate technology argued that, given the features of third-world countries and in particular their abundance of cheap labor, most governments should have encouraged the development of comparatively small, labor-intensive production units. These could have been located throughout the country, where they would have developed close linkages to the economy, instead of being concentrated in one or a few large cities.[58] However, the lessons of appropriate technology were not apparent to the drafters of postwar development plans. To them, industrialization and urbanization went together. The growth of the city symbolized the advance of modernity. The costs borne by the peasantry were considered legitimate sacrifices to make for the building of a nation, and the benefits of ISI were readily apparent.

▍ Conclusion

Certainly not all the news from the third world was bad. Many countries eradicated the ancient problem of famine, nutrition and access to health care frequently improved, infant mortality rates declined, and literacy rates rose. However, the difficult truth was that in many places, economic growth barely kept pace with population growth and inflation, and progress was much slower than had been hoped. In real per capita terms, a significant portion of humanity ended the twentieth century poorer than when it welcomed political independence.

Yet against this backdrop of disappointment, some exceptions stood out. A small number of newly industrialized countries, or NICs, managed to attain very high rates of growth, particularly over the last three decades of the century. Not only did industrial development boom in these countries, but their governments managed to build strong export industries, thereby altering not only the structure of production but of exports as well. These economies became models of efficiency, innovation, and rising prosperity among the citizenry. Chief among these stars were the Four Little Tigers or Dragons of East Asia: Hong Kong, Taiwan, Singapore, and South Korea. Since the 1960s these economies experienced annual growth rates of over 10 percent in some years; in the latter three countries, manufacturing grew even more quickly, and the profile of manufactured goods in exports rose dramatically. In per capita terms, these were the world's fastest-growing economies in the latter decades of the twentieth century.[59] Yet these economies were not necessarily specially privileged or pegged from an early date to boom. South Korea, for example, is a densely populated country with limited natural resources that traditionally inspired "poets and painters more than engineers or economists."[60] It suffered at the hands of Japanese colonialism and from the ravages of the Korean War.

Why, then, did South Korea belie the general rule of the third world? That question provoked one of development studies' most vigorous debates in recent years. Agreement has yet to be reached, but as will be shown in Chapter 3, a resurgent school of economic thought, neoclassical theory, believed that the lessons of the East Asian NICs vindicated what it had maintained all along: that, left unfettered, the market would bring about economic growth and development.

Time would soften the harsh assessment of ISI, or at least of some of its components. But by the late 1970s, those who favored an interventionist role for the state had become so discredited by the excesses and abuses of statist experiments, not to mention the growing intellectual and political weaknesses of the left, that they would be swamped in a tide of right-wing criticism.

I Notes

1. Charles Issawi, *An Economic History of the Middle East and North Africa* (London: Methuen, 1982).

2. This discussion is taken from Mete Pamir, *Determinants of Late Development: A Study of Turkey's Late Industrialisation Attempt Until 1946* (Bergen: Chr. Michelsen Institute Report 1993).

3. Economist Intelligence Unit, *Chile to 1991* (London: Economist Publications, 1987), p. 5.

4. Roger Owen and Şevket Pamuk, *A History of the Middle East Economies in the Twentieth Century* (London: I. B. Tauris, 1998), part 2.

5. Specifically, a Sinhalese (and Buddhist) nationalism, which stood in opposition to the Tamil (and Hindu) minority.

6. See Nurul Islam, *Development Planning in Bangladesh* (New York: St. Martin's Press, 1977).

7. See John Wong, *ASEAN Economies in Perspective: A Comparative Study of Indonesia, Malaysia, the Philippines, Singapore, and Thailand* (Philadelphia: Institute for the Study of Human Issues, 1979).

8. Crawford Young, *Ideology and Development in Africa* (New Haven and London: Yale University Press, 1982), p. 155.

9. Ibid., p. 158.

10. See Killick in Young, *Ideology and Development*, pp. 151–152.

11. Whether these strategies were effective would become a bone of contention among competing schools of theorists. For recent statements on the role of indigenous capitalists in Africa, see Bruce Berman and Colin Leys, eds., *African Capitalists in African Development* (Boulder and London: Lynne Rienner Publishers, 1994), in particular the contributions by David Himbara and John Rapley.

12. Pamir, *Determinants of Late Development*, p. 119.

13. Owen and Pamuk, *History of Middle East Economies*.

14. See Celso Furtado, *Economic Development of Latin America* (Cambridge: Cambridge University Press, 1970). See also Werner Baer, *Industrialization and Economic Development in Brazil* (Homewood, Ill.: Richard D. Irwin, 1965), p. 69; Economist Intelligence Unit, *Chile to 1991*, p. 7.

15. Judith Adler Hellman, *Mexico in Crisis*, 2d ed. (New York and London: Holmes and Meier, 1983), p. 59.

16. Dietmar Rothermund, *An Economic History of India* (London: Croom Helm, 1988), pp. 133–136.

17. Young, *Ideology and Development*, p. 156.

18. Ibid., p. 157.

19. John Cole, *Development and Underdevelopment* (London and New York: Routledge, 1987), p. 40.

20. Donald K. Freebairn, "Did the Green Revolution Concentrate Incomes? A Quantitative Study of Research Reports," *World Development* 23 (1995): 265–279.

21. Between 1948 and 1952, the United States injected $17 billion into Western Europe, especially into Britain, France, West Germany, and Italy. This helped to kickstart the Western European economies, and by the time the plan ended in 1952 their recoveries were self-sustaining.

22. Paul Kennedy, *The Rise and Fall of the Great Powers* (London: Unwin Hyman, 1988), p. 358.

23. Whereas the war strained much of Africa and Asia by restricting their trade with Europe, Latin America reaped the same benefits of the wartime leap in demand as did the United States. The end of the war, and the resumption of trade throughout the world economy, eroded Latin America's privileged position as a supplier.

24. The United States ran balance-of-payments deficits all through the golden age, but this was as a result of the outflow of money due to foreign aid and investment. Its balance of trade was continually positive.

25. Rosemary Thorp, Economics of Development Lecture Series, University of Oxford, 18 November 1992.

26. As Ragnar Nurkse once said, "progress depends largely on the use of capital," not on more appropriate labor-intensive means of production. See Ragnar

Nurkse, "Balanced and Unbalanced Growth," in *Equilibrium and Growth in the World Economy,* edited by Gottfried Haberler and Robert M. Stern (Cambridge, Mass.: Harvard University Press, 1961), p. 249. This focus on savings and investment and the creation of physical plant arose largely in response to the work during the 1940s of the economists R. F. Harrod and Evsey Domar, who emphasized the role investment played in growth.

27. World Bank, *World Development Report 1981,* pp. 150–151.

28. Furtado, *Economic Development of Latin America.*

29. See the introduction to Martin Fransman, ed., *Industry and Accumulation in Africa* (London: Heinemann, 1982). The figures used cover the 1960–1975 period.

30. Armand Gilbert Noula, "Ajustement structurel et développement en Afrique: L'expérience des années 1980," *Africa Development* 20, no. 1 (1995): 5–36.

31. Ian Little, Tibor Scitovsky, and Maurice Scott, *Industry and Trade in Some Developing Countries: A Comparative Study* (London: Oxford University Press, 1970).

32. World Bank, *Kenya: Into the Second Decade* (Baltimore and London: Johns Hopkins University Press, 1975), chapter 4.

33. On this subject see Luc Soete, "Technological Dependency: A Critical View," in *Dependency Theory: A Critical Reassessment,* edited by Dudley Seers (London: Frances Pinter, 1981).

34. Sanjaya Lall, *The New Multinationals: The Spread of Third World Enterprises* (Chichester: John Wiley & Sons, 1983), pp. 255–256, and Sanjaya Lall, *Multinationals, Technology and Exports* (London: Macmillan, 1985), pp. 179–181.

35. One should note that transfer pricing is becoming more difficult to get away with. The Swiss General Superintendence Company, a private consulting firm, can effectively monitor prices and determine when firms are overpricing, and it can sell this information to governments that suspect firms of overinvoicing.

36. For example, Indian firms had low capital-output ratios: investments were allegedly not as productive as they would have been in more open economies. See Ashok V. Desai, "Factors Underlying the Slow Growth of Indian Industry," *Economic and Political Weekly* 16, nos. 10, 11, 12 (Annual Number, March 1981): 381–392; "The Slow Rate of Industrialisation: A Second Look," *Economic and Political Weekly* 19, nos. 31, 32, 33 (Annual Number, August 1984): 1267–1272.

37. This problem of inefficient use of production technology has been widespread in Africa. See Howard Pack, "Productivity and Industrial Development in Sub-Saharan Africa," *World Development* 21, no. 1 (1993): 1–16.

38. Rothermund, *Economic History of India,* pp. 135–136.

39. J. Knight, Economics of Development Lecture Series, University of Oxford, 2 December 1992.

40. Côte d'Ivoire, Ministère du Plan, *Plan quinquennal de développement économique, social et culturel 1981–85,* pp. 49–50.

41. Gavin Williams, "Why Structural Adjustment Is Necessary and Why It Doesn't Work," *Review of African Political Economy* 60 (June 1994): 214–225.

42. Thomas L. Vollrath, "The Role of Agriculture and Its Prerequisites in Economic Development," *Food Policy* 19 (1994): 469–478.

43. Stanley A. Kochanek, *Business and Politics in India* (Berkeley: University of California Press, 1974), chapter 4.

44. The estimate was made by the Philippine government's ombudsman; Reuters, 3 October 1995.

45. David I. Steinberg, *Burma's Road Toward Development* (Boulder, Colo.: Westview Press, 1981), p. 144.

46. John S. Reshetar Jr., *The Soviet Polity,* 2d ed. (New York: Harper and Row, 1978), p. 240.

47. Young, *Ideology and Development,* p. 158.

48. Carmelo Mesa-Lago, "Economics: Realism and Rationality," in *Cuban Communism,* 4th ed., edited by I. L. Horowitz (New Brunswick, N.J.: Transaction, 1981).

49. Marina Ottaway, "Mozambique: From Symbolic Socialism to Symbolic Reform," *Journal of Modern African Studies* 26 (1988): 211–226; Mulatu Wubneh and Yohannis Abate, *Ethiopia: Transition and Development in the Horn of Africa* (Boulder, Colo.: Westview; and London: Avebury, 1988), chapter 4.

50. See Goran Hyden, *Beyond Ujamaa in Tanzania* (Berkeley: University of California Press, 1980), and Henry Bernstein, "Notes on State and Peasantry: The Tanzanian Case," *Review of African Political Economy* 21 (1981): 44–62.

51. For examples, see Edward S. Greenberg, *The American Political System,* 4th ed. (Boston: Little Brown, 1986); Ralph Miliband, *The State in Capitalist Society* (London: Weidenfeld and Nicolson, 1969); Wallace Clement, *Class, Power and Property* (Toronto: Methuen, 1983).

52. Bill Warren, *Imperialism: Pioneer of Capitalism* (London: New Left Books, 1980).

53. Ernesto Laclau, "Feudalism and Capitalism in Latin America," in *Politics and Ideology in Marxist Theory* (London: New Left Books, 1977).

54. G. B. Kay, *Development and Underdevelopment: A Marxist Analysis* (London: Macmillan, 1975).

55. Arghiri Emmanuel, "White Settler Colonialism and the Myth of Investment Imperialism," *New Left Review* 73 (1972): 35–57.

56. Bjorn Beckman, "Imperialism and the 'National Bourgeoisie,'" *Review of African Political Economy* 22 (1981): 5–19, and "Whose State? State and Capitalist Development in Nigeria," *Review of African Political Economy* 23 (1982): 37–51.

57. See Michael Lipton, *Why Poor People Stay Poor* (London: Temple Smith, 1977), on the advantages of rural over urban investment. Lipton's thesis anticipated the neoclassical new political economy of Robert Bates (see chapter 3). See also E. F. Schumacher, *Small Is Beautiful: A Study of Economics as If People Mattered* (London: Abacus, 1974).

58. See, for example, Frances Stewart, Henk Thomas, and Ton de Wilde, eds., *The Other Policy* (London and Washington, D.C.: Intermediate Technology Publications in association with Appropriate Technology International, 1990).

59. Only one country did better in this regard: Botswana. It is an interesting irony that the world's fastest-growing economy lay not in East Asia but in Africa, and as shall be seen in Chapter 6, it is a fact that provides much insight.

60. Jon Woronoff, *Korea's Economy: Man-Made Miracle* (Oregon: Pace International Research, 1983), p. 14.

3

The Neoclassical Answer
to Failure

IN MAY 1979 MARGARET THATCHER LED THE CONSERVATIVE PARTY TO VICTORY
in Britain's general election. Thatcher came to power with the intention of
profoundly altering Britain, purging it of socialism and returning it to its
Victorian golden age of individualist capitalism and free-market economics.

The next year, Ronald Reagan won the U.S. presidency. These events
heralded a shift to the right all over the Western world: further conservative
victories were to follow in other countries, and where leftist parties won or
retained power, they nevertheless moved right or formed coalitions with
right-wing parties. Convinced that the welfare state had become so generous
that it robbed individuals of discipline and initiative, and believing that the
growing intrusion of the state in the economy hobbled private enterprise,
conservative governments aimed to roll back the state and free the market.

This free-market ideology would eventually find its way into the cor-
ridors of the Western world's donor agencies, in particular the World Bank
and the IMF. To many observers, a new drummer was setting the world
economy's beat—a drummer that used its lending power to prod third-
world governments to radically alter their development policies, reducing
the role of the state in the economy and reemphasizing the market. It was,
in this interpretation, the start of the neoclassical assault. Yet this assault resulted not from first-world pressure only; even before first-world governments turned to the right, neoclassical theory had begun influencing third-
world policymakers because it seemed to offer practical solutions to the
problems facing the third world.

I The Neoclassical Tradition

Neoclassical economics dates back to the 1870s. At this time mathematics
was introduced into the study of economics, revolutionizing the discipline

51

and breaking it away from its parent, classical political economy. This created a fissure between the economic and political components of political economy, giving birth to the new disciplines of economics and political science. As time went by, economists devised more and more mathematical equations to explain and predict economic behavior. Guiding neoclassical economists in their theorizing was a fundamental assumption: individuals behave as rational utility maximizers. Put another way, people are self-interested, they know best what they want, and they also know best how to get it. In the pursuit of their goals, people act rationally and efficiently.

From this assumption it follows that the most productive economy will be one in which individuals are allowed the greatest freedom to engage in activities or enter into contracts as they choose, and to reap the full benefits of their labors. Neoclassical theorists thus argue not only against government regulation, but against taxation whose aim is to redistribute wealth. As argued by one of the doyens of neoclassical thought, Friedrich von Hayek, individualism ensured that more things would be tried, and the greater the number of things being tried, the more innovation and progress there would be. But, he maintained, individuals would only incur the costs of trying something new if they knew they would reap the benefits of any success they had; people were not altruistic. Taxing the rich to feed the poor hindered the most well-off, reduced initiative and thus innovation, and so hurt all of society.[1]

This conclusion points to a central tenet of neoclassical economics that dates back to Adam Smith and beyond:[2] if individuals are left to pursue their narrow self-interests, society as a whole benefits, whereas if individuals are compelled to pursue collective interests, society as a whole suffers. For example, creating a business in order to generate wealth for oneself nevertheless creates jobs for others, whereas taxing that business in order to redistribute its profits will discourage the owner from expanding it further and creating any more jobs. Accepting this "doctrine of unintended consequences," neoclassical economists conclude that free-market economies enable individuals to pursue their self-interest to the benefit of society, whereas command economies stifle self-interest and initiative and thus slow society's progress. One cardinal rule follows from this: the less state, the better.

Interestingly, the forerunners of contemporary neoclassical theory emerged at about the same time as Keynes. Friedrich von Hayek and the Chicago school of economists were publishing their ideas at the same time that Keynes put out his *General Theory of Employment, Interest and Money* in 1936. Yet so dominant was Keynes's thinking that neoclassical ideas remained confined to academic circles for a few more decades. It was only in the 1950s and 1960s that criticism of Keynes moved out of the margins of the academic community. Among the first critics to be given serious attention was Milton Friedman, who revived the quantity theory of money in the late 1950s, spurring considerable discussion in the academic literature over the next decade. In contrast to Keynes, who had argued that fiscal policy offered an effective means to manage capitalism's boom-and-bust cycles, Friedman contended that monetary policy was a more useful instrument. By tightening the money supply during bouts of high inflation, and loosening it during times of recession, governments could regulate aggregate demand and maintain economic growth. Money supply can be loosened by lowering interest rates, and tightened by raising them. When interest rates are high, people prefer to invest rather than spend their money, and the high cost of loans discourages people from buying on credit. Economic activity thus slows, less money chases after the same supply of goods, and prices rise more slowly or even fall. In times of recession, lower interest rates have the opposite effect: people withdraw money from savings and spend it; they even buy on credit because it is no longer expensive, and activity resumes. This, to Friedman, was a more effective means to deal with the boom-and-bust cycle than Keynes's proposed control of government purse strings.

Whereas Friedman assigned government a greater role in the economy than did traditional neoclassical theory, his was still an approach that implied a reduction in the size of the state. His proposal to remove many of the government's levers on fiscal policy went against much of the postwar Keynesian consensus, including such things as government investment and nationalization. As Friedman saw it, the task of the government was merely to create the right environment for businesses and individuals to maximize their potential. He argued that the government should concern itself merely with stabilizing monetary growth, which would "provide a monetary climate favorable to the effective operation of those basic forces of enterprise, ingenuity, invention, hard work, and thrift that are the true springs of economic growth."[3]

At first, Friedman's impact was modest. That changed in the 1970s, when stagflation hit the developed economies. As the decade progressed, first-world voters became more concerned with inflation than with unemployment. The latter, a devil the postwar generation had feared, had led people to see in Keynesian economics a powerful exorcist. By the 1970s, however, the working classes had diminished as a proportion of the population in first-world countries, and the middle classes had emerged to become the prominent constituency. They feared unemployment less than the high inflation that was eating into their standards of living and raising their mortgage payments. The monetarist recipe of tightening the money supply in order to reduce inflation appealed to them. By this time there had emerged an even more radical economic theory, known as rational expectations, whose essential claim was that people had learned to anticipate government policies and thus could effectively derail government attempts to make adjustments in the economy. The proposed solution was even more extreme than monetarism's hands-off approach: a complete retreat of the state from economic life.[4]

Along with neoclassical economics there arose a separate but related school of thought in political theory: neoclassical liberalism. Its origins lay in the work of John Locke, and its forefathers included Adam Smith, Jeremy Bentham, John Stuart Mill, and Alexis de Tocqueville. Since World War II, political philosophers such as Robert Nozick[5] and Ayn Rand, along with economists such as Friedman and Hayek, had revived the ideas of classical liberalism that had long been confined to the history books.

Classical liberalism stressed individualism above all else, seeing individuals as the building blocks of society. It believed the minimalist state produced not only a better economy, but a better society as well. Left with maximum freedom, people would not only realize their potential and pursue those things in life at which they were best, but would also become more responsible and self-reliant. They would form the institutions, such as families, churches, and neighborhoods, that would then look after the young, elderly, and weak. Expanding the state not only deprived people of freedom, but by usurping many of the tasks performed by society—as, for instance, social agencies replaced families, churches, and community associations—it robbed them of initiative and responsibility.

In the nineteenth century classical liberalism gradually gave way to modern liberalism. This judged that society was riven by so many historical inequalities that only state intervention could level the playing field to give to all the same degree of freedom and opportunity to realize their potential. However, especially after the 1960s, classical liberalism went through a renaissance in the first world, resulting in neoclassical liberalism. Although this school of thought did not have as direct an impact on third-world politics as did neoclassical economic literature, it did help to push the political agenda of the first world away from statism, profoundly influencing politicians such as Margaret Thatcher and Ronald Reagan. This in turn pushed the agendas of the donor agencies to the right, and prodded many third-world governments to reexamine their statist development practices. It was held that paring back the state would improve the operation of not only the economy but the state itself. Reducing the state's resources would at the same time reduce opportunities for corruption; eliminating civil-service jobs would encourage educated people to create their own opportunities for enrichment in the private sector rather than look to the state for advancement. Making the state "leaner and meaner" would improve its operation while at the same time releasing resources into the private sector.

I The Neoclassical Diagnosis of the Third World's Illness

By this time, critiques by neoclassical economists who focused their attention on the third world had begun to trickle in. Throughout the postwar period, dissenting voices were pointing to gaps or flaws in development theory, accumulating bits and pieces of evidence that could later be used in an
all-out assault on statist development theory. Prominent among these critics
was P. T. Bauer. Early in his career Bauer had studied Southeast Asian rubber farmers and West African traders. At the time, it was commonly assumed that third-world peoples, especially in rural areas, did not follow the
rules of market rationality. They were believed to be backward, uneducated,
and bound by cultural traditions that frowned on selfishness and individualism. This justified the state's playing the role as the economy's main entrepreneur, because there were too few private entrepreneurs to do the job.
From the late 1940s Bauer, following his studies, took direct aim at this
logic. He had found that his subjects did in fact behave as rational utility-
maximizing individuals, seizing new opportunities whenever they came
their way.[6] T. W. Schultz supported Bauer, arguing that when peasant farmers invested little time and capital in their farms it was not because their
cultural values or backwardness led them to ignore the market, but rather
that government policies deprived them of capital and kept returns on agriculture so low that it was neither possible nor worthwhile for them to become thrifty entrepreneurs.[7] Such arguments were later echoed by Harry G.
Johnson, who became convinced that "even the poorest producers are susceptible to price incentives" and doubted that the state could ever perform
economic functions better than could the market.[8] By the late 1960s, neoclassical writers believed that there was enough evidence to show that
peasants certainly responded to price incentives.[9]

This conclusion had profound implications. It questioned much of the
logic of state marketing boards, and challenged the principle of skimming
resources from agriculture to fuel industrial development. As time went by,
more and more voices would contend that state intervention had distorted
prices in such a way as to discourage production of potentially lucrative
primary goods, thereby slowing growth. Bauer argued strongly that individuals, not the state, should provide the economy's entrepreneurship, and
that too large a state stifled this entrepreneurship.

In the mid-1960s a rash of literature emerged by such neoclassical
economists as Jagdish Bhagwati, V. K. Ramaswami, H. G. Johnson, Bela
Balassa, W. M. Corden, and Anne Krueger. Much of it appeared in the
pages of the *Journal of Political Economy,* the publication of the Chicago
school. This literature drew attention to the costs of protection and exchange overvaluation, and began to explore ways of measuring the welfare

costs of these devices. Neoclassical writers also began to uphold the virtues of conventional economic theory, taking issue with the claims of structuralists and others that the peculiarities of the third world rendered traditional economics inapplicable.[10] This was the first intimation of what would become a sometimes vociferous claim that "development economics" was a waste of time because everything anyone needed to know was found in the conventional literature.[11]

In 1970 the Organization for Economic Cooperation and Development (OECD) published a study that did much to popularize neoclassical theory among development specialists.[12] This study looked at the trade regimes put in place in the postwar period by Argentina, Brazil, Mexico, India, Pakistan, the Philippines, and Taiwan, and concluded that in all these countries, ISI had done more harm than good. In their analysis the authors made a number of observations that would form a large part of the arsenal used in many neoclassical critiques of statism. To begin with, they pointed out that in trying to build new industries, ISI neglected the comparative advantages enjoyed by these economies. Given that these comparative advantages were often in agriculture, it was significant that industrialization had occurred at the expense of agricultural development. In large part this happened because currency overvaluation had discouraged exports, both industrial and agricultural. All in all, ISI was seen to be a wasteful strategy: industry accounted for more investment than output, its capital-intensive nature created too few jobs, and it gobbled up foreign exchange in its need for imported inputs. ISI's bulky state administration created bottlenecks in the economy, further wasting resources through capacity underutilization, corruption, and sluggishness. The authors expressed the doubt common to all neoclassical theory that bureaucrats could gain access to the information needed to effectively administer the economy, and they disliked the fact that the controls used in ISI appeared to curb private initiative.

As if this were not enough, the study concluded that ISI, which was often justified as a strategy that would benefit a whole economy and not just preserve the wealth of a lucky few, was actually worsening income distribution. While profit earners benefited from protection and skilled labor from currency overvaluation, farmers suffered and a large share of the urban population remained unemployed, forced to seek work in the marginal or informal sectors as bootblacks, peddlers, or prostitutes.

The proposed solution was for governments to shift from ISI to export industrialization, nurturing firms that could sell abroad rather than in the domestic market. For this purpose the study suggested promotional rather than protective policies to encourage industrialization—for example, subsidies over import restrictions. (As noted in later chapters, this preference for market-enhancing policies has now been accepted by most development theorists.) In line with its call for export industrialization, the study advocated more openness to foreign trade, less use of controls, more use of the "price mechanism," and currency devaluation. These recommendations would be repeated later, many times over, by other neoclassical theorists, but in hindsight the OECD study appears relatively moderate compared with some of the later volumes in the neoclassical library. It did not oppose public ownership, it accepted some role for price controls, it emphasized the state's role in building infrastructure and in human-capital formation, and it called for some degree of state activism in helping firms to capture export markets. Nor did the study repudiate ISI outright. It merely rejected its being used for too long.

Within a year the World Bank and the Inter-American Development Bank published a trade study, chaired by Bela Balassa, that strengthened the OECD study's findings.[13] This study assessed the impact of ISI's protectionism and currency overvaluation—or lack thereof, in some cases—on the economies of Brazil, Chile, Pakistan, Mexico, West Malaysia, the Philippines, and Norway. Its conclusions were damning to ISI. Protection, it said, entailed high costs in static (allocative) efficiencies, limited the scope for the introduction of large-scale production methods, provided few inducements to improve productivity, slowed the production and exports of primary commodities, and hindered the expansion of manufactured exports. ISI was, in sum, a policy that wasted resources and did too little to stimulate increases in exports. By contrast, in the countries with less-protective trade regimes agriculture and exports grew rapidly, new primary exports were developed, and exports of manufactured goods increased. Once again, while granting that protection was legitimate over set periods, the study called for devaluation coupled with disinflationary policies, the replacement of quotas by tariffs, and the use of subsidies rather than protection for the promotion of new manufacturing industries. So while the Balassa report recognized that the state had a role to play in economic development, its principal thrust was a call to roll back the state and streamline its procedures.

Stronger—some might say dogmatic—expressions of neoclassical thought were to follow, as critics gained confidence and grew convinced that their findings had thoroughly discredited the old statist development schools. Deepak Lal composed a scathing indictment of what he called "development economics,"[14] saying there was no need to articulate an economics for development, as "development economists" had tried to do, because all the answers could be found in conventional economic theory. Lal then gave to neoclassical theory the memorable aphorism that market failure was always preferable to state failure. Meanwhile, P. T. Bauer pilloried dependency theorists and claimed that imperialism had done no harm to the colonies but had, if anything, improved them. He insisted that the first world was in no way responsible for the poverty of the third world, and that the market offered the best mechanism for a poor country to develop.[15]

In 1983 the National Bureau of Economic Research (NBER) issued a trade study that would become so influential that some would call it the core of the neoclassical critique of statism.[16] Like the OECD study, the NBER study dealt with trade regimes, reaching similar conclusions. From it emerged a focus on export-oriented industrialization, which it set against ISI. In the view of the study's authors, the latter was statist while the former, said to be practiced in the most successful of the East Asian NICs, was market-oriented. Although few now dispute that export industrializers, particularly the East Asian NICs, have performed better than the import substituters, a great debate soon erupted over whether or not the export industrializers were free-market economies. Neoclassical theorists came to lean on the NBER study's claims that these economies illustrated the virtues of the free market and liberal trade regimes, and they brandished the success of such countries as South Korea as a lesson for those such as India.

The NBER study focused on the various market distortions caused by government intervention in the course of ISI. It argued that labor-market regulations, restrictive trade regimes, credit rationing, and social-insurance tax systems all combined to raise the domestic cost of hiring labor relative to capital. Meanwhile, currency overvaluation, the favorable treatment of capital-goods imports, and credit rationing at subsidized interest rates drove down the prices of capital services. The end result, relatively cheap capital and relatively expensive labor, clearly favored capital-intensive production. Although there is nothing intrinsically wrong with capital-intensive production, it normally arises in high-wage economies. When it develops in low-wage economies it excludes the mass of the population from the development process, because it creates relatively few jobs while eliminating traditional industries. The solution to this sort of problem appeared obvious: less distortion, which meant less government intervention in the economy. The trade regimes should be liberalized and there should be more "freedom" in the labor market.

The NBER study made another claim that drove to the heart of structuralist economics. Whereas structuralists had often argued that trade between first-world and third-world countries had worked to the detriment of the latter, and that intraregional trade offered more hope for development, the NBER study rejected this flatly. It argued that the gains from trade, including employment gains, would be maximized by trade with countries endowed with different characteristics. In other words, poor countries should trade with rich countries, not with other poor ones. Even if "collective self-reliance" had a nice ring to it, the study held that regional trade blocs in the third world would do little to benefit their member states. Given that postwar approaches to development were much influenced by trade pessimism, this argument, along with neoclassical claims that the terms of trade were not going against the third world, represented a remarkable attempt to refute that pessimism.

Throughout the 1950s and 1960s, other studies had been done that challenged the Prebisch-Singer thesis,[17] which had maintained that over time the value of primary exports relative to finished imports would decline. To bolster their arguments, neoclassical writers claimed that contrary to the trade pessimism that had underlain structuralism, the developing countries had actually gotten rich off selling their primary goods to the developed world.[18] Neoclassical writers were also citing other problems associated with state intervention. These included financial repression (interest rates kept low by government regulation), which had been intended to encourage investment by making it cheap but in fact discouraged it by dissuading people from putting their savings in banks, where the returns were so low. Neoclassical writers also criticized rules that restricted foreign investment in order to, among other things, stem the outflow of profits or prevent the importation of inappropriate technology. Critics of such policies claimed that the problems of capital outflow or the sale of inappropriate products were not as serious as structuralist theorists feared.[19]

The New Political Economy

In addition to this economic literature, there arose a new current in the political theory of development that challenged the statist approach. This was the new political economy. Pioneered by Anne Krueger,[20] the new political economy took the neoclassical assumption that humans are rational utility maximizers and applied it to politics. (In this it bore close ties to rational action or public choice theory, which had become popular in U.S. political science departments.)[21]

Krueger studied the effect of quotas on the behavior of firms. In any situation in which a government restricts the supply of a given good to a level that is below demand, the local price of that good will be bid up above the world price. The difference between the price paid by the importer (the world price) and the price the importer charges local buyers (the local price) is called economic rent. Because quotas create this windfall for importers, import licenses become hot commodities that are sought after for their own sake, not just because they offer access to needed inputs. Krueger found cases in which, with licenses being assigned to reflect firms' capacities, plant managers would invest to expand their plant even when they had idle capacity. (The problem with an idle plant is that though it generates no income, its owners must continue paying mortgage and other bills on it.) This enabled them to obtain bigger import licenses, which they could then sell to other managers at a profit. However, in the process their productivity dropped even further, as an even larger share of plant capacity went unused. Plant managers also tried to obtain licenses through bribery, hiring the relatives of officials in return for licenses, and so forth; such rent-seeking behavior consumed resources that could have been better spent elsewhere in the economy.

Jagdish Bhagwati later expanded this to look at tariff evasion, tariff seeking, and revenue seeking.[22] These were all, he said, directly unproductive, profit-seeking activities made possible by government controls. They were profitable, but produced no goods or services, and thus wasted valuable resources. Capital-gains tax treatment, for example, led to the overbuilding of apartments or uneconomic oil exploration. The policy implications of this new political economy were clear: less government control. If some kind of protection were required, tariffs were better than quotas, because tariffs created no opportunities for rent. In this regard, neoclassical theorists distinguished between discretion and rules. Quotas and licenses were applied in a discretionary manner by bureaucrats or politicians, who could abuse their powers to favor themselves or their friends. Tariffs, on the other hand, were rules: they applied equally to everybody, and so could not create opportunities for rent seeking. Neoclassical theorists tended to favor rules over discretion whenever some form of state intervention was deemed necessary.[23]

The new political economy was further elaborated in the work of Robert Bates on sub-Saharan Africa.[24] In the course of his research he had found that governments in Africa seemed biased against the farm sector. Currency overvaluation and pricing policies kept prices on farm products low, thereby subsidizing the urban population's food bill. At the same time, overvaluation also kept the prices on imported industrial inputs low, while protectionism kept profits high, which made life good for industrialists. Marketing boards, in turn, skimmed off revenue from the primary sector to fuel urban development. All in all, Bates found that the cities were squeezing the rural sector in order to fuel their own growth, dampening the dynamism of what should have been the economy's engine of growth—agriculture. Import substitution industries were gobbling up foreign exchange and earning none in return, while agriculture, the sector of the economy that did garner foreign exchange, was contracting. The unattractive prices prompted many farmers to resort to subsistence production or to pack up altogether and move to the city, where life was much better.

Puzzled by the apparent irrationality of this self-defeating policy, Bates turned to interest-group analysis to try to find an answer. Interest-group analysis has a long history in the study of industrial polities. Bates relied on the theory of one of its most influential practicioners, Mancur Olson,[25] whose approach he blended with a form of class analysis to produce a provocative and influential hybrid.

Olson had argued that individuals are self-interested, and so will rarely try to pressure the government if the sought-after policy brings them little benefit. A small group with a common interest will be more effective than a large one, because large groups are saddled with the problems of dispersed benefits and the free-rider effect. If a group has a million members, its weight of numbers may appear daunting; thus third-world farmers should be a force to be reckoned with. In fact, they seldom are. It is difficult for an individual to resist the temptation to stay at home tilling his or her plot while the million others go off to a demonstration to secure a policy that offers everyone an equal share of the gains. Of course, it is equally irresistible to all; the result is that very large groups often have a small number of activists doing all the work. When the work they have to do outstrips potential gains—after all, the gains are to trickle down equally to the million members—the rational incentive for action is lost. The opportunity cost is too high: the time and energy spent lobbying the government could be better spent on the farm. Consequently, in liberal democracies interest-group politics often lead to undemocratic outcomes, because small groups work to secure desired policies while large groups remain largely ineffectual.

Bates believed that this explained what was going on in much of Africa. Even if development policies were counterproductive, they nonetheless served the interests of the urban elite of industrialists and skilled laborers. This class alliance, suggested Bates, underpinned the power of modern Africa's regimes, and no government could afford to antagonize it. Whereas peasant farmers are often a dispersed and disorganized lot—so many potatoes in a sack, as Marx once referred to them disparagingly—the urban constituency is tight-knit and dangerous. The working class, living in densely packed neighborhoods, can easily take to the streets and threaten stability if it feels it has been pushed too far. As for the industrialists, their wealth and personal connections make them a desirable support base. Interventionist policies that distort markets create administratively generated rents that can be used to curry their favor or build up networks of political clients.

Bates considered this urban bias a key factor in Africa's underdevelopment. It had to be overcome. African governments had to be prodded to realize their static comparative advantages, which for the most part lay in agriculture. As other neoclassical theorists had argued, raising the prices for peasant farmers' products would lead them to increase their output and would bring more foreign exchange into the country. Producer prices could be raised easily through currency devaluation. Soon after Bates published his work, "getting the prices right" became a guiding concern of the World Bank in Africa.

The new political economy reached the following conclusions. Given that people behave in a self-interested manner, they will seek the available opportunities to maximize their gains. If those opportunities lie in the market, their self-interested behavior will create spinoff benefits for others— new jobs, products, and so forth. However, if those opportunities lie in a large and interventionist state, people will neglect the private sector and engage in activities that are detrimental to the welfare of society as a whole, such as corruption, rent seeking, and nepotism. The solution was obvious: reduce the size of the state and its role in the economy, so as to free up the market and make it attractive to entrepreneurs, and at the same time remove opportunities for corruption, rent seeking, and other economically harmful activities.

By the 1980s a formidable corpus of literature had come together that hobbled Keynesian economics and reasserted the primacy of neoclassical theory over the statism of the postwar generation of development economists. The recommendations pointed in one direction: less government intervention, more freedom in the market, and the abandonment of ISI in favor of outward orientation.

By "outward orientation" neoclassical theorists specifically mean not only export-led growth but a minimum of state control in this process. Other theorists, in particular the developmental-state theorists discussed in Chapter 5, talk of export-led growth that occurs behind a wall of state protection and sponsorship. Throughout this book, "outward orientation" will be taken to mean a development strategy that relies on export-led growth rather than domestic-led growth, and will not assume the neoclassical lack of control.

At any rate, underlying neoclassical theory was a sort of "trade optimism" that trade could be relied upon for growth. Economic planning was not needed to alter the structure of production, agriculture should be left free to flourish, and trade with the first world was a boon, not a hindrance. If this was not a revolution of the scientific sort, it was nevertheless a rebellion that critically weakened the old orthodoxy.

Meanwhile, in the politics of the first world, the postwar Keynesian consensus was about to be shattered by the rise of conservative governments and the rightward shift of virtually the entire political spectrum.

I From Theory to Practice

During the 1970s the public in many first-world countries had warmed to the neoclassical agenda. In part this arose from the apparent exhaustion and intellectual bankruptcy of the left. Well into the 1980s, when it was growing increasingly obvious that the state could not expand forever, socialist parties in many developed countries were still calling for increased government activism and expenditure as a remedy for social and economic problems. All the while, the left was fragmenting between its traditional support base in the working class and the new, more individualistic "post-materialist" voters of the baby-boom generation.[26] Related to this was the debilitating impact of postmodernism on leftist parties. Postmodernism, a current of thought that emerged in many disciplines, especially since the 1960s, rejected the modernist ambition of remaking and improving the world according to human design. Doubting that there is such a thing as progress, postmodern philosophers generally call for radical individual liberation that allows people to find their own truths in a world in which there is no objective reality. Postmodernist philosophers often gravitated to left-wing parties, to which they presented grave dilemmas. Their stress on individual autonomy, subjectivism, and relativism did not always sit well with the collective traditions of the left. Moreover, these values gave rise to calls for individual liberation, including gay liberation, that offended working-class supporters of the left, who were more inclined to be conservative on moral questions. The result was infighting on the left and erosion of its support base. The rise to political power of the right, with its neoclassical agenda, in large part arose from the crumbling of the opposition.

Even before the election of Margaret Thatcher in 1979, administrations with neoclassical economic agendas had come to power elsewhere in the first world. In a number of third-world countries, governments had already begun experimenting with ingredients of the neoclassical recipe to deal with their own problems. The best-known case was Chile, where the 1973 coup d'etat opened the country to a group of Chicago-educated monetarists who instituted a program of monetarist shock therapy even stronger than the IMF had recommended.[27] But as early as the late 1950s, governments had begun using short-term adjustment programs to deal with balance-of-payments problems.

One could liken the early experiments with adjustment to the early experiments with ISI. Both were responses to circumstances that were not necessarily thought to be long term, and neither was necessarily linked to an overarching and radically new vision of what development should entail. In the 1970s and 1980s these approaches would be formalized by theorists into long-term development programs. In the earlier period, the possibility of foreign borrowing lessened the need for major adjustment.[28]

The ascent of conservative governments in Europe and North America in the 1980s injected neoclassical policy into the international financial bodies of these states, in particular the World Bank. Initially, the new conservative governments were responding to recession by raising interest rates. Falling commodity prices and dwindling export revenue in the third world made the debt crisis an inescapable reality. The World Bank, whose Basic Needs approach of the 1970s had devoted itself to poverty alleviation, suddenly shifted to a neoclassical approach in 1980. Instead of investing in specific projects, the Bank began providing loans to governments facing balance-of-payments difficulties on the condition these governments agreed to implement structural-adjustment policies.

This rightward shift was intensified by the appointment of A. W. Clausen to the presidency of the World Bank in 1981, at which time the Bank began to incorporate the new political economy into its policy.[29] Meanwhile, the IMF, which by its nature advocated restrictive fiscal policies, gained influence during these years because more and more developing-country governments had to approach it for financing. In some cases the World Bank and, especially, the IMF virtually forced third-world countries into accepting neoclassical policies in return for funding. In the course of the 1980s developing countries increasingly implemented neoclassical recipes for development.

The way in which neoclassical theory worked its way onto the agendas of third-world countries varied from case to case. For the early implementers, such as Chile, Côte d'Ivoire, Turkey, and Sri Lanka, which had all adopted neoclassical reforms by 1980, the new development policies were largely internally generated, although these governments quickly won friends in the IMF. First-world pressure to implement neoclassical development strategies had not yet reached its highest point. The World Bank was at this time governed by a Basic Needs philosophy that aimed to relieve the misery of the world's poorest citizens through grassroots development projects. After the turn to the right in the politics of leading first-world countries, which filtered down into lending institutions and donor agencies, pressure on third-world countries grew. Those most dependent on these same agencies and governments, namely those whose debt was great and whose economies were in the worst shape, found it almost impossible to resist the neoclassical development strategies that were thrust upon them. Notable among the most vulnerable were the majority of sub-Saharan African countries.

Nevertheless, the neoclassical recipe for development did not lack local advocates. Third-world academics had since the 1950s been making key contributions to the neoclassical critique. When Mexico shifted to a neoclassical strategy in the 1980s, development planners agreed on the need for structural reform, and reformists were rising to power in the government.[30] Similarly, in Ghana, after Jerry Rawlings seized power for the second time in 1983, there was a growing conviction that the country had no choice but to turn to the West, so dire had the economic situation become. The original reform program was in fact drafted by Ghanaian authorities, not foreign lenders.[31] And in India, Rajiv Gandhi began in the 1980s to surround his government with technocrats who favored a reform process. However, the full weight of structural adjustment began to be felt only after the ascent to power in 1991 of P. V. Narasimha Rao, who enjoyed the backing of new and modernizing elements in the Indian business community.[32]

In all of these cases, what seemed to tip the local balance in favor of reform was the gravity of the economic situation. Mexico's early flirtation with reform in the 1970s and early 1980s had failed to stem economic decline. India was nearly bankrupt when it moved into the severe phase of structural adjustment in 1991. And Ghana had arguably been in an even worse position when Rawlings, who originally articulated a radical stance, made an about-face and imposed an IMF-sponsored reform package.

Foreign backing made structural adjustment all the more attractive. In contrast, countries that resisted pressure to implement the proposed reforms found it increasingly difficult to obtain development assistance at the time they needed it most.

This neoclassical "assault" rolled on through the 1980s. In both policy and intellectual circles, opposition to the assault was weak, just as opposition to the initial wave of Keynesian intervention had been. Socialist thought, which by now constituted the main opposition to neoclassical theory in the field of development studies, was dealt a severe blow by the collapse of Soviet and Eastern European communism after 1989. Few Western socialists continued to advocate the Soviet model by the time the Eastern European revolutions rocked the world. Yet for as long as it existed, the Soviet model stood as a reminder that it was possible to build an economy on principles other than capitalist ones. Its collapse seemed to show that history's great experiment with socialism had in fact been what detractors such as Friedrich von Hayek had said it was all along: a dangerously romantic delusion.[33] It became fashionable to say that the sweep of liberal capitalism across the globe was now inevitable.[34] Those who held this conviction found further confirmation for their views in several of the formerly communist states of the Soviet bloc, in which the neoclassical advance seemed most rapid now that communist objection had been swept aside. The Harvard neoclassical economist Jeffrey Sachs rocketed to center stage in the economic policymaking of several of these governments, notably in Poland and, for a time, in Russia. "Shock therapy" was embraced by the governments of several of these countries, signaling a complete rupture with past ways.

The political weakness and the theoretical schisms within the left prevented it from raising a coherent objection to the neoclassical advance. In this context the rightward shift in policy and the rollback of the state appeared beyond debate, at least in the first world. In the third world, if the concerns of policymakers differed from those of their first-world counterparts, they were often too weak politically to resist the pressure for change. Countries that had avoided the debt trap, such as those in East Asia, retained much autonomy; meanwhile, big economies such as Brazil's retained a certain amount of sheer economic might that gave them more leverage in negotiations with first-world agents. But a great many third-world countries could only tailor or soften the policies these agencies demanded as a condition for support,[35] and were seldom able to refuse outright the neoclassical recipe for development.

I   The Neoclassical Recipe for Development

In the third world, neoclassical theory has been embodied in structural adjustment. Essentially, structural adjustment seeks to make both the state and the market more efficient in such a way as to accelerate growth and eliminate waste. Structural adjustment embodies the goals of neoclassical theory: it places the market at center stage, assigns the state a secondary role in development, and puts its faith in the potential of unfettered individual initiative, creativity, and ingenuity.

Sensitive to the obstacles placed in the way of such individualism by an interventionist state, structural-adjustment programs (SAPs) aim to remove perceived structural blockages to the efficient operation of markets. To this end, SAPs have usually included such elements as fiscal austerity and disinflationary policies, the privatization of state-owned enterprises, trade liberalization, currency devaluation, and the general deregulation of the economy, including financial and labor-market deregulation. SAPs also try to attract new private foreign investment in industry. All in all, SAPs seek to increase the powers and freedoms of entrepreneurs and investors, increase pecuniary incentives and competition, lower costs, restore macroeconomic stability, and make the state leaner and reduce its presence in the economy. This represents a decisive shift away from the state and back toward the market in what has come to be seen as a market-state dichotomy.

I   Fiscal Austerity

Fiscal austerity has been an important component not only of structural adjustment, but of the government-retrenchment programs seen all over the first world in the 1980s and 1990s. Fiscal austerity, or "belt tightening" as it is sometimes known, refers to government reductions in spending.

The logic is straightforward: the more money the government spends, the more money it takes out of the economy. This money is removed directly, through taxes, or indirectly, by borrowing. When governments increase their borrowing they compete with private borrowers, such as banks and corporate bond issuers, for scarce capital. The quickest way to attract lenders is to raise the interest rates paid to them. When interest rates go up, not only do businesses and consumers cut spending—because the cost of credit, by which so much spending is done, gets too high—but people with money to spend are persuaded to put it in the bank, where returns are high, rather than spend it or invest in lower-yielding securities (stocks).

Furthermore, whereas government spending can be productive over the long term, for political and other reasons it often prompts inflation. Much government spending takes the form of short-term transfers, including salaries, welfare payments, subsidies, and grants. Salaries, in turn, are often increased regularly to retain the support of the civil service and the military, often important underpinnings of a third-world government. Although this money is pumped back into the economy, if it is spent rather than invested it contributes to inflation: when the amount of money in the economy is increased more rapidly than the economy's productive capacity, buyers bid up the prices of goods.

So the combined effects of excessive government spending are seen as follows. By withdrawing money from the economy, through taxes and borrowing, and by driving up interest rates, the government "crowds out" private investors. Businesses find it hard to attract savings, and so must restrict their investment. Economic activity therefore declines.

High inflation rates can further inhibit investment because they reduce business confidence and make profits unsure. When potential profits seem likely to be eroded by inflation, investment in new technology becomes unappealing. Investors are then more likely to prefer investments that promise high returns in the short run but may contribute little to long-term development, such as property speculation and trade. Under such conditions, big investors often find it safer to export their money to havens where the value of their investments is less likely to be eaten into by inflation.

The solution to all of these problems appears simple. By reducing spending, governments enable interest-rate cuts. By capping pay raises and slashing budgets, they reduce inflation. Private investment thus becomes cheaper, and the environment for business more attractive. Economic activity should therefore resume.

In addition to lowering inflation and borrowing costs and encouraging investment, fiscal austerity should achieve another goal: government-spending cuts and caps on salaries and transfers should lead to a fall in real wages, which in turn should reduce overall consumption in the economy. This so-called demand compression should leave a surplus of unsold goods that will then be available for export. Ideally, more foreign exchange should flow into the economy as a result, stimulating economic growth and rectifying any imbalances in the current account (that part of a nation's balance of payments that covers income and trade flows).

| Privatization

The idea behind privatization is self-evident. Any economic vision based on the virtues of a private market economy tends to frown upon the state performing the functions that can be taken on by private companies. The severe abuses and inefficiencies often associated with public firms in the third world provide added impetus to privatization. It is also believed that the owners of a private firm have a greater interest in maintaining its efficiency and profitability than do public-sector managers, who operate more like civil servants and so might be given to such strategies as "empire building." In theory, privatization should raise money for cash-starved governments, enhance the normal operations of the market economy, and improve the efficiency and financial performance of the firms privatized. It is worth noting, however, that the argument for privatization has often been expressed more strongly by the political wing of the neoclassical school than by its economists.

Trade Liberalization, Currency Devaluation, and the Abolition of Marketing Boards

Trade liberalization refers to the effort to reduce hindrances to trade, thus maximizing the free flow of goods and services. At a general level, there are two types of trade liberalization. First there is the liberalization of foreign trade by eliminating or reducing qualitative and quantitative restrictions on imports, especially quotas; streamlining taxes on imports; and devaluing overvalued currencies. Then there is the liberalization of domestic markets through the elimination of price controls and marketing boards. In addition, because it raises the price of export goods in local terms, devaluation has often been promoted as a means to give producers of export goods an incentive to increase production.

As a rule, ISI regimes limited imports of consumer goods but favored industrial producers when it came to the allocation of hard currency, whose price was kept down by overvaluation. This hard currency was then used to import the inputs and capital goods needed in the production process. When a currency is devalued, its purchasing power on international markets declines. Therefore, trade liberalization and currency devaluation doubly hurt firms that formerly relied on imported inputs to produce consumer goods for a protected market: their import costs jump just as imported consumer goods start entering the country, stiffening competition. These firms must find ways of lowering their costs, or else go out of business. Wasteful firms go under; efficient survivors then pick up the slack and thrive. In sum, trade liberalization and currency devaluation should stimulate an economy to realize its static comparative advantage. In other words, an economy should specialize in those industries in which it has the lowest opportunity costs, abandon those that are expensive for the economy to maintain, and rely on imports to fill the gap. This will ensure that the economy's resources are used with maximum efficiency.

In a third-world country, especially a less-developed one, much of the static comparative advantage lies in the agricultural sector. Devaluation boosts this sector by giving export-crop farmers a leap in income, because even if the world prices on their crops remain constant, the new exchange rate generates a greater amount of local currency. Their improved position should ordinarily encourage farmers to augment their output. This practice of "getting the price right" is a key concern of the new political economy. Given this school's belief that producer prices on primary goods were artificially distorted downward by an interventionist state, it follows that rolling back the state should, all other things being equal, lead to increased prices and thus output. Although domestic market liberalization is intended to improve the functioning of all domestic markets, in practice the concern of the new political economy has been to improve agricultural markets.

One way to liberalize domestic markets is to abolish marketing boards. This should introduce competition into local markets, thereby increasing the bargaining power of farmers and enabling them to obtain better prices on their sales. If a marketing board is to remain, it can be pressured by donor agencies into paying farmers better prices. However, given the sometimes terrible abuses wrought by marketing boards in Africa, where prices designed to extract maximum revenues from producers were so low they simply drove producers out of the market, dismantling marketing boards altogether made sense.

Retrenchment and Deregulation

At a general level, government retrenchment and deregulation should free up the market and reduce the inhibitions on private entrepreneurs. Deregulation should enable the market to function more effectively, reducing price distortions and allowing them to find levels that encourage efficient resource allocation. Wages may drop, encouraging investors to hire more workers and use more appropriate labor-intensive technology. Bankers will find the business environment more conducive, and will expand their operations and make more credit available.

An added concern in most third-world countries is the battle against corruption, in which retrenchment is said to be a useful weapon. Paring back the state reduces channels to resource accumulation in the public sector. Opportunities for rent seeking diminish, there are less patronage appointments to be used to gain political influence, and there are fewer chances to use public firms or marketing boards to skim resources from the economy. Ambitious individuals will therefore turn to the private sector to seek upward mobility. Whereas in the 1970s in Côte d'Ivoire people with university degrees most often entered the public service, by the 1980s most of them were driven into business by the low salaries, unappealing promotion prospects, and generally unpromising environment of the public service.[36] Similarly, trade liberalization should allow highly skilled managers who formerly lobbied for quota shares to turn their attention to productive endeavors.[37]

I   Conclusion

Neoclassical advocates of structural adjustment recognized that there would be losers along with gainers, but contended that this was not necessarily bad because the losers were gobbling up scarce resources in an inefficient manner. Their collapse would thus free up resources for more efficient producers. Losers would include large, protected industries producing for the home market and inefficient state firms. These would now have to compete with imports, lose state subsidies and protection, and pay more for imported inputs. Among the winners would be export industries, smaller firms, and farmers, especially export-crop farmers. They would benefit from currency devaluation, their goods becoming cheaper on export markets; they would gain more credit thanks to financial liberalization; and they would have fewer restrictions on their behavior.

By the 1990s very few holdouts remained against structural adjustment. Many experiments with structural adjustment were less than wholehearted. India approached it hesitantly at first, and in Zambia the government was forced to backpedal when riots broke out. But elsewhere shock therapy was and continues to be applied. Few if any other options presented themselves to governments facing economic stagnation and persistent balance-of-payments crises.

In the late 1980s the situation in the development debate was thus the mirror image of that which had prevailed in the late 1940s. Where neoclassical theory had once been a dissenting school, and Keynesianism and structural economics the orthodoxy, in both academic and policy circles, neoclassical theory was the new orthodoxy. Socialism was reeling, structuralism weak, and ISI discredited.

A great many third-world countries have implemented SAPs of one variety or another. As a result, most of the third world has become a laboratory for a huge experiment in neoclassical theory. The results are instructive. They shed a great deal of light on the strengths, but also the weaknesses, of neoclassical theory. Just as neoclassical critiques had trickled in steadily throughout the late 1940s and early 1950s, posing questions that orthodoxy could not answer or pointing to phenomena that orthodoxy had trouble explaining, so it goes today. Except that now it is the neostructuralists and new schools of statist theorists asking the prickly questions.

I   Notes

1. See F. A. Hayek, *The Constitution of Liberty* (London: Routledge, 1990), part 1.

2. The "doctrine of unintended consequences" was originally expressed in the early eighteenth century by Bernard Mandeville in *The Fable of the Bees,* newly edited (New York: Capricorn, 1962).

3. Milton Friedman, "The Role of Monetary Policy," *American Economic Review* 58 (1968): 17.

4. Michael Carter and Rodney Maddock, *Rational Expectations: Macroeconomics for the 1980s?* (London: Macmillan, 1984).

5. See Robert Nozick, *Anarchy, State, and Utopia* (New York: Basic Books, 1974).

6. P. T. Bauer, "Remembrance of Studies Past: Retracing the First Steps," in *Pioneers in Development,* edited by Gerald M. Meier and Dudley Seers (New York: Oxford University Press, for the World Bank, 1984).

7. T. W. Schultz, *Transforming Traditional Agriculture* (Chicago and London: University of Chicago Press, 1964).

8. Harry G. Johnson, *Money, Trade and Economic Growth* (London: George Allen and Unwin, 1964).

9. Ian M. D. Little, *Economic Development: Theory, Policy, and International Relations* (New York: Basic Books, 1982), p. 160.

10. Hla Myint, "Economic Theory and the Underdeveloped Countries," *Journal of Political Economy* 73 (1965): 477–491.

11. See, for example, Deepak Lal, *The Poverty of "Development Economics"* (London: Institute of Economic Affairs, 1983).

12. Ian Little, Tibor Scitovsky, and Maurice Scott, *Industry and Trade in Some Developing Countries: A Comparative Study* (London: Oxford University Press, 1970).

13. Bela Balassa et al., *The Structure of Protection in Developing Countries* (Baltimore: Johns Hopkins University Press, for the World Bank and Inter-American Development Bank, 1971).

14. Lal, *The Poverty of "Development Economics."*

15. P. T. Bauer, *Equality, the Third World and Economic Delusion* (Cambridge, Mass.: Harvard University Press, 1981).

16. Anne O. Krueger et al., *Trade and Employment in Developing Countries* (Chicago: University of Chicago Press, for the National Bureau of Economic Research, 1983). A neat summary of the report can be found in Anne O. Krueger, "Trade Strategies and Employment in Developing Countries," *Finance and Development* 21, no. 4 (June 1984): 23–26.

17. Little, *Economic Development,* p. 139.

18. Little, *Economic Development;* Hla Myint, "The Neo-Classical Resurgence in Development Economics: Its Strengths and Limitations," in *Pioneers in Development,* second series, edited by Gerald M. Meier (New York: Oxford University Press, for the World Bank, 1987).

19. Little, *Economic Development.*

20. See Anne O. Krueger, "The Political Economy of the Rent-Seeking Society," *American Economic Review* 64 (June 1974): 291–303.

21. For a comprehensive critique of the rational-actor model, with particular reference to its application to politics, see Kristen Renwick Monroe, ed., *The Economic Approach to Politics: A Critical Reassessment of the Theory of Rational Action* (New York: HarperCollins, 1991).

22. Jagdish Bhagwati, "Directly Unproductive, Profit-Seeking (DUP) Activities," *Journal of Political Economy* 90 (1982): 988–1002.

23. I am indebted to Sudhanshu Handa for clarifying this distinction for me.

24. Robert H. Bates, *Markets and States in Tropical Africa* (Berkeley: University of California Press, 1981).

25. Mancur Olson, *The Logic of Collective Action* (Cambridge: Cambridge University Press, 1965).

26. Ronald Inglehart, *The Silent Revolution* (Princeton, N.J.: Princeton University Press, 1977).

27. At one point the IMF complained that the Chilean government was cutting too deep into its spending program. It has been said that this was one of the few times the IMF found itself prodding a third-world government to take a more interventionist role in the economy. See the Economist Intelligence Unit, *Chile to 1991* (London: Economist Publications, 1991), pp. 23–24.

28. Eliana Cardoso and Ann Helwege, *Latin America's Economy: Diversity, Trends, and Conflicts* (Cambridge, Mass., and London: MIT Press, 1992), p. 99.

29. In spite of the growing influence of neoclassical liberals in its ranks, the World Bank "never became a neo-liberal monolith, even in its most doctrinaire years." See Paul Mosley, Jane Harrigan, and John Toye, *Aid and Power,* 2 vols. (London: Routledge, 1991), p. 24.

30. Eduardo A. Gamarra, "Market-Oriented Reforms and Democratization in Latin America: Changes of the 1990s," in *Latin American Political Economy in the Age of Neoliberal Reform,* edited by William C. Smith, Carlos H. Acuña, and Eduardo A. Gamarra (New Brunswick, N.J., and London: Transaction Publishers, 1994), p. 2; Nora Lustig, *Mexico: The Remaking of an Economy* (Washington, D.C.: The Brookings Institution, 1992).

31. Jonathan H. Frimpong-Ansah, *The Vampire State in Africa: The Political Economy of Decline in Ghana* (Trenton, N.J.: Africa World Press, 1992), p. 153.

32. Jørgen Dige Pedersen, "Explaining Economic Liberalization in India: State and Society Perspectives," *World Development* 28, no. 2 (2000): 265–282.

33. Hayek's 1988 book, *The Fatal Conceit* (London: Routledge), in some ways the summation of a life's work, provided a powerful critique not only of socialist central planning, but of the very principle of state intervention in the economy.

34. Francis Fukuyama, *The End of History and the Last Man* (London: Hamish Hamilton, 1992).

35. Stephan Haggard and Steven Webb point out that while the IMF and World Bank have at times appeared to impose their will on borrowing governments, in many cases they have still failed to secure full adoption of the policies they recommended as a condition for support. See "What Do We Know About the Political Economy of Economic Policy Reform?" *World Bank Research Observer* 8 (1993): 157.

36. See John Rapley, *Ivoirien Capitalism: African Entrepreneurs in Côte d'Ivoire* (Boulder and London: Lynne Rienner Publishers, 1993).

37. Sebastian Edwards, "Trade Liberalization Reform in Latin America: Recent Experiences, Policy Issues, and Future Prospects," in *Latin America's Economic Future,* edited by Graham Bird and Ann Helwege (London: Academic Press, 1994), p. 17.

4

Neoclassical Reform in Practice

AFTER MORE THAN TWO DECADES OF STRUCTURAL ADJUSTMENT, WE NOW HAVE ample data by which to judge neoclassical theory in action. Proponents of structural adjustment can point to test cases that illustrate the virtues of reforms that roll back the state and free up the market. Not surprisingly, they often draw their examples of successful reform from the same list of countries they held up as examples of unsuccessful or at least questionable state-led development, such as Mexico, India, and Ghana.

Overall, however, the results of structural adjustment have varied widely. From among the welter of cases one can draw the following general rule: SAPs have done the most good in Latin America, and the least good in Africa. Breaking structural adjustment into its various components and studying their results closely can help to explain this discrepancy. Upon such examination the theoretical weaknesses or oversights of the neoclassical approach come to light. In addition to the moral concerns raised by structural adjustment, namely that SAPs have worsened the plight of the poor and deepened injustices in third-world societies, there appear to be serious economic and political drawbacks to neoclassical reform. It appears that neoclassical theorists, in focusing on the virtues of rolling back the state, overlooked some of the problems this process would beget.

I The Dividends of Structural Adjustment

At first glance, the evidence that structural adjustment has done its job seems compelling. Mexico approached structural adjustment reluctantly, but a deepening economic crisis in the mid-1980s led the country to move fully into currency devaluation, tight fiscal and monetary policies, and trade liberalization. For the first couple of years, conditions worsened and gross domestic product fell, but not everyone was losing out. In the first year of

73

liberalization nonoil exports rebounded 41 percent. The economy began to turn around in 1988, and by 1991 inflation was down, investment and foreign-capital inflows were up, and growth was healthy.[1] The 1994 free-trade agreement with the United States and Canada then provided a further fillip to growth. In 1995, however, the booming stock market collapsed. This highlighted the risks of a recovery based largely on foreign investment. When foreign investors began to doubt the Mexican government's ability to sustain the political and economic situation, especially in light of rising political violence and instability, they retreated en masse, pulling the carpet out from under the peso and threatening the economy with collapse. The government responded with a strict austerity program, but survived the crisis only because foreign creditors, notably the United States, offered the government billions of dollars in credit to shore up the peso and restore investor confidence.

One Latin American country whose SAP depends less on foreign backing is Chile, and Chile is today considered the world's best advertisement for structural adjustment. Local investors dominate the stock market more than in Mexico, so Chile is relatively safe from a Mexican-style collapse. As in Mexico, the first years of its neoclassical experiment, begun in 1973, yielded misery and few signs of growth, but by the early 1980s matters started to improve. Subsequently, the growth rate became one of the world's highest. New jobs have materialized to replace those lost, and exports have increased. Nor have the gains been concentrated in the primary sector: new products make up much of the increase in exports. Agriculture is becoming more advanced as new technologies are adopted. To top it all off, Chile has managed to improve its social indicators.[2]

India was, comparatively, a late adjuster. After the assassination of Prime Minister Indira Gandhi in 1984, her son Rajiv Gandhi came to power and began appointing technocrats who shared a vision to remodel the economy. However, the reform process tended to stop and go for a few years, after which the Congress Party spent a few years out of office. It was only after the Congress Party returned to power in 1991, when the government faced a balance-of-payments crisis, that things really changed. P. V. Narasimha Rao succeeded Gandhi, and his finance minister, Manmohan Singh, instituted India's version of shock therapy. The country's notorious protective barriers began to tumble: the maximum import duty was cut from 250 percent to 50 percent and growth, which was almost stagnant in 1991–1992, was up to 5 percent a couple of years later.[3] By the late 1990s, parties right across the political spectrum had united behind the new economic agenda. Significantly, the agricultural economy, in which most of the country's population lives and operates, has been largely untouched by liberalization, which has targeted the industrial sector.

Ghana was one of Africa's early adjusters, and also one of those that remained most faithful to the IMF–World Bank recipe, thus earning itself generous aid and credit. By the late 1970s its economy was in dire straits. On the last day of 1981 Jerry Rawlings led a coup that brought a group of radical military officers to power, but the economy resisted his government's initial efforts to turn it around. The Rawlings government soon changed course and raised producer prices, phased out subsidies on agricultural inputs, increased tariffs on public utilities and services, devalued the currency, and cut government spending. Price controls were abandoned, import licensing was eliminated in 1989, privatization was begun, and the public sector was cut back. Results came right away: growth resumed and continued at more than 5 percent for the rest of the decade; investment and savings rose; and export volumes increased, with cocoa exports expanding by 15 percent from 1983 to 1988, and volumes for other commodities doing even better.[4]

Like Ghana, Turkey was a fairly early adjuster. While Tunisia and Egypt began trying ingredients in the neoclassical recipe as early as the late 1960s, by and large, serious reform would not begin in the Middle East for another generation, after the 1991 Gulf War.[5] However, in Turkey, a balance-of-payments crisis prompted the adoption of a structural adjustment program in the 1980s. The Middle East's most famous state-led development strategy was then transformed by devaluation, the liberalization of trade and payments regulations, the abolition of price controls, the elimination of subsidies for state economic enterprises, tax reform, and other policies that shifted economic activity toward exports and the private sector. Initial results were encouraging. The economy rebounded, inflation dropped, exports and especially manufactured exports rose, and the country's foreign-exchange constraint disappeared.[6]

These apparent successes aside, structural adjustment is not without its failures. Within a few years, Turkish economic growth fell back and the export boom was offset by even faster-rising imports. While to its boosters Ghana may be an African success story, to its detractors the data conceal more than they reveal. It has long been said that Ghana succeeded because it had to. As Africa's test case for structural adjustment it could not be seen to fail, so foreign backers pumped aid and credit into the Ghanaian economy in order to sustain its recovery. In the absence of this official foreign investment, it is unlikely its economy would have fared so well, because domestic investment remained rather flat[7] (much the same has been said of the "successful" structural adjusters of the Middle East).[8] Given that first-world governments have been slashing their aid budgets for years, it is unlikely that they will fill the gap in many other African countries as they did in Ghana. Ghana may find the odd imitator, such as Uganda, which after 1987 also received strong foreign backing for its equally successful retrenchment program, but these countries remain the exception rather than the rule in Africa.

Africanists have been among the harshest critics of structural adjustment, and they can draw upon a wealth of evidence to argue that it has done more harm than good in Africa. The aggregate evidence shows that during the 1980s, the decade when structural adjustment began across much of the continent, growth slowed and agricultural output failed to keep pace with population growth, leading in turn to increased food imports; manufacturing did not increase its share of total output, investment dropped, consumption plummeted, per capita incomes declined, and unemployment rose.[9] In fairness, neoclassical theory did anticipate that a decline would often precede a rebound, as economies weeded out their inefficiencies. Nevertheless, by the end of the century, a strong economic recovery had yet to materialize in Africa. The most sanguine assessment now appears to be that if structural adjustment did not cause Africa's current economic woes, nor did it cure them.[10]

However, proponents of structural adjustment contend that things might have gotten even worse had African governments not imposed structural adjustment. This is possible, but a glance at Nigeria, Africa's most populous country, reveals that SAPs, though positive in some respects, did not yield all their anticipated gains, and produced some unexpected and undesired consequences. Although cocoa production rose under structural adjustment, cocoa processing by local plants did not. This was because many of the inputs used by those plants, such as spare parts and technical expertise, are imported from abroad and thus had their prices boosted by currency devaluation. Any increase in Nigeria's gross domestic production resulted from expansion in the primary sector. Growth in manufacturing has, if anything, been held back: whereas in the early years a layer of new export manufacturers appeared to be developing,[11] this dynamism soon ran out of steam.[12] While industries enjoying comparative advantage did prosper, as anticipated by neoclassical theory, the gains were offset by retrenchment and an accelerated fall in capacity utilization.[13] Meanwhile, many large firms have closed down while small firms, despite improved access to credit, have fared poorly. They have suffered from rising input costs, the contracting domestic market, and the lack of linkages to large firms that might otherwise have shifted from imported inputs to local sources to reduce their input bills.[14]

That Nigeria has increased its primary production, but not the value added to that production in the local economy, is a finding echoed elsewhere in Africa.[15] There may be more farm output, but not more industrial processing of that output, the products being exported raw. Moreover, there is reason to expect the situation to get worse. Cuts in government spending are hindering human-capital formation, the development of the pool of skilled labor, managerial talent, and engineering capacity. This obviously jeopardizes future industrial development.

This bodes ill for the future, because it puts countries back in the syndrome they tried to break out of long ago when structuralists first identified the problem of declining terms of trade. Development theorists continue to debate hotly whether the terms of trade for third-world countries are declining,[16] but it seems clear that successful development usually arises when economies not only increase their exports but also alter the composition of those exports—that is to say, when they develop and build export industries. Demand for third-world primary commodities, especially those from Africa, is generally rather inelastic: as their prices go down, or as first-world incomes go up, demand for the goods does not increase very much, or increases only to a point. Therefore, increased output soon floods the world market. In this way, Ghana's increased cocoa exports were more than offset by falling world prices.[17] Future revenue will need to be generated by new industries, not just the primary sector, but these industries are apparently not emerging in Africa today. Furthermore, whereas in Africa the gains of structural adjustment have been concentrated in the primary sector, it is not even clear that those gains will last: investment has lagged, and in some cases increased production costs have led input consumption to decline.[18]

The question, then, is why did broadly similar policies yield apparently successful results in Latin America, yet do so little good in Africa? We can begin to tackle this question by dissecting structural adjustment and looking at its results.

I Fiscal Austerity

Fiscal austerity programs, which were designed to restore macroeconomic stability to economies sorely lacking it, generally succeeded in meeting this goal. As a rule, inflation and interest rates came down and local demand was cut.

However, neoclassical theorists may have been mistaken in assuming that such macroeconomic stability would necessarily lead to resumed growth; little evidence has emerged to justify the assumption.[19] Instead, economies often remain sluggish in spite of the propitious conditions. Even the World Bank now admits that SAPs can stabilize plummeting economies without necessarily putting them back on the road to growth.[20]

Neoclassical theorists may have placed too much faith in the potential of a free market. Inflation and high interest rates are not the only conditions that inhibit investment; lowering them appears to be necessary to increase economic activity, but not sufficient. Increasingly it appears that government spending often complements private spending, with private investors waiting for the government to make the first move. For instance, a private company might not build its planned factory until the government has built a road and provided electricity and plumbing to the site. Lance Taylor has shown that, whereas neoclassical theorists contended that government spending crowded private investors out of the market, at least some government spending seems to "crowd in" private investment. The trick is to maintain or increase that type of spending while reducing inflationary spending. In contrast, sweeping government cutbacks can do more harm than good to long-term development prospects, especially if they eat into infrastructure development. In many African countries highways have potholes large enough to swallow small cars, telephones only work part of the time and even then reaching your party is a hit-and-miss pastime, and the electricity might go off without warning. Running a business, let alone getting the goods to market or obtaining supplies, is frustrating and costly. Local investors eschew manufacturing, and foreigners avoid the country altogether. The neoclassical faith that "openness" would suffice to attract foreign investment now appears mistaken, as foreign capital tends to pursue those opportunities that, more often than not, are created by government policies.[21] Clearly more rather than less government spending is required, even if cuts can be made in other branches of government.

Demand compression, which in addition to lowering inflation was supposed to free goods for export, at times has had unintended consequences. In Niger demand compression not only caused a recession, but did not produce an appreciable increase in exports.[22] Bangladesh had similar problems.[23] The reason is that the goods produced by local firms could not find markets abroad. This is often the case in third-world countries, where goods made for local consumers are crude, simple, of low quality, or geared to local tastes and fashions. In some third-world countries, for instance, hand soap leaves a film in the water, lacks perfume, and is sold in big, unpackaged blocks. This makes it affordable to local consumers, but unattractive to consumers in richer countries who are less price-sensitive and have more sophisticated tastes. As for those firms that were exporting, in Bangladesh they produced exclusively for the export market, so reductions in local demand did not free any more goods for them to sell abroad.

I Privatization

Privatization has arguably been the least effective of the elements of structural adjustment. Unlike fiscal austerity, which can be useful when imposed in a discriminating manner (cuts in some budgets, increases in others), privatization seems to recommend itself only in relatively specific circumstances.

I The Weak Case for Privatization

The belief that privately owned firms will by definition operate more efficiently and productively owes more to ideology than to economic logic. There is no question that by the late 1970s many public-sector firms all over the world had become poor performers; but the causes of poor performance were largely circumstantial, and not a direct result of public ownership.

In any event, it is questionable that public firms should be judged by the same criteria as private firms. Efficiency—the ability to produce maximum output with minimum input—and financial performance—budget-related items like profitability—provide the standard measures of firm performance. In general these are fair standards and many third-world public firms, with their bloated staffs, high budgets, unused production capacity, heavy debts, and consistent losses on their operations have all too often stacked up poorly.

However, these measures often fail to capture some of the particular tasks taken on by public firms. To begin with, the state must often tackle market failures or deficiencies. Monopoly, when there is only one seller, and monopsony, when there is only one buyer, are common in the third world. For example, many peasant farmers deal with traders who are either monopsonists or organized into oligopsonies. These traders often offer producers low prices and provide credit at extortionate rates, raking in excess profits that may then be sent abroad or used for luxury consumption rather than investment. This raises concerns not only of justice, but also of economic efficiency, because the profits might be more productively invested by the farmers themselves. In such cases, the government can intervene by creating a public firm. Even if the firm does not meet ordinary standards of quality, it may improve the economy by fostering competition.[24]

State firms may also confer beneficial externalities on the economy. Such externalities emerge when the costs of a product or service are concentrated in one firm while its benefits are spread throughout the economy. Private firms will avoid such undertakings, investing in something only if there is reasonable assurance of eventually recovering their costs. A common example of such an externality is human-capital formation, which is largely neglected by private markets in the third world. Often, the best way to develop a pool of engineering talent is to create an engineering firm; technological capability can be improved by creating a firm that specializes in research and development. Especially in less-developed economies, the costs of such firms will often exceed their revenues. However, if in the meantime a pool of engineering or scientific talent is built up, which can then be exploited by the private sector, the net gain to the economy may well outweigh the investment. This occurred in Brazil, where poorly performing public firms helped create technological capability,[25] and in Taiwan, where they helped foster industrial development and diversification by building up new industrial sectors.[26]

A private firm will ignore a subsector that is important to national development if the returns are too low and the risks too high, or if the firm is simply too conservative to venture into new territory.[27] In Côte d'Ivoire, for instance, the Banque Ivoirienne de Développement Industriel's (BIDI) unrecovered loans eventually drove it into bankruptcy, but not before it had funded the creation and expansion of many successful local private ventures. These ventures would probably not have developed otherwise, because the foreign-dominated private banking sector avoided Ivoirien entrepreneurs in favor of safe investments in large multinational corporations.[28] In this case, the losses incurred by one firm, BIDI, were made up several times over by the gains of the firms to which it loaned money.

However, even if we ignore that there can be legitimate economic reasons for a government to maintain inefficient, loss-making firms, there is actually little evidence to suggest that public firms are intrinsically given to poor performance. It is not self-evident that private firms will be more efficient than public ones,[29] nor that private investment will be more productive than public investment,[30] and there are many cases of third-world public firms providing exemplary models of efficiency and productivity.[31] What seems to govern the quality of a firm's performance is less who owns it than who runs it, the conditions under which it is run, and the structure of the industry in which the firm is located. In most cases in which public firms perform poorly, their performance can be improved without privatization.

It may be that the managers of a public firm are incompetent political appointees. Privatization can help clean out such an administration, but so can changes in the way appointments are made. It may be that a public firm's mandate is so extensive, or its hands so tied by such things as price controls, that it cannot hope to recover its costs. African marketing boards have often been handicapped this way.[32] Deregulating such firms and allowing them to operate as private agents can improve their performance. Laxity on the part of a firm's administration may arise from a practice such as "soft budgeting." This occurs when the state covers the losses of a firm out of public revenue, thereby eliminating the careful spending habits imposed by fear of bankruptcy. Severing the firm's links to the state and fixing its budget can help impose such discipline. If the inefficient public firm in question is a monopoly, it can enjoy the laziness afforded any monopoly, public or private. In such a case, privatization merely shifts the monopoly from one agent to another who is even less accountable to the public. A more promising solution is sectoral reform, such as creating a rival company in order to inject competition into the industry. In all the above cases, public-sector reform seems at least as likely as privatization to improve the performance of the firm in question. Where reform has been used instead of privatization, the results have been positive.[33]

The Case Against Privatization

In general, reducing the public sector to expand the private sector appears to exercise little impact on development.[34] Not only does privatization do less than hoped to improve firm performance and accelerate economic development, it seldom raises much money for the governments selling them.[35] Public firms are sometimes sold cut-rate for political reasons, perhaps to favor friends of the government; this might encourage rent seekers and at the same time worsen income distribution within the economy.[36] Meanwhile, money-losing firms must be sold at a loss; profitable firms may earn the government a good price, but less than they might have earned over the long term in dividends.[37]

However, the argument against privatization does not rest solely on the claim that it seldom does much good. In some cases it may even hinder development. It may consume resources that could be used more productively for other purposes: the money that investors use to buy shares in privatized firms might do the economy more good if it were used to create new firms.[38] Especially in the case of large-scale privatization programs, attracting investors into the purchase of public firms may crowd out investment in private firms at a time when capital is in short supply. It is instructive that the former Soviet bloc's most dynamic private sector, in Poland, emerged not from privatization but from the creation of new firms.[39]

In principle, therefore, privatization seems to offer little to third-world countries. Public-sector reform, coupled with policies to encourage new private investment, seems the best policy. However, there are times when political conditions may preclude the implementation of such policies, and privatization emerges as the best option. This point has been made in reference to the former Soviet bloc, in particular to Russia. According to some scholars, governments there did not have the option of releasing firms into a market economy because they first had to create such an economy from scratch. Meanwhile, the immense bureaucracy of the state-industrial sector could not always be trusted to cooperate in any effort to reform the public sector and thus undermine its own power base. Faced with such conditions, several governments judged crash privatization programs to be the best means to leap rapidly from state socialism to a market economy.[40] In a similar vein, African elites who have used public corporations to distribute gains and thereby build up political support networks may be unwilling, or unable if they have extensive political commitments, to reform their public sectors.[41] There may also be situations in which public firms need fresh influxes of capital in order to complete their reforms, but are unable to obtain this capital without selling some or all of their shares. Even in these situations, however, it is best to reorganize public firms, turning them from state- to market-oriented enterprises before selling them off. Relying on the private sector to do this may be a mistake.[42]

I Trade Liberalization

Trade liberalization, which is meant to improve resource allocation and firms' efficiency while increasing exports, has produced more mixed results than privatization. Earlier neoclassical work argued for a strong link between trade liberalization and growth, but the more recent empirical research finds that, in general, the connection is ambiguous at best.[43] Comparing aggregate data to case studies, the best conclusion seems to be that trade liberalization can do some good to an economy, but only if carried out in a discriminating manner that takes account of both local and international demand and supply conditions.

For starters, the world economy is dominated by the highly protected and subsidized economies of the first world. First-world governments can go to great lengths to shelter their own industries, and will impose quotas on third-world exports if they undercut those of their own producers. Mahbub ul Haq has estimated that the revenue the third world loses to first-world protectionism may be ten times greater than what it gains from first-world aid.[44] Presently the IMF, the World Bank, and first-world donor agencies can compel third-world governments to liberalize their foreign trade when they apply for assistance. This opens the third world to trade but has little impact on the trade policies of first-world countries.

When import liberalization forms part of a coordinated worldwide strategy, as in GATT, the world economy is likely to grow in response. Poor economies may not fare so well, however, because they have not yet developed industries that can take advantage of the improved access to foreign markets, and the arrival of cheap imported goods may discourage local entrepreneurs from moving into industry. Moreover, when individual countries liberalize trade on their own, as SAPs prescribe, the benefits of trade liberalization become even more suspect. At best, it is unclear that liberalization of this sort improves economic performance;[45] even its proponents find a weak correlation between liberalization and increases in exports.[46]

Nevertheless, it seems that as a country develops, exports can further fuel its development, and trade liberalization can facilitate this process. Successful episodes of trade liberalization in Brazil, Chile, Argentina, and Uruguay, resulting in improved exports and productivity, seem to confirm this.[47] Equally, growth in India's manufacturing sector and in its exports have outstripped the already healthy economic growth rate achieved under trade liberalization; similarly, Turkey's exports, especially its manufactured exports, have surged under liberalization.[48] However, liberalization may not generate similar benefits everywhere. Whereas it exercises a positive impact on the efficiency with which firms operate, this effect apparently becomes negative when liberalization is begun at an early stage of a country's economic growth.[49] Evidence also suggests that trade liberalization will be most effective if it is implemented after a country has built up its industrial export sector.[50]

From this one may infer that trade liberalization is most effective in relatively industrialized economies. Moreover, liberalization will not itself bring about such industrialization: contrary to the neoclassical position that opening up to trade and exporting will accelerate development, it appears that increased exports do not so much cause development as result from it.[51] Increased output and the development of new goods and services seem not to be affected as much by trade policy as by other policies. It is telling, then, to contrast the successful instances of trade liberalization mentioned above with the experiences of African countries, where trade liberalization has been unsuccessful, and even harmful. Although the World Bank defends trade liberalization as applied to Africa against its many critics, arguing that evidence of deindustrialization is not yet conclusive, the Bank nevertheless admits that Africa's export performance has been disappointing.[52] What distinguishes the African experiences with trade liberalization from those of the Asian and Latin American cases mentioned earlier is that in the latter, liberalization followed a lengthy period of sheltered state-led industrialization; in the former, this period did not last very long and industry remained relatively immature.

This sheds new light on the role of the state in economic development, partially redeeming import substitution's protection and subsidizing of industry. The policy of sheltered industrialization, as advocated by the import-substitution model, may not have sufficed to develop third-world economies, but it did build firms and industries that could later take advantage of the shift to liberal trade policies. The principle of nurturing industries that will later export is often referred to as the infant-industry model (IIM). IIM differs from import substitution in its attempt to build up an industrial base not to supply the local market but to move into the export market.

IIM and the neoclassical model differ in their conceptions of comparative advantage. Neoclassical theorists see trade liberalization as the best way for an economy to realize its comparative advantages, but they tend to concern themselves only with static comparative advantage, that is, the comparative advantages existing in the economy at present. In contrast, IIM aims to develop new skills and capacities, and thus focuses on what is called dynamic comparative advantage—comparative advantage that does not presently exist but could be developed by the state.

IIM will be discussed further in the next chapter. Yet even if one rejects IIM and argues that governments should only concern themselves with realizing static comparative advantage, it still may not follow that trade liberalization will on its own accomplish this. For example, Lesotho, a small mountain kingdom surrounded by South Africa, enjoys a comparative advantage in the production of wool and mohair. However, Lesotho's rugged landscape has a much less developed infrastructure than does South Africa. Moreover, the streets of Lesotho's capital, Maseru, are lined with stores belonging to South African retail chains. South African producers therefore enjoy better access to markets and distribution outlets, which lowers their costs of production. For Lesotho to realize its comparative advantage in the production of wool and mohair would probably require that the government invest in infrastructure and facilitate distribution.[53]

Critics of trade liberalization do not usually advise against pursuing it at all, but rather against pursuing it too soon. Before producers in poor countries can take advantage of trade liberalization the government must first improve the operation of markets, develop infrastructure and human capital, and possibly foster new firms or industries. Otherwise, trade liberalization will have little positive impact, as illustrated by the Nepalese case.[54] Worse yet, there is a risk that in such circumstances trade liberalization may do what it has done in much of Africa: drive budding firms out of business.[55] Even after these developments have been effected, the government should retreat from the economy slowly and cautiously, ensuring that investment does not drop and infrastructure does not deteriorate.[56] India's liberalization of its television industry offers a successful example of this kind of phased or selective withdrawal. The government liberalized trade, but at the same time assisted small producers in order to keep the industry from getting oligopolized by a few large producers.[57]

| Domestic Market Liberalization

If the benefits of import liberalization in the correct circumstances are clear, domestic market liberalization, or getting the prices right, has been a different matter. The new political economy argued that third-world output of primary products was sluggish because farmers were paid too little for their products, the state having skimmed off so much for urban and industrial development. According to this logic, reducing state involvement in the economy, liberalizing trade, and devaluing the currency would cause producer prices to rise and output to increase. Today, few theorists dispute the basic principle put forth by the new political economy that peasants respond positively to price incentives, all other things being equal. The problem is that all other things rarely are equal in much of the third world, and certainly not in Africa, where the new political economy was considered most relevant.

Policies of domestic market liberalization have been adopted all over the third world, so that there is a substantial pool of evidence by which to evaluate the experiment in getting the prices right. By and large, the results have not been encouraging: the desired results either did not materialize, or produced unforeseen and damaging consequences.

It is now clear that farmers will not respond to price increases unless they have access to a good transportation infrastructure: better prices for their products mean little to farmers if they cannot get those products to market. In addition, farmers need inputs that might not be available on a free market. Among these are affordable credit, cheap land and labor, and subsidized seed and fertilizer. Poor farmers frequently lack the capital to make the initial investment in export crops, and will continue to rely on subsistence production unless the government assists them in the transition. Once the transition is made, government-sponsored research and development—whereby extension workers in field stations promote the adoption of new technologies and train farmers in their use—are needed to further development. Farmers also need incentives to expand their output or shift from subsistence to cash-crop farming: increasing one's income does little good if there is nothing to spend that extra income on, and readily available consumer goods are among the important incentives to production.[58]

Too great a withdrawal by the state can reduce the availability of all these inputs and incentives and worsen already inadequate infrastructures. While it retreats in some areas, such as marketing and price setting, the government may need to advance in others, such as infrastructure development, credit provision, and extension. For instance, in several African countries market liberalization brought new traders into the economy, which heralded greater competition and thus higher prices for farmers. However, because capital was hard to obtain, few traders could make the leap from petty to large-scale trade, and the risk was that a few traders would oligopolize or even monopolize the market: a few families, rather than the state, would skim off revenue.[59] Much as India did with its television-manufacturing industry, African governments may need to intervene to assist the development of their markets and help traders to acquire capital, if they want domestic market liberalization to work.

On balance it appears that responses to price factors are greater in more-developed than in less-developed countries,[60] and Africa's experiences seem to confirm this. In general, export-crop production did not respond as favorably to price increases as had been hoped, and most of the increase in agricultural output resulted from food production, which is less expensive for farmers. Structural adjustment was not necessarily bad, but it needed more state intervention to become effective. As things stand, production costs remain too high for many farmers; intermediaries, free from competition or effective regulation, are absorbing price increases.[61] All in all, it is in the least-developed economies that the state will have to intervene most effectively if domestic market liberalization is to have any positive impact.

I Currency Devaluation

The new political economy advocated currency devaluation as one means to raise producer prices. At first glance the benefits of devaluation to agricultural output appear unquestionable. In Ghana, for example, the 1980s devaluations prompted remarkable increases in exports. However, closer examination reveals the gains to be less than they at first appear, and devaluation can in the meantime create problems.

To begin with, by raising the prices of imported inputs, devaluation can hurt urban industry. This may not be all bad. Those industries that rely heavily on imported inputs and produce for the local market will suffer, but one can argue that they place a drain on the economy and offer it few spin-off benefits because they are so little connected to it, buying few of their inputs locally. On the other hand, those firms that finish local inputs for export will become more competitive; they may expand their output, increase demand for local inputs, and thereby benefit the economy as a whole.

Nevertheless, each firm will factor the increased cost of its imported inputs into the prices of its finished goods. If, for example, a firm that makes plastic goods has to pay more for imported petroleum, it will recover its increased costs by raising the prices on the plastic goods it sells. This causes a shift in society's revenue. Urban consumers and food-producing farmers will pay higher prices but get little compensation in the form of higher incomes; their condition will worsen. Meanwhile, profit earners and export-crop farmers will be better off. The former are obviously rich to begin with, the latter tend to be so since, as was discussed above, farmers usually need to be relatively well off before they can become involved in export farming. This matters because profit earners and prosperous farmers often have a lower propensity to consume than do the other groups. This shift of income may reduce overall consumption and cause the economy to contract.[62]

This is still not so bad, if we assume that if instead of consuming more, these higher earners will invest more, presaging future development, and that in the meantime export revenue will make up for the contracting domestic economy. This, after all, is what devaluation is meant to do: shift resources to more efficient producers who will increase export revenue.

In sub-Saharan Africa, this is where the sequence appears to stop. Devaluation appears to have done little to stimulate exports from the region; the markets for its goods lie primarily in the first world, where demand is relatively inelastic. Devaluation increases output, and increased output lowers world prices, but these lower prices do not translate into increased demand the way they might for other goods.[63] Meanwhile, devaluation and/or the removal of subsidies on inputs causes inflation, owing to the jump in import costs. This effect is accentuated when farmers use a good deal of imported inputs, such as fertilizer.[64] Inflation may then erode the gains in producer prices. In 1994, for example, Côte d'Ivoire's currency was devalued and coffee and cocoa prices rose 50 percent, but the price of insecticides rose 60 percent. Similarly, studies in Kenya, Tanzania, and Zimbabwe found that rising input prices offset producer-price increases, dampening hopes that market liberalization would bring substantial increases in output.[65]

It also appears that the new political economy overestimated the degree of currency overvaluation prevailing under old regimes,[66] given the existence of parallel and black markets. Many travelers to third-world countries have experienced the hectoring of black-market currency traders offering better exchange rates than those set by the government. In other words, the official exchange rate prior to devaluation may not have been the rate prevailing in all of the economy. The same goes for output figures. Of the increases in output attributed to devaluation, some if not most result not from new production, but from the reentry into formal circulation of goods previously smuggled.[67] During the 1970s, for example, many Ghanaian cocoa farmers smuggled their crops across the border into Côte d'Ivoire, because the Ivoirien marketing board offered higher purchase prices than did the Ghanaian board. Once devaluation took effect in Ghana in the 1980s, not only did all these farmers begin selling to the Ghanaian board again, but many Ivoirien farmers joined the cross-border flow. Given our growing knowledge of informal and parallel markets,[68] it seems the new political economy overstated the detrimental impact of government policies on agriculture.[69] Such policies might not have decreased output so much as increased secrecy. In sum, the apparently positive changes produced by currency devaluation and state withdrawal may be exaggerated.

Should one conclude from all this that devaluation does no good? Perhaps not. In India, although devaluation hurt domestic industrial producers, for whom the cost of imported inputs rose, it led to a spurt in industrial exports.[70] As with other elements of the neoclassical strategy, it appears that devaluation can yield positive gains, but perhaps only in economies with strong industrial bases, and then only if the government intervenes to mitigate the effects of inflation or decreased consumption,[71] as well as to help producers take advantage of price changes. Still, all things considered, it appears that the benefits of devaluation are, in most cases, modest at best.[72] Given, too, that one of its key effects is to undercut the prices on the goods sold by competitors in other third-world countries, there is a case to be made that its chief beneficiaries are consumers in the first world. Seen this way, devaluation begins to emerge as one of the less effective weapons in the neoclassical arsenal.

▌ The Abolition of Marketing Boards

Abolishing marketing boards sometimes helps to liberalize domestic markets, and sometimes does not. African marketing boards were often monopsonies under no pressure to bid up the prices they offered farmers. In Ghana and Nigeria, marketing boards underpriced the goods they were buying, which led farmers either to stop growing cash crops or to smuggle those they produced. In theory, abolishing such monopsonies would allow a competitive market to emerge, increasing the prices paid to farmers and in turn encouraging them to increase their output.

To be fair, not all African marketing boards performed so badly. For example, Côte d'Ivoire's cocoa and coffee marketing board offered its farmers sufficiently attractive prices to keep them raising output year after year, even while it was skimming off revenue used by the government to build up the industrial sector. But such success stories were the exception rather than the rule in Africa. Nigeria's experience with abolition, which gave way to a competitive market that raised prices and pleased farmers, seems to affirm the virtue of state withdrawal from marketing.[73]

However, other countries lack Nigeria's history of competitive private trade. State withdrawal does not always give way to a free and competitive market: small and immature in comparison to those of the first world, third-world markets are more likely to be distorted and imperfect.[74] A traditional or family network, operating as a monopsony, may dominate trade; this problem is common in Africa.[75] Even in one of the more developed African countries, Côte d'Ivoire, a small number of distributors dominates the large market for printed cloth (*pagnes*), and their conservative behavior vis-à-vis suppliers serves as a sort of "private protectionism" against market entry by outsiders.[76] Equally, in rural India the crumbling bureaucracy does not enforce the laws governing agricultural contracts, so entrepreneurial families fall back on trust and reputation when entering contracts. Given that these can take generations to form, and rely on personal acquaintances working together, only those potential entrepreneurs within established family or caste networks can enter the market as traders.[77] At the same time, farmers can be especially weak. If they live in outlying regions, far from markets, they may have to sell to intermediaries who can charge high transport fees. The poor can be especially vulnerable on grain markets: unable to wait for a better price, they must sell during harvest time when prices are low and buy later in the season when prices are high.[78] In such cases, price increases might not reach the producers but are instead absorbed by small, privileged groups, who might even deposit their gains abroad.[79] When there is such pronounced market imperfection, "reregulation" offers more promise than deregulation.[80] In all such cases, what is needed is not less but more effective government. Whereas proper regulation is essential, even small interventions, such as providing a bicycle to an outlying village so that someone can go to a market center and negotiate with traders in a competitive environment, can make big differences.

It is difficult to say how widespread these sorts of market imperfections are in the third world, because little research exists on the subject.[81]

What does exist suggests mixed results,[82] and the safe rule would probably be to err on the side of caution and assume that all markets, at least in the less-developed countries, are guilty until proven innocent. Yet aside from their role in reducing market distortion, marketing boards can perform other important functions. One is the marketing of goods eschewed by private traders: in Africa, private traders often find subsectors such as cotton and bulk-food crops unappealing, so it falls to the state to market them.[83] A second function is market integration. Markets in poor areas are often highly segmented, again a common problem in Africa: price changes in one region will not work their way into others, so price incentives might not always reach the people they are intended to benefit. By establishing uniform national standards, marketing boards can help to integrate national markets.[84]

One of the most important functions of all is price stabilization. A completely free market in primary goods will reflect the vagaries of world commodity markets, with their sometimes violent price swings. Peasant producers are often more concerned with risk than with price, and will avoid growing crops whose price fluctuations are great, because they may not be able to take the risk of a bad year from fear of indigence or even starvation. By narrowing price fluctuations into a predictable range, marketing boards can encourage farmers to begin growing export crops that will earn the country foreign exchange.[85] For example, in India a marketing board stabilizes coffee prices, whereas cardamom is sold on a free market. Attracted by price stability, farmers have consistently augmented their investments in coffee production, thereby expanding output; in contrast, the cardamom market has remained sluggish.[86]

Admittedly, marketing boards are not always the best means to stabilize commodity prices.[87] Even when they are, they need not be the monolithic structures they have sometimes been in Africa. In Indonesia, the rice board purchases or releases less than a tenth of marketed output in any given year, and this modest intervention suffices to mop up excesses or keep the market stocked, effectively stabilizing prices.[88] The Indonesian approach may not work in many African countries,[89] but the Ugandan government employed a similar strategy in retaining the coffee marketing board after 1986 while allowing other marketing firms to compete with it. Producer prices rose and services to farmers improved, output picked up as a result, and today the state marketing board controls only 30 percent of the market.[90] However, as Kenya's experience shows, in the absence of selective state interventions to facilitate market entry, new firms might have a hard time entering into competition with a marketing board, even after liberalization,[91] in which case monopsony power will persist.

In short, marketing boards can still play an effective role in third-world economies, albeit on a smaller scale than was often the case in the past.

And to encourage the growth of competitive markets, a measure of state intervention may be needed.

I   Retrenchment and Deregulation

Neoclassical theory holds that retrenchment and deregulation should improve the economy's operation. Reduced spending should minimize the crowding-out effect on private investment, and financial deregulation should increase the availability of credit. Deregulated labor markets should also function more effectively. In addition, paring back the state should reduce opportunities for corruption, resulting in the economy's resources being used more effectively than in such unproductive activities as rent seeking.

I   *Crowding Out Versus Crowding In*

Lance Taylor has cast doubt on the crowding-out hypothesis by arguing that not all government spending crowds out private investment. Some crowds it in. Moreover, when public investment does crowd out private investment, it does not always do so in a one-to-one ratio.[92] Because of the new demands it creates in the private sector, public investment can in many cases provide an economy with net gains—a boost in economic activity greater than an unregulated market might have achieved.

Although the term "crowding in" belongs to Taylor, the idea that government investment can spur private investment goes back to Keynes, and recent studies have lent weight to his hypothesis.[93] In particular, research in several third-world countries has revealed public investment to be a key, and sometimes *the* key, determinant of growth in agriculture; retrenchment has had negative effects.[94] However, this is not an argument for across-the-board spending increases: Taylor himself acknowledges that not all government spending spurs private investment.[95] Nevertheless, it is mistaken to assume that reducing the state will always expand the market. Moreover, when governments choose to invest, it is best if they raise money through taxation rather than borrowing, and thereby soften the impact on interest rates.[96]

Another cautionary note is in order. Third-world governments have often cut their investment budgets by reducing their education spending, which often consumes a large share of a government's budget. However, it appears that future growth in world trade may favor goods with a higher human-capital content than in the past—in other words, sophisticated products rather than unprocessed primary goods.[97] Cutting education spending may save money today, but slow a country's development and thus cost it dearly.[98]

Financial Deregulation

Financial deregulation can raise rather than lower credit costs if banks choose to lend money to firms rather than invest in them. Requiring banks to invest directly in firms, and possibly also in long-term bonds rather than stocks, as Germany does, will cause capital to be used more efficiently.[99] When financial institutions make direct and long-term investments in firms, they encourage long-term development rather than short-term ventures geared to high dividends. Deregulation must also take account of the international environment. In the 1980s, deregulation in Latin American financial markets resulted in a massive flight of capital abroad, until domestic interest rates rose above those of first-world countries. But because the latter rates were at historic highs, the consequent leap in the cost of credit depressed investment.[100] Additionally, deregulation will yield few gains if the institutional framework to mobilize domestic savings is either absent or immature. In most African countries the private sector remains too immature to generate sufficient investment locally,[101] so the state must fill the breach. Finally, "crash" deregulation, as tried by Chile in the 1970s, can produce an overheated credit market, leading to a crisis and at worst a crash.[102] As we shall see in the next chapter, financial liberalization of this variety has been held at least partly responsible for the 1997–1998 Asian crisis, which caused so much pain in third-world countries. As with other aspects of structural adjustment, the lessons of all these cases are that effective reregulation is preferable to blanket deregulation, and that whatever deregulation takes place must be accompanied by state interventions to develop local credit institutions and maintain competition.[103]

There is an added drawback to financial deregulation. Like so many other structural-adjustment measures, it appears to worsen income and wealth distribution. It is common knowledge that in any country, rich borrowers with well-established credit ratings get "prime," whereas ordinary borrowers, particularly first-time borrowers with no credit history, must pay a premium on the interest rates at which they borrow. But where the differential in a first-world country might be a few percentage points, in the third world it can be huge. In Zimbabwe, for instance, thanks to credit deregulation, established businesses have been able to borrow on foreign markets: first-world creditors are happy to lend to well-capitalized third-world investors because they can earn higher returns there than they do lending to investors at home. Consequently, such established borrowers have been able to obtain interest rates as low as 5 percent, whereas small entrepreneurs borrowing locally pay in the order of 50 percent.[104] The purpose of state banks, even poorly performing ones like the Ivoirien development bank, has often been to provide credit to such small and medium-sized entrepreneurs, who can be very efficient but suffer from their lack of access to credit.

| Labor Market Deregulation

Labor market deregulation is expected to depress wage rates by reducing controls on them. Lower wage costs should in turn attract new investment and increase employment. However, if wages drop too low, local demand can follow, reducing demand for firms' output and erasing some of the gains lower wages are meant to bring investors.[105] The answer seems to be to find an optimum level at which firms preserve their advantages on both the local and international markets. This may require some form of wage regulation, but this need not be harmful. One literature survey on the subject concluded that minimum-wage rates in the developing world have caused little in the way of labor-price distortions.[106] Indeed, there appear to be cases in which minimum-wage rates actually reduce distortions.[107]

| Tackling Corruption

Although it seems logical that reducing the state should in turn reduce opportunities for rent seeking and corruption, this seems to be a case of "it depends." Barbara Harriss-White has done research in India that may provoke a second look at the new political economy's theory of rent seeking.[108] It may be, as the new political economy presumes, that rent seeking is economic and top-down: governments create regulations, like quotas, that offer opportunities for rent, and entrepreneurs pursue them. In that event, rolling back the state will eliminate such opportunities. Entrepreneurs will give up their rent seeking and devote their resources to other, preferably more productive activities.

However, it may be that instead of originating within the state, some types of rent seeking may emerge from society. Rather than being top-down and economic, rent seeking may be bottom-up and political. It may arise at times from a competition for power in which people bid for resources controlled by the state. In such cases, rolling back the state will not reduce rent seeking but will drive up the prices of the resources or positions of power being sought, because their greater scarcity will stiffen competition for them. This may change the balance of power within the state and strengthen the position of the wealthy and well-connected. Along these lines, Jean-François Bayart maintains that corruption in Africa is indeed bottom-up: even if a politician wants to be honest, the pressure from his or her supporters is so great that political survival, and in some cases physical survival, depends on using his or her position in the state to dole out favors.[109] Reducing the size of the state might not eliminate the competition for its resources, but rather make it keener and possibly violent.

The findings are too tentative to offer any basis for conclusions, but they do raise intriguing questions that deserve study. It may come to light that rent seeking is related more to a certain type of politics than to a mal-functioning economy. If so, this would certainly prompt a rethinking of the new political economy's theory of rent seeking and directly unproductive activities.

Why the Failures?
Theoretical Perspectives on Structural Adjustment

At the heart of the failings of structural adjustment lie some weaknesses in neoclassical theory. Some of the foundations on which the theory is built are questionable, particularly its microeconomic principles.[110] For example, neoclassical theory is rooted in the assumption that humans are rational, self-interested, profit-optimizing creatures. Yet there is growing evidence that individuals in third-world countries may be more likely to "satisfice" than maximize. This means they satisfy some minimum requirement, there-after turning their time and resources to other pursuits. If this is so, basing policies on the assumptions of profit maximization may backfire. For ex-ample, freeing up the market in order to maximize returns might not attract new entrants, because a free market might present not only high returns, but also high risks. Potential entrants who fear that their basic goals might not be reached may then stay away. In this case, government intervention to minimize risk, as in the example of the marketing board given earlier, may be more desirable than a completely free market.

Humans as Rational Actors

The assumptions that humans are rational and self-interested remain con-troversial as well.[111] There is good cause to doubt that people are consis-tently rational, and people may well behave in a self-interested manner less frequently than neoclassical theory assumes. The new political economy at-tributed the urban-biased industrialization strategies of third-world coun-tries to the interests of governing elites, but the development policies adopted by postcolonial states were often influenced as much by ideology as by self-interest.[112] A fallback position that Robert Bates has used is to acknowledge such influences while trying to incorporate them into a ra-tional-choice perspective.[113] An example is to suggest that an individual with altruistic desires is still making rational calculations in the way he or she seeks to satisfy those desires. This recalls the views of philosophers such as Ayn Rand who insist that individuals who enjoy sacrificing them-selves for others are no less selfish for it: after all, they only do what brings them pleasure. This, however, is dubious logic. For example, research on the motives of those who sheltered Jews during the Holocaust has revealed that they did not employ any kind of moral calculus in making their decision but were motivated by principles that stood above calculation and compelled them to act with little second thought.[114] Although there may not be an economy of affection, there certainly appears to be a society of one, whose rules will at times clash with those of the economy. Basing policies on the assumption that humans behave in a rational and self-interested manner may yield undesirable consequences. For example, in recent years some first-world governments have instituted performance targets with financial and other rewards to improve the performance of their civil servants. However, older civil servants complain that this weakens the sense of service that used to be strong in the state bureaucracy, because employees are rewarded not for looking out for the taxpayer but for themselves.

Many sociologists and anthropologists contend that humans do not behave as individuals, but as members of collectivities. For example, a person's cultural background is often said to influence the way he or she behaves.[115] Such academics resist grand theories and argue that each community will develop its own rules of operation: what works in the West will not necessarily work elsewhere. In particular, they often consider rational utility maximizing to be a learned behavior inculcated in Western societies, whereas third-world peoples are more likely to operate in an "economy of affection"[116] in which other goals—family and community obligations among them—take precedence and can even conflict with those of individual advancement.

Furthermore, add such theorists, just as we cannot expect other peoples to behave the way we do, we cannot apply the same principles to judge their behavior. For example, an influential school of thought has grown up around the French writer Jean-François Bayart, who maintains that corruption in Africa is not such a bad thing, but merely forms part of the practice of politics in Africa.[117] As disorganized, harmful, and immoral as corruption seems to the Western observer, Bayart suggests it is just the African way of settling questions over who gets what, which is the crux of politics. Moreover, he adds, it actually works pretty well in drawing most people into the political system. Structural reform to eliminate state inefficiency and improve the operation of the market will therefore probably be futile, because the behavior it is trying to eliminate is not dysfunctional and the goals of reform may not be feasible.

However, the views that humans are products of their cultures, and that cultures differ so widely that it is not possible to generalize about human behavior, do not go uncriticized. The suggestion that neoclassical theory engages in a sort of intellectual imperialism that pays little attention to the peculiarities of third-world cultures must be balanced against the fact that many third-world academics reject such an assessment. Indeed, many third-world economists are themselves neoclassical theorists. And Bayart's position has been condemned for endorsing a sort of fatalism, or even an admiration for severe abuses of power.[118] Nevertheless, these cultural perspectives do raise questions that development theory must always keep in mind.

Differences Between the First and the Third Worlds

Neoclassical theory also tends to assume that there is a fundamental similarity between first- and third-world economies, and this may be a mistake. In the third world there are arguably more serious market imperfections,[119] and there is more dualism. Highly modern urban industrial sectors coexist with backward rural areas, where the same economic rules do not apply. There is also more market fragmentation, as was mentioned in the discussion of market integration.[120] The combined effects of dualism and fragmentation can be seen in the operation of third-world urban labor markets. Ordinarily, high wages attract job seekers. As the supply of job seekers increases, the market reaches equilibrium, wages drop, and job seekers must look elsewhere. However, in many third-world countries, where the level of education is low, few people have the training necessary to perform difficult manufacturing jobs. Thus, increasing the supply of labor does not affect wages, and one finds the peculiar third-world phenomenon of what has been called cities of peasants: large numbers of people leaving the countryside and flooding into cities, looking for jobs that do not exist, while a small number of skilled workers continue to earn relatively high wages.[121] Such problems often demand government action to integrate markets, build up human capital, and encourage the development of labor-absorbing production technologies.

Third-world countries also must deal with the problems peculiar to technological latecomers.[122] Most production technologies originated in the first world, where consumers demand highly differentiated, highly promoted, and highly packaged goods. Supermarkets stock dozens of brands of toothpaste, all fundamentally the same but with cosmetic and packaging differences. However, third-world consumers need cheap, relatively undifferentiated goods: one toothpaste, abundant and inexpensive, will do. New types of technology may be needed to produce such goods, but this may necessitate market protection during an evolutionary period.

Perhaps most important, in the third world capitalist firms are not the only, or even the principal economic agents. Whereas firms respond to price incentives, other agents behave differently. For example, third-world households respond to price incentives, but they filter these incentives through traditional or structural arrangements. To cite one case, in parts of sub-Saharan Africa women cultivate food but men decide how the farm's revenue will be spent. In such circumstances, increasing producer prices might not cause women farmers to increase their output, because they will not see the fruits of their labors, and could better devote their energies to other tasks.[123] Not surprisingly, feminists have written some of the most vigorous criticisms of neoclassical theory, arguing among other things that neoclassical assumptions about individual behavior overlook the laws and customs that often restrict third-world women's control of money, property, and their own employment.[124]

| Non Sequiturs in Neoclassical Theory

In addition to flawed assumptions, there are also problems in the way neo-classical theorists put together their critique of statism. Some neoclassical theorists have been given to building straw men that they then set out to burn down, in the process not doing justice to the statist schools with which they took issue. For instance, Deepak Lal used the Indian case of planning to pillory development economics, but almost everyone agrees that the Indian case was one of bad planning, and few development economists stand by it.[125] Thus, to infer from instances of bad planning that planning is intrinsically bad is a non sequitur. John Toye puts it aptly that evidence of bad planning in some countries does not constitute "a general case against the use of economic controls, any more than a leaky pipe constitutes a general case against water engineering."[126]

Other non sequiturs in neoclassical theory result from deducing practical prescriptions from idealized models, which is always a risk in economics. For example, whereas perfect competition increases efficiency and productivity, it does not follow that in the real world, which is never perfect, more competition is better than less.[127] Even some neoclassical writers admit that the faith in competition lacks empirical justification.[128] Rather, it appears that the government must manage competition if it is to be made effective.[129] Therefore in the third world, switching to a market-oriented development strategy may require not a reduction in the state but an alteration of it.[130] In contrast to the neoclassical assumption that the economy is characterized by a public-private competition for resources, with any increase in one sector's activities necessitating a decrease in the other's, it now appears that under some circumstances the two increase or decrease together. State and market are often symbiotic rather than conflictual.

| Flaws in the New Political Economy

Finally, the new political economy, which seemed to offer a persuasive explanation for the failures of state-led development strategies in Africa and Asia, is now seen to be riven with flaws. In arguing against state exploitation of agriculture to build up urban industry, it overlooked those cases in which such a rural-urban transfer actually managed to build up industry without retarding agriculture, as in South Korea or Côte d'Ivoire. The new political economy overstated the cohesion and power of urban interest groups in their defense of protectionist development strategies. Sometimes it also misjudged the actual interests of those groups, expecting urban industrialists to favor inward-looking development strategies and rural elites to favor reform, whereas in fact sometimes the opposite relationship prevailed. The rural-urban dichotomy also captured little of the reality of African society, where much of the population lives in two economies simultaneously, young men in cities sending money back to their farming families in the country.[131]

Presented with such critiques, even initial proponents of the new political economy came to see that interest groups exercised less influence on policy than they supposed, and they accepted the role of such things as ideology.[132] Nationalism, in particular, can be used to prod people to forgo the material benefits of development for a time in order to allow a nation to build up its wealth.

Yet interest groups do have influence. At times they have frustrated reform policies that went against their perceived interests.[133] As Chapter 6 shows, there have also been times when interest groups have played key roles in underpinning shifts to reform. However, the common thread through all these cases appears not to be the geographic group identity—urban versus rural—put forth by the new political economy, but a class identity. Some rural groups, such as commercial farmers who produce export crops, might favor reform; others, such as small food producers, might not. Some urban groups, such as public-sector corporations and uncompetitive firms that produce for the home market and rely on imported inputs, might oppose reform; others, such as export manufacturers who purchase mainly local inputs, might not. And even when they share common interests, such groups must be organized in such a way that they recognize their common interests and act upon them in a coherent manner. What emerges from this view of political economy is not an urban-rural dichotomy but a more complex melange of classes and class factions, the alliances they form, the positions of influence they obtain within the state, and the hierarchy of power within the bureaucracy. As we will see in Chapter 6, studying such class politics may help us go further in understanding the way governments behave and the effectiveness with which they do it.

I The Moral Critique of Structural Adjustment

On New Year's Day 1994 the world woke to the news that a small, hitherto unknown band of peasant rebels had begun an uprising in Mexico. Here, in the midst of one of the supposed success stories of structural adjustment, was a throwback to a revolutionary age many had presumed dead. For the

Zapatista National Liberation Army, named after Mexico's great revolutionary hero Emiliano Zapata, the suffering of Mexico's peasantry had apparently become unbearable.

Though unique, the Zapatistas found parallels elsewhere. Almost every country that has pursued structural adjustment has seen its own share of strikes and riots in response to deteriorating living standards and rising unemployment. In a few cases, unrest became so serious that governments had to retreat from their adjustment programs. This points us in the direction of one of the most contentious issues related to structural adjustment. Whatever its overall results in any given place, structural adjustment is profoundly, even traumatically altering the economies of the third world. Although there is some debate about this,[134] most observers believe that poverty in the third world is worsening, at least in the short term. Education cutbacks have driven many students out of school; market liberalization has raised food prices, worsening malnutrition;[135] rapid growth rates have coexisted with high indigence rates.[136] In these and other ways, conditions for the world's poor seemed to worsen in the dying years of the twentieth century.

Yet all the while, many grow rich. It is not that structural adjustment reinforces existing divisions by helping the rich and hurting the poor. Rather, SAPs reshape society: some poor, such as peasant farmers selling export crops, rise while some rich, such as rent seekers, fall.[137] On balance, however, the results of most studies seem to point to a worsening in the distribution of wealth.[138]

Neoclassical theory can live with this. As Friedrich von Hayek always argued, income inequality leads to innovation and investment, whereas income redistribution hinders these activities. Thus, heightened inequality is the price that must be paid for development. One may add that Hayek, and other neoclassical liberals such as Robert Nozick, do not even see income inequality itself as a bad thing; they hold that leftist critics rely on an unjustified assumption that material inequality is unjust.

Assuming material inequality to be morally neutral, leftist theorists would still condemn it for its economic drawbacks. Whether income inequality raises investment and hence growth in rich countries, it appears to have the opposite effect in poor ones.[139] Furthermore, it not only reduces the size of the local market, but may equally hinder human-capital formation because poor families cannot afford to give their children full educations. Leftist theorists tend to believe that there is no trade-off between growth and welfarism, often citing Sri Lanka as a country that achieved growth with redistribution.[140] However, their arguments seldom convince skeptics, who maintain that over the long term investment yields more growth than does welfare expenditure, and thereby brings greater benefits to future generations. Yet the growing inequality of wealth and income all over the world provokes the question: For whom is development being engineered? If development is measured by such indicators as increases in gross domestic product, the gains of structural adjustment may be beyond dispute, at least in some cases. Yet most development theorists have long agreed that economic growth must translate into gains for the population at large to be considered development.

Defenders of structural adjustment argue that not all the economic ills of the last two decades can be blamed on structural adjustment. They refer to the problem of the counterfactual, namely, the possibility that things would be even worse had structural adjustment not been implemented.[141] As to the unequal distribution of wealth caused by structural adjustment, its defenders maintain that over the long term, the gains in economic productivity these policies produce, assuming they materialize, will trickle down to the population. In answer to the question, development for whom?, neoclassical thinkers such as Hayek have always answered, for future generations.

This answer poses a couple of problems. One is the apparent paradox in development theory that assumes that individuals are motivated by self-interest, but relies on their forgoing that interest for the sake of future generations. As for the trickle-down hypothesis, this may not be valid in the third world. Given, for example, dualism and the operation of labor markets, in many cases gains do not work their way down. A more likely scenario is that which unfolded in recent years in South Korea. Once the country attained a relatively high level of development, the population began to demand that the gains of development be redistributed by the government. This was a political rather than a market-driven distribution process. In any case, it takes a generation or more for the gains of development to percolate down to the mass of the population.

Nations or other groups may well choose to make such sacrifices for future generations. The South Korean government, for one, used nationalist ideology to appeal for self-denial on the part of its people. But such a recourse to public opinion has seldom preceded structural adjustment. Whereas in the first world, elections prompted the shift to neoclassical economic policies,[142] in the third world such policies were often imposed from above, often under donor pressure and in the face of popular anger. In India and in some Latin American countries, governments must at least win continued electoral support to stay their course, but others, especially in Africa, have not mobilized public support for the changes taking place.

As we will see in Chapter 5, it is not only morally and politically just for such policies as structural adjustment to arise from the demands of the people they affect, but it also makes sound economic sense. When a consensus in favor of reform is established, a program is more likely to yield positive results.

There are, finally, sociological and political dimensions to the moral critique of structural adjustment. Some political scientists have watched the retreat of the state with anxiety. In much of Africa, traditional structures have reappeared to fill the breach and perform such tasks as policing. Some Africanists regard this trend favorably, seeing in it a return to the traditional African village-centered way of doing things.[143] But in more urban settings, especially where such traditional community structures are long dead, state retreat has produced less benign effects. Rising inequality appears to be threatening the consolidation of democracy in the third world. And in some Latin American and Caribbean countries it seems to have fed the rise of drug gangs and increased lawlessness. In many countries, growing marginalization and the increasingly unequal distribution of wealth appear to have fueled ethnic conflict and/or the rise of Islamic fundamentalism, especially if certain groups perceive others to benefit at their expense.[144] Such results not only threaten the quality of life for many people, but the rising instability is arguably starting to jeopardize future development.

I Conclusion

Several conclusions can be made about neoclassical reform. The first is that the state must be brought back into development, even if only to make structural adjustment more effective. Second, the less developed a country is, the greater appears to be its need for state intervention. Rather than set the state against the market, as the development debate has traditionally done, the two need to be made to complement one another. It seems that statist policies, properly implemented, can help a country in the early stages of its development, after which a gradual opening to the market, enhanced by selective state interventions, should follow. In a rough analogy, the state should perhaps behave like a parent, who nurtures a child best not by stifling it, but by preparing it to go off into the world on its own.

Third, one of the lessons of neoclassical theory is that state interventions must enhance rather than repress the market. They must work with the market, improve its operation, and help it to reach its potential, rather than undermine it as some earlier statist policies tended to do. Fourth, material incentives such as high producer prices are important, though perhaps not as important as supposed by neoclassical theory, which considered them the key stimulus to economic development. Other factors, such as a national consensus in favor of development, and organization within those groups underpinning the state's change in policy direction, are likely to play a key role in successful development. All in all, we can say that the neoclassical critique provided a useful rejoinder to the statist theories it targeted, but that neoclassical theory is now itself being transcended.

Recent evidence suggests that there is no reason to assume that less government leads to faster growth. In fact, if there is any relationship between the two, it may be that in the aggregate, more government leads to more growth.[145] This is hardly a new claim—structuralists, among others, have been making it for years. Although they may have been inclined to think of themselves as Cassandras during the heyday of the neoclassical assault in the 1980s, those who advocate a strong state role have come back in from the cold.

I Notes

1. Nora Lustig, *Mexico: The Remaking of an Economy* (Washington, D.C.: Brookings Institution, 1992).

2. On Chile's experiences with structural adjustment, see A. R. M. Ritter, "Development Strategy and Structural Adjustment in Chile, 1973–1990," *Canadian Journal of Latin American and Caribbean Studies* 15, no. 30 (1990): 159–195, and Polo Diaz and Tanya Korovkin, "Neo-Liberalism in Agriculture: Capitalist Modernization in the Chilean Countryside During the Pinochet Years," *Canadian Journal of Latin American and Caribbean Studies* 15, no. 30 (1990): 197–219.

3. *Newsweek,* 13 February 1995.

4. Douglas Rimmer, *Staying Poor: Ghana's Political Economy, 1950–1990* (Oxford: Pergamon Press, 1992), chapter 8.

5. Roger Owen and Şevket Pamuk, *A History of the Middle East Economies in the Twentieth Century* (London: I. B. Tauris, 1998); Joel Beinin, "The Working Class and Peasantry in the Middle East: From Economic Nationalism to Neoliberalism," *Middle East Report* 29, no. 1 (spring 1999): 18–22.

6. Owen and Pamuk, *History of Middle East Economies,* chapter 5; Birol A. Yeşilada and Mahir Fisunoğlu, "Assessing the January 24, 1980, Economic Stabilization Program in Turkey," in *The Politics of Economic Reform in the Middle East,* edited by Henry J. Barkey (New York: St. Martin's Press, 1992).

7. Newman K. Kusi, "Ghana: Can the Adjustment Reforms Be Sustained?" *Africa Development* 16, nos. 3–4 (1991): 181–206. Slow growth in the domestic-savings pool has also been a problem in Malawi; see Ben Kaluwa, ed., *The Structural Adjustment Programme in Malawi: A Case of Successful Adjustment?* (Harare: Southern Africa Political Economy Series books, monograph series No. 3, 1992).

8. Karen Pfeifer, "How Tunisia, Morocco, Jordan and Even Egypt Became IMF 'Success Stories' in the 1990s," *Middle East Report* 29, no. 1 (spring 1999): 23–27.

9. Armand Gilbert Noula, "Ajustement structurel et développement en Afrique: L'expérience des années 1980," *Africa Development* 20, no. 1 (1995): 5–36.

10. David E. Sahn et al., *Structural Adjustment Reconsidered* (Cambridge: Cambridge University Press, 1997); Farhad Noorkabash and Alberto Paloni, "Structural Adjustment Programs and Industry in Sub-Saharan Africa: Restructuring or De-industrialization?" *Journal of Developing Areas* 33 (summer 1999): 549–580.

11. See Katharine P. Moseley, "Seizing the Chance: Economic Crisis and Industrial Restructuring in Nigeria," in *Beyond Structural Adjustment in Africa: The Political Economy of Sustainable and Democratic Development,* edited by Julius E. Nyang'oro and Timothy M. Shaw (New York: Praeger, 1992).

12. Tom Forrest, personal communication, 22 June 1995.

13. Anthony Enisan Akinlo, "The Impact of Adjustment Programs on Manufacturing Industries in Nigeria, 1986–1991: A Sample Study," *African Development Review* 8, no. 1 (June 1996): 61–96.

14. For details on the impact of structural adjustment in Nigeria, see T. Ademola Oyejide, "Adjustment with Growth: Nigerian Experience with Structural Adjustment

Policy Reform," *Journal of International Development* 3 (1991): 485–498; "Structural Adjustment and Its Implications for Financing Small Enterprises in Nigeria," *Small Enterprise Development* 2, no. 4 (1991): 31–39; Bola Akanji, *Cocoa Marketing Under Nigeria's Structural Adjustment Programme* (Ibadan: Nigerian Institute of Social and Economic Research monograph series No. 1, 1992); Yusuf Bangura, "Structural Adjustment and De-industrialisation in Nigeria: 1986–1988," *Africa Development* 16, no. 2 (1991): 5–32; Jonathan Dawson, "Responses to Adjustment: The Marginalization of Small Enterprises in Nigeria," *Small Enterprise Development* 5, no. 2 (1994): 18–24.

15. See, for example, Kusi, "Ghana." Also, in Tanzania, agriculture has grown but capacity utilization in the industrial sector remains low. See Ibrahim Shao, *Structural Adjustment in a Socialist Country: The Case of Tanzania* (Harare: Southern African Political Economy Series books, monograph series No. 4, 1992).

16. For recent contributions to this debate, see Pasquale L. Scandizzo and Dimitris Diakosavvas, "Trends in the Terms of Trade of Primary Commodities, 1900–1982: The Controversy and Its Origins," *Economic Development and Cultural Change* 39 (1991): 231–264; John T. Cuddington, "Long-Run Trends in 26 Primary Commodity Prices: A Disaggregated Look at the Prebisch-Singer Hypothesis," *Journal of Development Economics* 39 (1992): 207–227; Michael Bleaney and David Greenaway, "Long-Run Trends in the Relative Price of Primary Commodities and in the Terms of Trade of Developing Countries," *Oxford Economic Papers* 45 (1993): 349–363; Prabirjit Sarkar, *Terms of Trade of the South Vis-à-Vis the North: Are They Declining?* (Brighton: Institute of Development Studies Discussion Paper No. 304, 1992); Dragoslav Avramovic, *Developing Countries in the International Economic System: Their Problems and Prospects in the Markets for Finance, Commodities, Manufactures and Services* (New York: Human Development Report Office Occasional Paper No. 3, 1992); Timothy M. Shaw, *Reformism and Revisionism in Africa's Political Economy in the 1990s* (New York: St. Martin's Press, 1993), chapter 5. See also Syed Nawab Haider Naqvi, "Development Economics: The Winds of Change," *The Pakistan Development Review* 31 (1992): 341–363.

17. Donald Rothchild, ed., *Ghana: The Political Economy of Recovery* (Boulder and London: Lynne Rienner Publishers, 1991), p. 10.

18. This appears to have been the case in both Kenya and Ghana. See Peter Gibbon, "A Failed Agenda? African Agriculture Under Structural Adjustment with Special Reference to Kenya and Ghana," *Journal of Peasant Studies* 20 (1992): 66–71; Peter Gibbon, Kjell J. Havnevik, and Kenneth Hermele, *A Blighted Harvest: The World Bank and African Agriculture in the 1980s* (London: James Currey, 1993), pp. 29, 39.

19. See Khosrow Doroodian, "Macroeconomic Performance and Adjustment Under Policies Commonly Supported by the International Monetary Fund," *Economic Development and Cultural Change* 41 (1993): 849–864. See also Jacob A. Frenkel and Mohsin S. Khan, "Adjustment Policies of the International Monetary Fund and Long-Run Economic Development," *Bangladesh Development Studies* 20, nos. 2–3 (1992): 1–22.

20. See the World Bank's 1994 report, *Adjustment in Africa* (New York: Oxford University Press).

21. John Rapley, "Convergence: Myths and Realities," *Progress in Development Studies* 1, no. 4 (2001).

22. Patrick Guillaumont and Sylviane Guillaumont, *Ajustement structurel, ajustement informel: Le cas du Niger* (Paris: L'Harmattan, 2000); Kiavi Liman Tinguiri, "Crise économique et ajustement structurel (1982–1988)," *Politique Africaine* 38 (1990): 76–86.

23. Sultan Hafeez Rahman, "Structural Adjustment and Macroeconomic Performance in Bangladesh in the 1980s," *Bangladesh Development Studies* 20, nos. 2–3 (1992): 89–125.

24. Indonesia's rice marketing board provides a successful example of this. See Frank Ellis, "Private Trade and Public Role in Staple Food Marketing: The Case of Rice in Indonesia," *Food Policy* 18 (1993): 428–438.

25. Philippe Faucher, "Public Investment and the Creation of Manufacturing Capacity in the Power Equipment Industry in Brazil," *Journal of Developing Areas* 25 (1991): 231–260.

26. George T. Crane, "State-Owned Enterprises and the Oil Shocks in Taiwan: The Political Dynamics of Economic Adjustment," *Studies in Comparative International Development* 24, no. 4 (1989–1990): 3–23.

27. Morrelo de Paiva Abreu, *Journal of Economic History* 52 (1992): 496–497, suggests that many public firms in Latin America were established not because of a programmatic commitment to statism, but rather because private investors lacked interest.

28. John Rapley, *Ivoirien Capitalism: African Entrepreneurs in Côte d'Ivoire* (Boulder and London: Lynne Rienner Publishers, 1993), pp. 135–136.

29. Lance Taylor, "The Rocky Road to Reform: Trade, Industrial, Financial, and Agricultural Strategies," *World Development* 21 (1993): 586; Pranab Bardhan, "Economics of Market Socialism and the Issue of Public Enterprise Reform in Developing Countries," *Pakistan Development Review* 30 (1992): 566; Tony Killick, *A Reaction Too Far: Economic Theory and the Role of the State in Developing Countries* (London: Overseas Development Institute, 1989), p. 26; John Toye, *Dilemmas of Development* (Oxford: Basil Blackwell, 1987), p. 58; Al Bavon, "Does Ownership Matter? Comparing the Performance of Public and Private Enterprise in Ghana," *Journal of Developing Areas* 33 (1998): 53–72, and especially the literature review pp. 54–58.

30. Rati Ram, "Productivity of Public and Private Investment in Developing Countries: A Broad International Perspective," *World Development* 24, no. 8 (1996): 1373–1378.

31. For a few examples, see Crane, "State-Owned Enterprises and the Oil Shocks in Taiwan," and Syed Nawab Haider Naqvi and A. R. Kemal, "The Privatization of the Public Industrial Enterprise in Pakistan," *Pakistan Development Review* 30 (1991): 105–144. See also the conclusion to *State-Owned Enterprises in Africa,* edited by Barbara Grosh and Rwekaza S. Mukandala (Boulder and London: Lynne Rienner Publishers, 1994), which highlights successful public firms and the conditions underlying their performance. On the other hand, Roger Tangri argues that, on balance, public firms have performed poorly in Africa by "virtually any measure of economic performance." See "The Politics of Africa's Public and Private Enterprise," *Journal of Commonwealth and Comparative Politics* 33, no. 2 (1995): 169–184.

32. Nevertheless, there have been cases of marketing boards that were simply badly run, or were used largely for personal accumulation, as in Nigeria, Ghana, and Zambia.

33. See, for examples, Kaluwa, *The Structural Adjustment Programme in Malawi;* Jane Harrigan, review in *Journal of African Economies* 1 (1992): 151–162; Alan Whitworth, "Public Enterprise Reform in Papua New Guinea," *World Development* 20 (1992): 69–81; George Irvin, "Vietnam: Assessing the Achievements of Doi Moi," *Journal of Development Studies* 31 (1995): 725–750.

34. Richard A. Yoder, Philip L. Borkholder, and Brian D. Friesen, "Privatization and Development: The Empirical Evidence," *Journal of Developing Areas* 25 (1991): 425–434.

35. For details, see Paul Cook, "Privatization and Public Enterprise Performance in Developing Countries," *Development Policy Review* 10 (1992): 403–408; Naqvi and Kemal, "The Privatization of the Public Industrial Enterprise"; Ravi Ramamurti, "Privatization as a Remedy for State-Owned Enterprises," in *Latin America's Turnaround: Privatization, Foreign Investment, and Growth*, edited by Paul H. Boeker (San Francisco: Institute for Contemporary Studies, 1993); Armando Castelar de Pinheiro and Ben Ross Schneider, "The Fiscal Impact of Privatisation in Latin America," *Journal of Development Studies* 31 (1995): 751–776.

36. See, for example, Paul Cook and Colin Kirkpatrick, *The Distributional Impact of Privatization in Developing Countries: Who Gets What and Why?* (Bradford: Development and Project Planning Centre, University of Bradford, new series discussion paper No. 51, 1994).

37. In Sri Lanka, privatization apparently yielded the government net gains, partly because the firms in question became more efficient and so contributed tax revenues rather than drawing state subsidies; see Howard White and Saman Kelegama, *The Fiscal Implications of Privatisation in Developing Countries: The Sri Lankan Experience* (The Hague: Institute of Social Studies Working Paper No. 179, 1994). However, had it been possible to make the firms more efficient while keeping them in state hands, they would have contributed profits directly to the state's accounts.

38. Peter Murrell, "Privatization Complicates the Fresh Start," *Orbis* 36 (1992): 323–332; Barry Ickes and Randi Ryterman, "Credit for Small Firms, Not Dinosaurs," *Orbis* 36 (1992): 333–348.

39. United Nations Department for Economic and Social Information and Policy Analysis, *The World Economy at the End of 1993: Short-Term Prospects and Emerging Policy Issues* (December 1993), p. 7.

40. Barbara W. Lee and John Nellis, "Enterprise Reform and Privatization in Socialist Economies," *Public Enterprise* 11 (1991): 101–117. On the resistance of the Russian bureaucracy to reform, see Juliet Johnson, "Should Russia Adopt the Chinese Model of Reform?" *Communist and Post-Communist Studies* 27 (1994): 59–75; Leonid Gordon, "Russia at the Crossroads," *Government and Opposition* 30, no. 1 (1995): 3–26.

41. Tangri, "The Politics of Africa's Public and Private Enterprise."

42. For examples, see Jacques Alibert, "Le temps de l'ajustement: Chères ambiguités," *Afrique Contemporaine* 164 (1992): 109–119; David S. Young, "Going to Market: Economic Organization and Transformation in a Hungarian Firm," *World Development* 21 (1993): 883–899; Sultan Hafeez Rahman, "Structural Adjustment and Macroeconomic Performance"; Miriam Gervais, "Les enjeux politiques des ajustements structurels au Niger, 1983–1990," *Canadian Journal of African Studies* 26 (1992): 226–249; Gérard Roland, "On the Speed and Sequencing of Privatisation and Restructuring," *Economic Journal* 104 (1994): 1158–1168.

43. Rhys Jenkins, "Trade Liberalization and Export Performance in Bolivia," *Development and Change* 27 (1996): 693–716; Ann Harrison and Gordon Hanson, "Who Gains from Trade Reform? Some Remaining Puzzles," *Journal of Development Economics* 59 (1999): 125–154; Kishor Sharma et al., "Liberalization and Productivity Growth: The Case of Manufacturing Industry in Nepal," *Oxford Development Studies* 28, no. 2 (2000): 205–221; Francisco Rodriguez and Dani Rodrik, *Trade Policy and Economic Growth: A Skeptic's Guide to the Cross-National Evidence* (Cambridge, Mass.: National Bureau of Economic Research Working Paper No. 7081, 1999); David Greenaway et al., "Trade Liberalization and Growth in Developing Countries: Some New Evidence," *World Development* 25, no. 11 (1997): 1885–1892.

44. Mahbub ul Haq, *Human Development in a Changing World* (New York: Human Development Report Office Occasional Paper No. 1, 1992).

45. R. Adhikari, C. Kirkpatrick, and J. Weiss, *Industrial and Trade Policy Reform in Developing Countries* (Manchester and New York: Manchester University Press, 1992).

46. David Greenaway and David Sapsford, *Exports, Growth and Liberalisation: An Evaluation* (University of Nottingham Centre for Research in Economic Development and International Trade, Credit Research Paper No. 93/1, 1993); cf. Robert Wade, *Governing the Market: Economic Theory and the Role of Government in East Asian Industrialization* (Princeton, N.J.: Princeton University Press, 1990).

47. Sebastian Edwards, "Trade Liberalization Reforms in Latin America: Recent Experiences, Policy Issues, and Future Prospects," in *Latin America's Economic Future,* edited by Graham Bird and Ann Helwege (London: Academic Press, 1994). Edwards finds the results more ambiguous in Mexico and Brazil, hence John Weiss cautions against overstating the extent of these benefits. See Weiss, "Trade Policy Reform and Performance in Manufacturing: Mexico 1975–88," *Journal of Development Studies* 29 (1992): 1–23; Donald A. Hay, "The Post-1990 Brazilian Trade Liberalization and the Performance of Large Manufacturing Firms: Productivity, Market Share and Profits," *Economic Journal* 111 (2001): 620–641.

48. In India in 1995, the industrial sector grew 10 percent, and exports were up 27 percent; in Turkey, during the first half of 1995 exports were up 29.9 percent, and industrial exports were up 36.6 percent (*Indolink,* 31 December 1995; Wire Ltd., *Economic and Business Analysis* [Internet newsletters]). The downside, however, is that in both countries imports exceeded exports.

49. Hiroki Kawai, "International Comparative Analysis of Economic Growth: Trade Liberalization and Productivity," *The Developing Economies* 32 (1994): 373–397. Cf. Hans Singer, who argues that outward orientation works better in middle-income countries than in low-income countries: H. W. Singer and Sumit Roy, *Economic Progress and Prospects in the Third World* (Aldershot, England: Edward Elgar, 1993), p. 21.

50. Manuel R. Agosin and Ricardo Ffrench-Davis, "Trade Liberalization and Growth: Recent Experiences in Latin America," *Journal of Interamerican Studies* 37, no. 3 (1995): 42.

51. Behzad Yaghmaian, "An Empirical Investigation of Exports, Development, and Growth in Developing Countries: Challenging the Neoclassical Theory of Export-Led Growth," *World Development* 22 (1994): 1977–1995.

52. World Bank, *Adjustment in Africa,* p. 150. Critics contend that this report, the World Bank's defense of structural adjustment in Africa, is not sufficiently persuasive. See, for example, Paul Mosley, Turan Subasat, and John Weeks, "Assessing *Adjustment in Africa,*" *World Development* 23 (1995): 1459–1473; Peter Lewis, "The Politics of Economics," *Africa Report* (May-June 1994): 47–49.

53. See G. G. Storey, ed., *Agricultural Marketing in Lesotho* (Ottawa: International Development Research Centre, 1992).

54. Sharma et al., "Liberalization and Productivity Growth."

55. Frances Stewart, "Are Adjustment Policies in Africa Consistent with Long-Run Development Needs?" *Development Policy Review* 9 (1991): 413–436; Sanjaya Lall, *Building Industrial Competitiveness in Developing Countries* (Paris: OECD Development Centre, 1990), p. 66.

56. See Miguel D. Ramirez, "Stabilization and Trade Reform in Mexico, 1983–1989," *Journal of Developing Areas* 27 (1993): 173–190, on the case of Mexico.

57. Subhrajit Guhathakurta, "Electronics Policy and the Television Manufacturing Industry: Lessons from India's Liberalization Efforts," *Economic Development and Cultural Change* 42 (1994): 845–868.

58. On these points, see Jonathan Barker, *Rural Communities Under Stress* (Cambridge: Cambridge University Press, 1989), p. 203; Taylor, "The Rocky Road to Reform," pp. 588–589; Rahman, "Structural Adjustment and Macroeconomic Performance," p. 122; Helmke Sartorius von Bach, Johan van Zyl, and Nick Vink, "An Empirical Analysis of the Role of Prices and Access to Markets on Beef Numbers in Namibia: A Regional Approach," *Quarterly Journal of International Agriculture* 30 (1991): 224–235; Maarten Janssen and Dirk Perthel, "Seasonal and Regional Differences in Agricultural Supply Response in Bénin," *European Review of Agricultural Economics* 17 (1990): 407–420; David E. Sahn and Jehan Arulpragasam, "The Stagnation of Smallholder Agriculture in Malawi: A Decade of Structural Adjustment," *Food Policy* 16 (1991): 219–234; Richard C. Crook, "State Capacity and Economic Development: The Case of Côte d'Ivoire," *IDS Bulletin* 19, no. 4 (1988): 19; P. J. Gunawardana and E. A. Oczkowski, "Government Policies and Agricultural Supply Response: Paddy in Sri Lanka," *Journal of Agricultural Economics* 43 (1992): 231–242; Gun Erikkson, *Peasant Response to Price Incentives in Tanzania* (Uppsala: Scandinavian Institute of African Studies, Research Report No. 91, 1993); Howard White and Saman Kelegama, *External Shocks, Adjustment Policies and the Current Account: The Case of Sri Lanka, 1971–1991* (The Hague: Institute of Social Studies Working Paper No. 138, 1992); Dimitris Diakosavvas and Colin Kirkpatrick, "Exchange-Rate Policy and Agricultural Exports Performance in Sub-Saharan Africa," *Development Policy Review* 8 (1990): 29–42; Juan Antonio Morales, "Structural Adjustment and Peasant Agriculture in Bolivia," *Food Policy* 16 (1991): 58–66; Riccardo Faini, "Infrastructure, Relative Prices and Agricultural Investment," in *Open Economies: Structural Adjustment and Agriculture,* edited by Ian Goldin and L. Alan Winters (Cambridge: Cambridge University Press, 1992); Bola Akanji, *The Changes in the Structure of Export-Crop and Food-Crop Production Under the Structural Adjustment Programme: The Case of Cocoa and Yams* (Ibadan: Nigerian Institute of Social and Economic Research monograph series No. 11, 1992); E. Leigh Bivings, "The Seasonal and Spatial Dimensions of Sorghum Market Liberalization in Mexico," *American Journal of Agricultural Economics* 79 (May 1997): 383–393; Nlandu Mamingi, "The Impact of Prices and Macroeconomic Policies on Agricultural Supply: A Synthesis of Available Results," *Agricultural Economics* 16 (1997): 17–34; Awudu Abdulai and Wallace Huffman, "Structural Adjustment and Economic Efficiency of Rice Farmers in Northern Ghana," *Economic Development and Cultural Change* 48, no. 3 (April 2000): 503–520; Christopher B. Barrett, "The Effects of Real Exchange Rate Depreciation on Stochastic Producer Prices in Low-Income Agriculture," *Agricultural Economics* 20 (1999): 215–230.

59. Stephen Jones, *Agricultural Marketing in Africa: Privatisation and Policy Reform* (Oxford: Food Studies Group, International Development Centre, Queen Elizabeth House, 1994); Vanessa Scarborough, *Domestic Food Marketing Liberalisation in Malawi* (Ashford, England: Wye College, Agrarian Development Unit, Occasional Paper No. 13, 1990).

60. Faini, "Infrastructure, Relative Prices and Agricultural Investment."

61. Gibbon, Havnevik, and Hermele, *A Blighted Harvest;* C. S. L. Chachage, "Forms of Accumulation, Agriculture and Structural Adjustment in Tanzania," in *Social Change and Economic Reform in Africa,* edited by Peter Gibbon (Uppsala: Scandinavian Institute of African Studies, 1993); V. Seshamani, "The Impact of

Market Liberalization on Food Security in Zambia," *Food Policy* 23, no. 6 (1998): 539–551.

62. Kigane Mengisteab, "Export-Import Responses to Devaluation in Sub-Saharan Africa," *Africa Development* 16, nos. 3–4 (1991): 27–43. See also Paul Krugman and Lance Taylor, "Contractionary Effects of Devaluation," *Journal of International Economics* 8 (1978): 445–456.

63. Mengisteab, "Export-Import Responses to Devaluation"; Kigane Mengisteab and Bernard I. Logan, "Africa's Debt Crisis: Are Structural Adjustment Programs Relevant?" *Africa Development* 16, no. 1 (1991): 106.

64. As a rule, small farmers use fewer imported inputs than do larger ones, but this is not universal. Illustrating what sorts of proportions of inputs are imported, one study in Kenya found that imported inputs accounted for up to 34 percent of the ex-factory value of pineapples. At the low end of the scale, some export crops grown on small farms absorbed less than 8 percent of their ex-factory cost in imported inputs. See Jennifer Sharpley, "The Foreign Exchange Content of Kenyan Agriculture," *IDS Bulletin* 19, no. 2 (April 1988): 16–27.

65. Shahla Shapouri, Margaret Missiaen, and Stacey Rosen, *Food Strategies and Market Liberalization in Africa: Case Studies of Kenya, Tanzania and Zimbabwe* (Washington, D.C.: United States Department of Agriculture, 1992); Shao, *Structural Adjustment in a Socialist Country;* Chachage, "Forms of Accumulation."

66. Mengisteab, "Export-Import Responses to Devaluation."

67. Patrick Guillaumont, "Politique d'ajustement et développement agricole," *Économie Rurale* 216 (1993): 20–29; Chachage, "Forms of Accumulation"; Gibbon, Havnevik, and Hermele, *A Blighted Harvest.*

68. See, for example, Janet MacGaffey, *The Real Economy of Zaire* (London: James Currey, 1991); Alex de Waal, "The Shadow Economy," *Africa Report* (March-April 1993): 24–28.

69. Sara Berry, "Understanding Agricultural Policy in Africa: The Contributions of Robert Bates," *World Development* 21 (1993): 1055–1062.

70. United Nations Department for Economic and Social Information and Policy Analysis, *The World Economy at the End of 1993: Short-Term Prospects and Emerging Policy Issues* (December 1993), p. 10.

71. For his conclusion on the Jamaican experience, see Rupert G. Rhodd, "The Effect of Real Exchange Rate Changes on Output: Jamaica's Devaluation Experience," *Journal of International Development* 5, no. 3 (1993): 291–303.

72. Steven B. Kamin and Marc Klau, *Some Multi-Country Evidence on Effects of Real Exchange Rate on Output* (Basle: Bank for International Settlements Working Paper No. 48, 1997); Steven B. Kamin and John H. Rogers, "Output and the Real Exchange Rate in Developing Countries: An Application to Mexico," *Journal of Development Economics* 61 (2000): 85–109; Barrett, "Effects of Real Exchange Rate Depreciation."

73. Akanji, *The Changes in the Structure of Export-Crop and Food-Crop Production.*

74. Barry Lesser, "When Government Fails, Will the Market Do Better? The Privatization/Market Liberalization in Developing Countries," *Canadian Journal of Development Studies* 12 (1991): 159–172.

75. Guillaumont, "Politique d'ajustement et développement agricole."

76. Kouassy Oussou, personal communication, Abidjan, February 1994.

77. Barbara Harriss-White, *Agricultural Markets and Agro-Commercial Capitalism: Masters of the Countryside?* (Delhi and London: Sage, 1995), chapter 6.

78. Barbara Harriss and Ben Crow, "Twentieth-Century Free Trade Reform: Food Market Deregulation in Sub-Saharan Africa and South Asia," in *Development*

Policy and Public Action, edited by Marc Wuyts, Maureen Mackintosh, and Tom Hewitt (Oxford: Oxford University Press, in association with The Open University, 1992), p. 206.

79. See Cynthia Hewitt de Alcantara, "Introduction: Markets in Principle and Practice," *European Journal of Development Research* 4, no. 2 (1992): 1–16; Barbara Harriss, "Real Foodgrain Markets and State Intervention in India," *European Journal of Development Research* 4, no. 2 (1992): 61–81. Frank Ellis also argues that in the case of the Indonesian rice market, a liberalized market would end up being less free than one in which the state maintains a presence; see "Private Trade and Public Role."

80. Harriss and Crow, "Twentieth Century Free Trade Reform."

81. Ibid., p. 210.

82. See, for example, Emmanuel Grégoire, "L'état doit-il abandonner le commerce des vivres aux marchands?" *Politique Africaine* 37 (1990): 63–70; Jean-Paul Azam, "The Agricultural Minimum Wage and Wheat Production in Morocco (1971–89)," *Journal of African Economies* 1 (1992): 171–191; Jonathan Beynon, *Market Liberalization and Private Sector Response in Eastern and Southern Africa* (Oxford: Queen Elizabeth House, Food Studies Group Working Paper No. 6, 1992).

83. Gibbon, "A Failed Agenda," p. 58.

84. Harriss and Crow, "Twentieth-Century Free Trade Reform."

85. Guillaumont, "Politique d'ajustement et développement agricole"; Beynon, *Market Liberalization and Private Sector Response,* p. 7; Barker, *Rural Communities Under Stress,* p. 210.

86. D. Narayana, "Coffee Trade in India: Is There a Case for Privatisation?" *Economic and Political Weekly* 28 (1993): 1853–1856.

87. See the example of Papua New Guinea in Chinna A. Kannapiran, "Commodity Price Stabilization: Macroeconomic Impacts and Policy Options," *Agricultural Economics* 23 (2000): 17–30.

88. Ellis, "Private Trade and Public Role."

89. Jones, *Agricultural Marketing in Africa.*

90. E. A. Brett, "Rebuilding Organization Capacity in Uganda Under the National Resistance Movement," *Journal of Modern African Studies* 32, no. 1 (1994): 73.

91. Steven J. Staal and Barry I. Shapiro, "The Effects of Recent Price Liberalization on Kenyan Peri-Urban Dairy," *Food Policy* 19 (1994): 533–549.

92. Sebastian Edwards, "Why Are Latin American Savings Rates So Low?" Paper presented to First Annual World Bank Conference on Development in Latin America and the Caribbean, Rio de Janeiro, 12–13 June 1995.

93. See, for example, Eliana Cardoso, "Private Investment in Latin America," *Economic Development and Cultural Change* 41 (1993): 849–864.

94. Shenggen Fan et al., *Linkages Between Government Spending, Growth, and Poverty in Rural India* (Washington, D.C.: International Food Policy Research Institute Research Report No. 110, 1999); Jorge Fernandez-Cornejo and C. Richard Shumway, "Research and Productivity in Mexican Agriculture," *American Journal of Agricultural Economics* 79 (August 1997): 738–753; Thomas J. Kelly, *The Effects of Economic Adjustment on Poverty in Mexico* (Aldershot, England: Ashgate, 1999); K. N. Selvaraj, "Impact of Government Expenditure on Agriculture and Performance of Agricultural Sector in India," *Bangladesh Journal of Agricultural Economics* 16, no. 2 (December 1993): 37–49; Mark W. Rosegrant et al., "Output Response to Prices and Public Investment in Agriculture: Indonesian Food Crops," *Journal of Development Economics* 55 (1998): 333–352; Shenggen Fan and Philip G. Pardey, "Research, Productivity, and Output Growth in Chinese Agriculture," *Journal of Development Economics* 53 (1997): 115–137.

95. Lance Taylor, ed., *The Rocky Road to Reform: Adjustment, Income Distri-*

bution, and Growth in the Developing World (Cambridge, Mass., and London: MIT Press, 1993), p. 5.

96. Cardoso, "Private Investment in Latin America."

97. Juan Luis Londono, "Inequality, Poverty, and Social Participation." Paper presented to First Annual World Bank Conference on Development in Latin America and the Caribbean, Rio de Janeiro, 12–13 June 1995.

98. See, for example, Sudhanshu Handa and Damien King, "Structural Adjustment Policies, Income Distribution and Poverty: A Review of the Jamaican Experience," *World Development* 25, no. 6 (1997): 915–930.

99. Taylor, "The Rocky Road to Reform," pp. 585–586.

100. John Weeks, "Fallacies of Competition: Myths and Maladjustment in the Third World" (London: Professorial Lecture, School of Oriental and African Studies, University of London, 13 October 1993).

101. Charles Harvey, *The Role of Commercial Banking in Recovery from Economic Disaster in Ghana, Tanzania, Uganda and Zambia* (Brighton, England: IDS Discussion Paper No. 325, 1993).

102. Jose DeGregorio and Pablo E. Guidotti, "Financial Development and Economic Growth," *World Development* 23 (1995): 433–448.

103. See also Stephan Haggard, Chung H. Lee, and Sylvia Maxfield, *The Political Economy of Finance in Developing Countries* (Ithaca, N.Y.: Cornell University Press, 1993); Rob Vos, *Financial Liberalization, Growth and Adjustment: Some Lessons from Developing Countries* (The Hague: Institute of Social Studies, Sub-Series on Money, Finance and Development Working Paper No. 51, 1993).

104. BBC World Service, 1 March 1995. Case studies that made similar findings include Kailas Sarap, "Transactions in Rural Credit Markets in Western Orissa, India," *Journal of Peasant Studies* 15, no. 1 (October 1987): 83–107; Ade S. Olomola, "Changes in Rural and Agricultural Credit Policies Under Structural Adjustment in Nigeria," *Quarterly Journal of International Agriculture* 33, no. 1 (1994): 23–34. In Kenya, small and medium-size enterprises got easier access to credit, but could afford less of it because its cost rose, so the total volume of credit to them did not increase: see Penniah W. Kariuki, "The Effects of Liberalization on Access to Bank Credit in Kenya," *Small Enterprise Development* 6, no. 1 (1995): 15–23.

105. Taylor, "The Rocky Road to Reform," p. 587; E. V. K. Fitzgerald, "The Impact of Macroeconomic Policies on Small-Scale Industry: Some Analytical Considerations," in *The Other Policy,* edited by Frances Stewart, Henk Thomas, and Ton de Wilde (London and Washington, D.C.: Intermediate Technology Publications in association with Appropriate Technology International, 1990), pp. 385–386.

106. Steve Haggblade, Carl Liedholm, and Donald C. Mead, "The Effect of Policy Reforms on Non-Agricultural Enterprises and Employment in Developing Countries: A Review of Past Experiences," in *The Other Policy,* edited by Frances Stewart, Henk Thomas, and Ton de Wilde (London and Washington, D.C.: Intermediate Technology Publications in association with Appropriate Technology International, 1990), p. 67.

107. Azam, "The Agricultural Minimum Wage and Wheat Production in Morocco."

108. Barbara Harriss-White, personal communication, Oxford, May 1994.

109. See Jean-François Bayart, *The State in Africa* (London: Longman, 1993).

110. Killick, *A Reaction Too Far,* pp. 38–42.

111. For a critical examination of these issues, see the edition of *Political Psychology* (16, no. 1, March 1995) dedicated to an evaluation of rational-choice theory.

112. G. M. Meier concludes that rational-choice self-interest explains only some of the decisions that have been attributed to it by the new political economy. See "The New Political Economy and Policy Reform," *Journal of International De-*

velopment 5 (1993): 381–389.

113. See Bates's reply to critics in World Development 20 (1993): 1077–1081.

114. See Kristin R. Monroe, Michael C. Barton, and Ute Klingemann, "Altruism and the Theory of Rational Action: An Analysis of Rescuers of Jews in Nazi Europe," in The Economic Approach to Politics: A Critical Reassessment of the Theory of Rational Action, edited by Kristen Renwick Monroe (New York: Harper-Collins, 1991).

115. See, for example, Ian Boxill, "Science in the Social Sciences: A View from the Caribbean," Journal of Human Justice 6, no. 1 (autumn 1994): 100–110.

116. This term is associated with a school of development theorists known as the moral economists. See, for example, James C. Scott, The Moral Economy of the Peasant (New Haven: Yale University Press, 1976), and Goran Hyden, Beyond Ujamaa in Tanzania (Berkeley: University of California Press, 1980).

117. See Bayart, The State in Africa; cf. Patrick Chabal and Jean-Pascal Daloz, Africa Works: Disorder as Political Instrument (Oxford: James Currey, and Bloomington: Indiana University Press, 1999).

118. See, for example, Colin Leys, "Confronting the African Tragedy," New Left Review 204 (1994).

119. Killick, A Reaction Too Far, pp. 24–25, 50.

120. Frances Stewart, "The Fragile Foundations of the Neoclassical Approach to Development," Journal of Development Studies 21 (1985): 282–292; Killick, A Reaction Too Far, pp. 49–50.

121. Bryan Roberts, Cities of Peasants (London: E. Arnold, 1978).

122. Stewart, "The Fragile Foundations," pp. 285–286.

123. Harriss and Crow, "Twentieth-Century Free Trade Reform," p. 222.

124. On this subject, see Pamela Sparr, "Feminist Critiques of Structural Adjustment," in Mortgaging Women's Lives: Feminist Critiques of Structural Adjustment (London: Zed Press, 1994).

125. Toye, Dilemmas of Development.

126. Ibid., p. 77.

127. Weeks, "Fallacies of Competition"; see also Killick, A Reaction Too Far, pp. 44–46.

128. See Dwight H. Perkins and Michael Roemer, Reforming Economic Systems in Developing Countries (Cambridge, Mass.: Harvard Institute for International Development, 1991), p. 3.

129. Weeks, "Fallacies of Competition."

130. Killick, A Reaction Too Far, p. 28.

131. On these points, see Berry, "Understanding Agricultural Policy in Africa"; Thandika Mkandawire, "The Political Economy of Development with a Democratic Face," in Africa's Recovery in the 1990s: From Stagnation and Adjustment to Human Development, edited by Giovanni Andrea Cornia, Ralph van der Hoeven, and Thandika Mkandawire (New York: St. Martin's Press, and London: Macmillan, for UNICEF, 1992); Stephan Haggard and Steven B. Webb, "What Do We Know About the Political Economy of Economic Policy Reform?" World Bank Research Observer 8 (1993): 144; John Toye, "Interest Group Politics and the Implementation of Adjustment Policies in Sub-Saharan Africa," Journal of International Development 4 (1992): 183–197; Tor Skålnes, "The State, Interest Groups and Structural Adjustment in Zimbabwe," Journal of Development Studies 29 (1993): 401–428; Iyanatul Islam, "Political Economy and East Asian Economic Development," Asian-Pacific Economic Literature 6, no. 2 (1992): 84; Joan M. Nelson, "Poverty, Equity, and the Politics of Adjustment," in The Politics of Economic Adjustment, edited by

Stephan Haggard and Robert R. Kaufman (Princeton, N.J.: Princeton University Press, 1992).

132. See Robert H. Bates and Anne O. Krueger, *Political and Economic Interactions in Economic Policy Reform* (Oxford: Basil Blackwell, 1993), p. 456; Anne O. Krueger, *Political Economy of Policy Reform in Developing Countries* (Cambridge, Mass., and London: MIT Press, 1993), chapter 3.

133. See Chris Edwards on Malaysia, Ramesh Adhikari on Sri Lanka, and J. Keith Johnson on the Philippines in *Industrial and Trade Policy Reform in Developing Countries* (Manchester and New York: Manchester University Press, 1992); see also York W. Bradshaw, "Perpetuating Underdevelopment in Kenya: The Link Between Agriculture, Class and State," *African Studies Review* 33, no. 1 (1990): 1–28; Baldev Raj Nayar, "The Politics of Economic Restructuring in India: The Paradox of State Strength and Policy Weakness," *Journal of Commonwealth and Comparative Politics* 30 (1992): 145–171.

134. See Elliott Berg et al., *Poverty and Structural Adjustment in the 1980s: Trends in Welfare Indicators in Latin America and Africa* (Washington, D.C.: Development Alternatives, 1994); Lawrence Haddad et al., "The Gender Dimensions of Economic Adjustment Policies: Potential Interactions and Evidence to Date," *World Development* 23 (1995): 890–891; Kelly, *Effects of Economic Adjustment.*

135. For examples, see Aloysius C. Nwosu, *Structural Adjustment and Nigerian Agriculture: An Initial Assessment* (Washington, D.C.: United States Department of Agriculture, 1992); Francis Akindès, "Dévaluation et alimentation à Abidjan (Côte d'Ivoire)," *Cahiers de la Recherche Développement* 40 (1995): 24–42; Bocar Diagana et al., "Effects of the CFA Franc Devaluation on Urban Food Consumption in West Africa: Overview and Cross-country Comparisons," *Food Policy* 24 (1999): 465–478.

136. See, for example, Rothchild, *Ghana,* pp. 9–12, and Stephanie Barrientos, "Economic Growth Versus Poverty and Inequality in Chile: A Dualist Analysis" (Brighton, England: Development Studies Association Conference, 8 September 1993).

137. David E. Sahn and Alexander Sarris, "The Evolution of States, Markets, and Civil Institutions in Rural Africa," *Journal of Modern African Studies* 32, no. 2 (1994): 299.

138. Harald Beyer et al., "Trade Liberalization and Wage Inequality," *Journal of Development Economics* 59 (1999): 103–123; Harrison and Hanson, "Who Gains from Trade Reform?"; Sonia R. Bhalotra, "The Puzzle of Jobless Growth in Indian Manufacturing," *Oxford Bulletin of Economics and Statistics* 60, no. 1 (1998): 5–32; Kelly, *Effects of Economic Adjustment.* Results from Pakistan are more ambiguous, though. See the debate in the *Pakistan Development Review* 37, no. 4, part 2 (winter 1998), in particular the articles by Zafar Siqbal and Rizwana Siddiqui, "The Impact of Structural Adjustment on Income Distribution in Pakistan: A SAM-Based Analysis," pp. 377–397, and Rashid Haq, "Trends in Inequality and Welfare Consumption Expenditure: The Case of Pakistan," pp. 765–779, along with the comments that follow each paper.

139. Robert J. Barro, *Inequality, Growth and Investment* (Cambridge, Mass.: National Bureau of Economic Research Working Paper No. 7038, 1999); see also chapter 5 of Vito Tanzi and Ke-young Chu, eds., *Income Distribution and High-Quality Growth* (Cambridge, Mass.: MIT Press, 1998), and Klaus Schmidt-Hebbel and Luis Servén, "Does Income Inequality Raise Aggregate Saving?" *Journal of Development Economics* 61 (2000): 417–446.

140. On this discussion, see S. R. Osmani, "Is There a Conflict Between Growth

and Welfarism? The Significance of the Sri Lanka Debate," *Development and Change* 25 (1994): 387–421.

141. See, for example, Tony Killick, "Structural Adjustment and Poverty Alleviation: An Interpretive Survey," *Development and Change* 26 (1995): 305–331. Killick does not deny that structural adjustment is hurting the poor; he simply cautions against overstating the case, suggesting for example that in sub-Saharan Africa adjustment appears to have had little to do with worsening poverty. Cf. Werner Baer and William Maloney, "Neoliberalism and Income Distribution in Latin America," *World Development* 25, no. 3 (1997): 311–327.

142. Killick, *A Reaction Too Far.*

143. See, for example, Basil Davidson, *The Black Man's Burden* (London: James Currey, 1992).

144. See Jeremy Salt, "Nationalism and the Rise of Muslim Sentiment in Turkey," *Middle Eastern Studies* 31, no. 1 (1995): 24–25; J. 'Bayo Adekanye, "Structural Adjustment, Democratization and Rising Ethnic Tensions in Africa," *Development and Change* 26 (1995): 355–374; Alyson Brysk and Carol Wise, "Liberalization and Ethnic Conflict in Latin America," *Studies in Comparative International Development* 32, no. 2 (1997): 76–104. Structural adjustment has also been cited as a contributing cause to rising ethnic tension in Mexico and Rwanda. See Neil Harvey, *The Chiapas Rebellion: The Struggle for Local Land and Democracy* (Durham, N.C., and London: Duke University Press, 1998), and David Newbury, "Understanding Genocide," *African Studies Review* 41, no. 1 (April 1998): 73–97.

145. Zaidi Sattar, "Public Expenditure and Economic Performance: A Comparison of Developed and Low-Income Developing Countries," *Journal of International Development* 5 (1993): 27–49.

5

Development Theory in the Wake of Structural Adjustment

In the 1990s the World Bank began to show its concern over the negative effects of structural adjustment. In so doing it typified the way in which neoclassical theorists have tried to digest the lessons of structural adjustment. However, while neoclassical theorists were left to square uncomfortable facts with their theories, the left began advancing again—though not quite the same left as before. The radical left, though reinvigorated, is still engaged in academic debates, and much of the earlier statist development theory remains discredited. But a new version of statist thought has emerged to fill the breach that draws ideas from such sources as the new institutional economics and historical research on the twentieth century's development success stories in the Far East. From this has emerged a new school of thought, developmental-state theory, that in fact revives a very old idea: the infant-industry model. While this model appeared temporarily to have been eclipsed by the Asian crisis, which drew it into question, it retains its popularity.

1 Change at the World Bank

Even the World Bank, into which neoclassical theory made deep inroads in the 1980s, has come to accept the need for an increasing state role in economic development.[1] Many neoclassical theorists share this changing attitude,[2] recognizing not only that the market requires state management to realize its potential, but also that there may be some things that cannot be left to the free market, such as environmental protection.[3] Fundamentally, however, the neoclassical confidence in the market remains unshaken. Although they accept that a greater state role may be needed in the economy, neoclassical theorists differ from their colleagues on the left when it comes to specifying this role. Whereas leftist theorists tend to conceive a long-term vision of the state's role in the economy, neoclassical theorists are still anxious to minimize the scope and duration of state intervention, and above all to ensure that any intervention does not interfere with market forces.

Their proposed solution to the harmful social effects of structural adjustment illustrates this. Although they still believe that in the long run structural adjustment will produce a growth rate that will bring benefits to the entire population, they recognize that there is a bridging period during which many suffer. To sustain support for reforms during these difficult times, neoclassical theorists propose measures to target aid to affected groups. They prefer targeted aid to broader interventions such as price controls or subsidies on food, because the latter would reintroduce the problems of drains on government budgets and distortions in the market.

Take, for example, the problems caused by rising food prices, which are believed to have worsened malnutrition. Reimposing price controls would lower price incentives to farmers and drive down production, thereby forcing the government to import food, which would in turn bring back the balance-of-payments problems that structural adjustment set out to correct. The neoclassical solution is to maintain the market mechanism—no government intervention in price setting—while tackling those parts of the market that are failing consumers. According to this logic, most urban consumers might not like price rises but they can live with them. They will stop eating rice and start eating cassava, or stop buying bread made from higher-quality imported wheat. Grumbling as they eat, they will eat nonetheless, and in the meantime local producers will get the benefit of an increased demand for their goods. However, the poorest urban consumers, who simply cannot absorb the price increase and so will reduce their consumption, need to be relieved. The trick is to identify them and to target food aid at them alone.

Such targeting, which the World Bank favors,[4] has been used to direct to the poorest of society not only food, but also jobs, health care, and even help with school fees. Experiments in targeting have produced mixed results. In Jamaica, Chile, and India, food targeting allegedly reached the most needy without distorting the operation of the market at large,[5] but targeting in Zimbabwe and Ethiopia appears to have been less effective.[6] One survey of programs found that while there were positive results, in some cases they reached only a tiny proportion of the affected population. Significantly, such programs have tended to benefit men more than women,[7] an obvious cause for concern.

Critics of targeting contend that it alleviates the misery of the worst-off but does little to reduce poverty; it keeps people alive but does not improve their condition, which has already been worsened by structural adjustment.[8] For this improvement neoclassical theorists still place their faith in the long-term workings of the market. However, the World Bank's motives for supporting targeted aid reveal an innovation on its part: it is concerned less with market imperfection than with political stability. The hard truth is that, provided the urban working class remains well fed, no matter how unhappy, the market can tolerate the miseries of the poor. Those who are marginalized operate largely outside the market, and are a surplus labor force, so their worsening plight is not necessarily an economic problem. However, the problem, as Bob Marley once put it, is that a hungry mob is an angry mob. Anger at the policies drafted by bureaucrats in luxury hotels has often given way to violent protest, which can undermine structural adjustment. The World Bank, often criticized for being too economistic, now recognizes that there is also a political dimension to reform.[9] Economic reform depends on regime stability, and this in turn relies upon sheltering society's poorest from reform's harshest effects.[10]

I The Return of the Left

Whereas neoclassical theory still trusts in the long-term potential of the market, Chapter 4 showed that research on structural adjustment calls into question this potential in the absence of significant state intervention. Furthermore, there now exists a body of historical and political-economic research, which is discussed in this chapter, that presents a serious challenge to neoclassical theory. For these reasons the left has returned after a journey through the academic wilderness. It is not the old left of structuralism or dependency theory, but a new generation of leftist development thought that is forming in the wake of structural adjustment.

Neoclassical ideas still dominate in development practice. Yet as the "governing party," neoclassical theory must defend itself against uncomfortable questions being posed by the opposition; its defenses are not always persuasive.[11] The fallback position that strategies have failed only because they were not properly implemented can at times sound like the old radical-leftist disclaimer that one could not judge socialism for its failures because true socialism had never been practiced.

I The Radical Left

The radical left—those who have traditionally repudiated capitalism and searched for alternative development strategies—has had to shed its orthodoxies and toy with new ideas. The existence of the Soviet bloc, pernicious as it was, nevertheless fostered hope that there was another way to build an economy than capitalism. The collapse of the system at first demoralized the radical left, and some renounced the faith. Others hit the books and began to consider new ideas that were unthinkable before, which invigorated leftist debates.

Postmodernism, with its hostility to authority and its stress on individual autonomy, has worked its way into both the radical left and its development theory, largely because of the influence of poststructuralism in the social sciences. Rejecting grand revolutionary struggles as authoritarian, and seeking instead to grant individuals maximum power to determine their environment, radical postmodernists typically look for popular struggles in grassroots politics and activism centered on social movements such as women's and environmental groups. In development studies, this gave rise in the 1990s to a new school of thought known as postdevelopment theory.

Postdevelopment theorists make varying claims that, however, share a family resemblance. For starters, they take issue with the economism and materialism of mainstream development theorizing, and suggest that the definitions of development employed within the discipline are arbitrary ones designed to serve the interests of their practitioners. Seen this way, development is a Western concept imported into the third world in order to consolidate the power of dominant groups and draw more people into their orbit of control by, for example, bringing more human activity into commodity circulation. From this angle, the many failures of development are seen in a novel light. Created to serve the interests of the powerful, development was never intended to ameliorate the conditions of the poor.[12]

However, critics are quick to note the many successes of development—such as the near-doubling of life expectancy in the third world in the last century—that postdevelopment theorists choose to overlook.[13] Equally, they point to the irony that while postdevelopment theory rejects development as a Western concept or for its essentialist claims, its own postmodern discourse is both essentialist[14] and thoroughly Western.[15] If anything, development arguably originated in the third world itself when Latin American governments implemented policies to effect development in the first half of the last century. It was those policies that then helped to shape development theory, not the other way around.[16] The problem with radical postmodernism, as more traditional leftists point out, is that such activists can sound a bit like hippies who become stockbrokers yet insist they are still radical because they support gay rights. Although it advances the cause of the poor and downtrodden, radical postmodernism may not offer them a practical means to lift themselves from their poverty. Furthermore, more traditional minds on the left decry such postmodernism as closet conservatism that resigns itself to the existing order and redefines old-style resistance to change as opposition to authority.[17] Several critics argue that postdevelopment thought, like all postmodern theory, is closer to neoclassical economics than it is to traditional leftist principles.[18]

Nevertheless, if postdevelopment theory fails to provide answers to the pressing needs of today's third world, it remains useful for the questions it raises. Whether Western or not, it originates outside the traditional boundaries of development theory, and has thus launched a salutary broadside to the discipline. In particular, its focus on culture and its resistance to the commodification of all things is arguably helping to shake the complacency of theorists whose basic, materialist assumptions have until now been broadly shared by its various subschools.

An alternative path being charted by some Marxists is to further develop the idea of market socialism, with which the formerly communist regime in Hungary had experimented. One such school of thought is rational-choice Marxism.[19] Rational-choice Marxism adopts many of the practices of capitalism, such as markets, individual autonomy, and property, but grounds them in a system of public ownership in which all people are given a share of society's wealth through tradable stocks, which revert to the state upon a person's death, to then be redistributed to new generations.

Intriguing as they may be, such radical ideas will probably take a long time to work their way out of academic circles and onto the public agenda. For the time being, most of the left, in both the first and the third worlds,[20] has resigned itself to capitalism, and is concerned with finding ways to make it not only more just, but more efficient. For these purposes, it still foresees an important role for the state.

| The Contribution of the New Institutionalism

The left arguably has been vindicated in its suspicion of unfettered markets by the research of the new institutional economics. The neoinstitutionalists stress the regulatory role the state must play in a capitalist economy.[21] Markets do not exist in a vacuum, but require a detailed institutional framework. In the absence of this framework economic agents will resort to improvisation, which may damage the economy. In Russia, for example, the absence of contract law in the wake of communism's collapse quickly forced businesspeople to turn to criminal gangs to enforce their agreements.[22] This not only created new costs for businesspeople, but spurred harmful phenomena such as protection rackets and extortion, which discouraged potential investors from entering the market. Equally, structural adjustment seems to have done poorly in Central America because the state did not foster essential preconditions to the effective operation of markets, such as access to information, formal equality of economic agents, and free entry and exit to market contracts.[23]

Neoinstitutionalists also draw our attention to an economy's cultural milieu, highlighting the way this affects both the economy and the state's ability to regulate it. Individualist cultures tolerate innovation and give rise to generalized morality and formal contract enforcement; collectivist cultures, suspicious of difference, rein in innovation and foster in-group moralities that develop trust within communities but mistrust between them. In such cases the state must intervene to correct the "trust failure"[24] and replace enforcement of contracts by traditional in-groups with impartial enforcement by state agencies. Otherwise, a freely flowing economy will have difficulty emerging, as agents restrict their business contacts to other members of their in-group.

To the neoinstitutionalists, markets arise from human design. They do not emerge spontaneously, as such neoclassical theorists as Friedrich von Hayek argued. The state is seen as the best, if not the only agent for managing the creation of a market order in a third-world country. Yet in spite of the insights of the new institutional economics, most leftist development theorists have reentered the development debate not from the reference point of lands of capitalism gone mad, such as Russia, but of lands in which capitalism has blossomed, such as East Asia.

The Lessons of East Asia

One of the global economy's most significant postwar developments has been the rise of East Asia. For a long time Japan held everyone's fascination, but in the 1990s it came to be eclipsed by China; the Four Little Tigers or Dragons of Hong Kong, Singapore, Taiwan, and South Korea; and eventually the Southeast Asian economies, including Indonesia and Malaysia. These economies have filled the top ranks of the world's economies in terms not only of their overall growth rates, but also of their industrial and export growth rates. Today, if they have not already done so, these economies are leaving the third world and entering the industrial age—a remarkable accomplishment when one considers that in 1960 South Korea was on a par with Ghana in terms of its gross domestic product per capita.

This development provokes two questions: Why, and how? In accounting for success in East Asia, neoclassical theorists have argued that these governments employed market-based development strategies coupled with outward orientation, or essentially a noninterventionist trade strategy.[25] However, the experiences of East Asia seem to have dealt critics of neoclassical theory a stronger hand. This is because an inescapable ingredient in the East Asian development recipe has been an interventionist state, typically one that plays a more active role in the economy than that ordinarily preferred by neoclassical theory. With the possible exception of Hong Kong, intrusive states guided the development of these economies. In South Korea, for instance, the state protected selected industries through tariffs and quotas and nurtured them through export subsidies and subsidized credit, steered firms toward new forms of production, set export targets and rewarded those firms that met or surpassed them, owned and controlled all commercial banks and used them to direct funds toward favored industries, limited the number of firms allowed to enter an industry, set controls on prices and capital outflows, and distorted prices to favor certain industries. Moreover, when hit by external shocks the South Korean government did not use IMF-style adjustment policies, but borrowed its way out of crises, thereby keeping its development strategy on track.[26] Even the World Bank has admitted that state intervention was crucial to East Asian development.[27]

Added to this are the lessons of successful structural adjustment discussed in Chapter 4. Successful adjustment appears to have followed upon long periods of sheltered industrialization. This has led many theorists to conclude that an initial state-led phase should precede opening onto the market.

Such lessons have given rise to a new theory of the state, known as the developmental state. Originated by Chalmers Johnson, the concept of the developmental state has come to be closely, though by no means exclusively, associated with a group of theorists at the Institute of Development Studies of the University of Sussex. Influential figures in the developmental-state school include Gordon White, Robert Wade, Manfred Bienefeld, and Alice Amsden.[28]

The developmental state includes the following features. First, the state makes development its top priority, encourages the people to forgo the benefits of growth so as to maximize investment, and uses repression if need be to achieve this goal. Second, the state commits itself to private property and markets, even if only in the long run, as in China or Vietnam. Third, the state redistributes land, if necessary, to expand the national market and sweep aside the potential opposition of landed oligarchies to industrialization, and represses labor to keep wages low and thereby attract investment. Fourth, the state insulates itself against society, giving a highly skilled, technocratic bureaucracy the autonomy it needs from societal interest groups to impose discipline, at times harsh, on the private sector. Fifth, and most important, the state guides the market extensively, exercising strict control over investment flows (developmental states can be ardently nationalistic in restricting foreign investment in preferred sectors), using multifaceted import restrictions, regulating the terms of interaction between industry and agriculture, altering the incentive structure of the economy (getting some prices wrong if this is seen to benefit an emerging sector), promoting technological change, and protecting selected infant industries. At the same time, having chosen which industries it will protect and nurture, the developmental state opens the rest of the economy to foreign competition and penetration, even allowing poorly performing firms within the favored industries to wither on the vine. Finally, developmental states invest heavily in human-capital formation, in particular targeting the development of the technical and engineering corps necessary to modern industry.

| The Infant-Industry Model

In focusing on selected industries and intervening extensively to build them up not to supply the local market, but to export, the developmental state draws upon the infant-industry model. IIM has a long history. One of its earliest proponents, Friedrich List, developed his ideas in the mid-nineteenth century. List separated political economy from what he called the "cosmopolitical" economy of Adam Smith and his followers, arguing that Smith was wrong to generalize his conception of the entrepreneur operating with maximum freedom under a minimalist state to the outer world. Although it would have been appropriate in a world of economic equals, List argued, in the world economy of his time the conception would have led to British domination. He maintained that other states needed to protect and nurture their economies until they caught up with Britain. Only then could the world open up to unregulated competition.[29] List was not an economist by training, and some of his ideas seem simple to contemporary economists, but the tradition he started has proved popular ever since and has been added to many times, the developmental-state model being the latest innovation.

In its focus on statism and protection, IIM shares characteristics of the import-substitution model. Both are founded on the principle that conditions in the third world differ so markedly from those in the first world that the neoclassical model cannot be used to develop an economy whose conditions call for state intervention. To raise industry from the ground requires sums of capital beyond the reach of the private financial sector, but the state can gather these through borrowing, taxation, and the sale of primary exports. To build up its human capital—its engineers, technicians, managers, and skilled workers—the state must invest heavily in educating not just the children of an elite who might otherwise afford education, but the population at large. To acquire, adapt, and alter production technologies imported from the first world, firms must be given a learning period during which the state protects them from foreign competition. To make it possible for firms to move onto a market in which penetration and brand loyalty favor established producers, the state may need to reserve its domestic market to local producers for a set period of time. By these and other means, proponents of IIM suggest, the state can level the playing field between the third and the first worlds.[30]

Varieties of IIM have proved popular in practice. Indeed, List's theory was influential in Germany in the late nineteenth century, when that country embarked on an industrialization strategy that leaned heavily on state intervention. Several European countries used similar models, but in recent years the countries that have elicited the most interest in IIM have been Japan, South Korea, Taiwan, and Singapore.[31] Yet the list of countries that one could argue used IIM in one form or another is extensive and could even include a few African countries, such as Botswana[32] or Côte d'Ivoire. Even Chile, touted by neoclassical theorists as a great success story of the liberal, free-market model, would not likely have benefited as it has from structural adjustment had it not first passed through a phase of sheltered development: some of the industries that performed the best under liberalization were those nurtured by the state during its interventionist years.[33]

The variety of IIM epitomized by the developmental state differs from ISI in two important regards. First, rather than build an industrial base to satisfy local demand, it focuses on building an economy's export industries. Second, rather than provide local industry with relatively indiscriminate protection, as in ISI, governments enacting IIM "choose winners," selecting a few industries to nurture and relying on imports to satisfy the remainder of local demand. Within these favored industries, state bureaucrats decide which firms they will raise to maturity, and which will be left to die. It is a model that plans to alter the structure not only of the economy, but of its exports; the government intervenes not only to expand exports, but also to expand the share of manufactured goods in exports. In short, this model seeks to foster new comparative advantages, and so concerns itself with dynamic rather than static comparative advantage.

Those who favor such infant-industry protection are not advocating a state economy. Nor do they usually want the pervasive role adopted by the state in the initial phases of industrial development to persist over the long term. Contrasting the favorable experiences of protection in East Asia with the less favorable cases in South Asia, particularly India, and in Latin America, recent proponents of IIM seem to have coalesced around a general approach. Accepting the principle of outward orientation, they agree there should be a time limit on protection. This enables plant managers to know how long they have to build up their capabilities before their companies will be thrown onto the world market. In addition, IIM advocates maintain that government interventions should be in support of the market, or market-enhancing, rather than against the market, or market-repressing.[34] For example, although it is acceptable to assist the growth of a competitive firm, an inefficient one should be left to die. In countries that practiced ISI this was seldom done. Officials implementing an IIM model must be willing and able to impose discipline on private entrepreneurs—hence the need for the state to be somewhat insulated from societal pressures, to be "strong" or "hard."

The East Asian experiences offer one other interesting lesson to development theorists. Neoclassical theory, in particular the new political economy, criticized ISI for its urban bias—the way it transferred resources from the rural sector to urban industry, when in fact third-world economies' comparative advantages often lay in the rural economy. However, East Asian states also followed this practice.[35] By the same token, until the end of the 1970s the state in Côte d'Ivoire successfully fostered the growth of agriculture, using the surpluses from this sector to fuel a very rapid expansion in urban industry.[36] Therefore, it may be wrong to think of rural-urban transfer as a zero-sum game. In many countries the drift of people and income from countryside to city did slow economic growth, but in both South Korea and Côte d'Ivoire, states nurtured agriculture *and* industry, even if on balance more resources went to the urban economy.[37] In principle, third-world governments can exploit agriculture, or the primary sector in general, in order to fuel industrial development. However, the strategy will fail if they do not develop the primary sector as well—a shortcoming of which ISI strategies were often guilty.

Furthermore, it appears that the gains of such development must be distributed broadly. If a small share of the population controls most of the property and income, a small but rich class of consumers develops a taste for a wide range of products, which will be either imported or produced locally in such small numbers that their prices will be high (given economies of scale). This results in inefficient firms that cannot compete on foreign markets, which hinders the country's move into export industry. On the other hand, a large class of consumers with moderate incomes will create demand for large numbers of a narrower range of products. The narrow range of products allows firms to specialize, and the large demand allows them to take advantage of economies of scale and become internationally competitive.[38] One of the problems of ISI strategies was that they tended to concentrate the gains of development in the urban sector, a result exacerbated in many countries by an uneven distribution of land and income. This explains why developmental-state theorists advocate land redistribution as a key ingredient in development; it is a policy that requires a very hard state because it makes enemies of a privileged population.

The Asian Crisis:
The Eclipse of the Developmental State?

Just as the developmental state was in the ascendant in development studies, and was gaining in popularity outside of its heartland—for example, with the end of apartheid, many South Africans were calling on their country to adopt the model [39]—it fell suddenly from grace. The Asian financial crisis both shook its legitimacy and forced an abandonment of some of its precepts. The irony is that there is a strong case to be made that neoclassical reforms helped cause the crisis in the first place. It should thus not surprise us if some critics portray this as a situation in which a villain orchestrates an emergency so that he can ride to the rescue. Of course, the reality was not so simple.

Financial liberalization in the 1980s suddenly opened the world's markets to foreign investment. Today, there is arguably no sector as globalized as the financial one, with over a trillion dollars moving across international boundaries each day. That is roughly the gross domestic product of France.[40] But while most foreign investment still moves among rich countries, the third world was not left out of this new current. So-called emerging markets—third-world countries that provided attractive investment opportunities to foreign capital—drew in influxes of capital that greatly surpassed previous inflows. However, there was a new pattern to the investment. Instead of direct investment by foreign companies seeking either to establish branch plants or to globalize parts of their domestic operations, much of the new money was in the form of portfolio investment–seeking opportunities for rapid turnovers on the property, bond, and stock markets of the third world. With capital controls gone, they no longer feared being locked into investments in countries in which they had lost confidence, and the flow of funds helped spur a boom on the markets of several third-world countries, particularly those in East and Southeast Asia.

For a time, this seemed to speak to the virtues of neoclassical reform. But there was a storm cloud gathering. The investments created speculative bubbles in several countries, producing such excesses as that of the Bangkok property market. Due to the relatively large inflow of funds, they also led to a rise in the value of the currencies of the recipient countries. In the short term, this boosted the prosperity of the recipient countries, and so helped feed the rapid growth of the early 1990s in East Asia. But over the longer term, it weakened the competitiveness of exports from these countries. Eventually, when investors feared that the future growth of these countries would be threatened as a result, they began to withdraw their investments.

Matters were compounded by the fact that many of the managers of emerging market funds were not necessarily specialized in the politics and economics of the regions in which they were investing. They tended instead to treat the third world as an entity. So when the withdrawal of funds from a small number of East Asian countries began, the panic was not long to spread. It started in Thailand in the summer of 1997, where the bursting of the property bubble caused the value of the Thai currency, the bhat, to decline sharply. Investors eager to lock in their gains thus sought to pull out before the currency fell further, thereby eroding the value of their investments. In the process they created a self-fulfilling prophecy: fearing the decline in the currency's value, they withdrew their funds, which led to further declines in currency value and so further liquidations. The virtuous cycle that had accelerated the last few years of the East Asian boom thus turned into the vicious cycle underlying the bust.[41] Before long, other East Asian countries were affected by the contagion. By the summer of 1998, it had spread right through the world, leading to plunges in the value of the

Brazilian market and sharp rises in Russian bond yields. Faced with such pressure, several governments had to announce moratoriums on debt payments, and the world was staring at a fresh financial crisis.

Old Keynesians might have smiled wryly and said, What did you expect? Precisely because he saw capitalism as given to such boom-and-bust cycles, Keynes had called for state management to smooth their effects. But the time for Keynesian remedies was past. Those governments that were most likely to advocate such responses were in Europe and Japan. In either case, their economies were themselves only just emerging from recession, as in Europe's case, or mired in it, as in Japan's. Their countries thus enjoyed neither the resources nor the confidence to impose themselves on the situation. The situation was compounded by the fact that even were an alternative response available, the Europeans would have been unlikely to articulate it, since they were still working through the quasi-federal arrangements of the emergent European Union, and had yet to find a way to speak with one voice on any matter.

It thus fell to the U.S. government, whose booming economy gave its model unprecedented legitimacy, to lead the charge. And unlike the East Asian and European governments, it was squarely committed to the principles of neoclassical economics (despite its left-leaning rhetorical flourishes, the Clinton administration's policy was as governed by neoclassical thinking as that of its Republican predecessors). Once the Asian crisis began dragging down U.S. equity markets in the autumn of 1998, President Clinton persuaded congressional Republicans who were otherwise reluctant to bail out foreign governments to inject fresh credit into the coffers of the International Monetary Fund. This credit was then made available to governments suffering capital outflows in order to restore confidence to their markets. At the same time, faced with the global slump in demand resulting from East Asia's recession, the central banks of the Western countries began cutting interest rates, thereby encouraging investors to invest and consumers to spend.

In the event, the massive intervention served to restore stability to global financial markets, at least for a time. The significant thing, though, is that it also imposed neoclassical reforms on those countries that had held out against them in pursuit of the Asian model. The price for IMF assistance was policies that rolled back the powers of the state. Although East Asian politicians and intellectuals maintained that the solutions were inappropriate to their contexts, they were hardly in a position to hold out for better. Even though liberalization helped cause the crisis and many critics maintained that the IMF exacerbated it—for example, its insistence that capital controls would worsen the crisis was essentially proved false by those countries that employed them[42]—the U.S. government blamed it instead on the "crony capitalism" of the Asian model. It did so in spite of the fact that earlier in the decade, liberalization in different settings, such as Mexico and Turkey, yielded substantially similar outcomes.[43] The end result is that at just the time the neoclassical model was coming in for increasing criticism in intellectual circles, in policy circles, circumstances made it all but global in its reach. The East Asian model, on which many third-world scholars had pinned their hopes, was put on the defensive on its own home turf. The question is: Is the East Asian model dead, or merely sleeping? For that matter, has the spread of the neoclassical model to the far reaches of the globe really heralded the end of history, as some of its most ardent proponents claimed?

The triumph of the neoclassical model could not prove anything more than temporary, though, for the simple reason that the problems associated with it, which were identified in the previous chapter, persist. It is thus worth noting that the period after the imposition of the new neoclassical reforms in the wake of the crisis, compounded by the recession that followed the crisis and the consequent resource scarcities that saddled third-world governments, produced a wave of political instability across the third world. It is perhaps not coincidental that the years after 1998 saw a dramatic upsurge in street protests at international gatherings associated with the major economic powers or the forces identified with neoclassical reform. This "antiglobalization" movement stands, paradoxically, in the vanguard of globalization, having exploited the Internet to foster effective transnational links. Opposed thus more to the neoclassical model of the world favored by the U.S. Treasury Department—an arch-villain in the minds of activists—than to globalization as such, the antiglobalizers appear above all to be issuing a cultural critique of the homogenizing, economizing thrust of neoclassical reforms and their alleged goal of assigning prices to all things. This may explain why conventional economists and policymakers have been so mystified by these protesters, who often approach the world with a different template, more akin to that found in postdevelopment thought.

The rebound from the Asian crisis proved to be temporary. The new challenges facing poor countries continue to multiply. Meanwhile, the sharp ending of the U.S. boom at the turn of the century drew its free-market–based approach back into question. The search for alternative development models, with particular attention to an expanded state role, thus goes on.

I Conclusion

Just as the first generation of statist development models were not created by leftist theorists, but were soon taken up by them, so the developmental state has originated outside the left, but has become popular among many within it. Among other things, it vindicates their long-held suspicion of laissez-faire capitalism. A few have even been tempted to dust off socialist central planning and maintain that it is, after all, the most effective way to create a capital-goods base.[44] Although the argument has merits, most who favor infant-industry protection stop well short of state socialism.

Yet even if one shies away from the developmental-state model or infant-industry protection, it seems clear that successful development demands a greater state role in the economy than neoclassical theory has foreseen. If the market is to function effectively, it requires elaborate state guidance. Furthermore, if and when any kind of state retreat is made, it appears it should be done gradually. Hard and fast cuts in the state may do more harm than good in the long run. State retrenchment in some domains should be accompanied by advances in others. One or two steps forward may make a step backward more effective. For example, governments can enhance measures to liberalize domestic commodity markets by building roads to agricultural areas, providing credit and inputs to farmers, and so forth.

Proponents of shock therapy contend that in the former Eastern bloc, those countries that implemented deep reform most quickly, especially Poland, emerged in the best position. However, critics of shock therapy maintain that China's more gradual move away from socialist central planning has yielded even greater success.[45] Even those not so wedded to the idea of a strong state agree that gradual reform of state-socialist systems is preferable to the Russian approach,[46] even if gradual reform may not have been an option in Russia itself (a state that appeared beyond reform at the time of communism's collapse).[47] More telling, perhaps, is the Chilean experience, in which the initial phase of shock liberalization, from 1974 to 1981, yielded poor results. When Chile altered its strategy in 1982, maintaining liberalization within a context of greater regulation and state intervention, the real successes began.[48]

Today an active and effective state role seems critical in the least-developed countries, found mostly in Africa, in which poor infrastructure and market structure are causing producers to slide backward. For example, high transportation costs, due to poor infrastructure and monopolies that extract high profits, ate into many of the price gains that devaluation was meant to bring to coffee producers. As a result, West African producers lost market share to Indonesian and Vietnamese producers.[49] Only a greater state role will tackle such problems.

Whether or not such an expanded state role can emerge in these countries, let alone whether developmental states can emerge in many third-world countries, is a different matter altogether. As Chapter 6 shows, the developmental state may simply not be an option for many of the countries most in need of it.

I Notes

1. See, for example, the World Bank's 1991 *World Development Report,* p. 9, which recognized the necessary roles for the state in the economy, and the paper by Paul Krugman at the 1992 annual World Bank conference on development.

2. See, for example, Dwight H. Perkins and Michael Roemer, eds., *Reforming Economic Systems in Developing Countries* (Cambridge, Mass.: Harvard Institute for International Development [HIID], 1991). Associated for some time with the neoclassical school, the HIID authors in this volume call for a strengthened state role, including even a role in price setting.

3. See, for example, Fengkun Zhao, Fred Hitzhusen, and Wen S. Chern, "Impact and Implications of Price Policy and Land Degradation on Agricultural Growth in Developing Countries," *Agricultural Economics* 5 (1991): 311–324.

4. Marcelo Selowsky, "Protecting Nutrition Status in Adjustment Programmes: Recent World Bank Activities and Projects in Latin America," *Food and Nutrition Bulletin* 13 (1991): 295.

5. Margaret E. Grosh, "The Jamaican Food Stamps Programme: A Case Study in Targeting," *Food Policy* 17 (1992): 23–40; Stephanie Barrientos, "Economic Growth Versus Poverty and Inequality in Chile: A Dualist Analysis" (Brighton, England: Development Studies Association Conference, 8 September 1993); G. Chellaraj, B. Brorsen, and Paul L. Farris, "Effects of Subsidized Wheat Consumption by the State in India," *Agricultural Economics* 7 (1992): 1–12.

6. Guy C. Z. Mhone, "The Social Dimensions of Adjustment (SDA) Programme in Zimbabwe: A Critical Review and Assessment," *European Journal of Development Research* 7, no. 1 (1995): 101–123. Daniel C. Clay et al., "Food Aid Targeting in Ethiopia,: A Study of Who Needs It and Who Gets It," *Food Policy* 24 (1999): 391–409.

7. Jessica Vivian, "How Safe Are 'Social Safety Nets'? Adjustment and Social Sector Restructuring in Developing Countries," *European Journal of Development Research* 7, no. 1 (1995): 1–25.

8. Barrientos, "Economic Growth Versus Poverty."

9. With the appointment of James Wolfensohn to the presidency in 1995, the World Bank moved further away from the steadfast commitment to neoclassical theory it had made in the 1980s. Shortly after his appointment, the Bank's annual development report came out in support of trade unions, a move that would have made a neoclassical purist such as Friedrich Hayek shudder.

10. Rob Davies and David Sanders, "Economic Strategies, Adjustment and Health Policy: Issues in Sub-Saharan Africa for the 1990s," *Transformation* 21 (1993): 81.

11. In his 1994 review of the World Bank's recent assessment of structural adjustment in Africa, Peter Lewis suggests that the Bank makes a good case for structural adjustment. However, he then adds that "as the 'strong case' for the bank's commitment to structural adjustment, this study provides lukewarm evidence of the efficacy or sustainability of orthodox reform." See "The Politics of Economics," *Africa Report* (May-June 1994): 49.

12. For examples of postdevelopment thought, see Arturo Escobar, *Encountering Development: The Making and Unmaking of the Third World* (Princeton, N.J.: Princeton University Press, 1995); Gilbert Rist, *The History of Development: From Western Origins to Global Faith* (London and New York: Zed Books, 1997); James Ferguson, *The Anti-Politics Machine: Development, Depoliticization and Bureaucratic Power in Lesotho* (Cambridge: Cambridge University Press, 1990). See also

M. P. Cowen and R. W. Shenton, *Doctrines of Development* (London and New York: Routledge, 1996), which, while not an example of postdevelopment thought, nonetheless argues for development as a process of control. For reference, see also Gail Omvedt, *Reinventing Revolution: New Social Movements and the Socialist Tradition in India* (New York: M. E. Sharpe, 1993), and Stuart Corbridge, "Post-Marxism and Development Studies: Beyond the Impasse," *World Development* 18 (1990): 623–639.

13. Jan Nederveen Pieterse, "After Post-Development," *Third World Quarterly* 21, no. 2 (2000): 175–191.

14. Ray Kiely, "The Last Refuge of the Noble Savage? A Critical Assessment of Post-Development Theory," *European Journal of Development Research* 11, no. 1 (June 1999): 30–55.

15. N. Shanmugaratnam, "Encountering Postdevelopment and the End of the Third World," *Forum for Development Studies* 2 (1997): 329–339.

16. Marc Edelman, *Peasants Against Globalization: Rural Social Movements in Costa Rica* (Stanford, Calif.: Stanford University Press, 1999).

17. For a critique of the postmodern left, see Tom Brass, "Old Conservatism in 'New' Clothes," *Journal of Peasant Studies* 22 (1995): 516–540.

18. Pieterse, "After Post-Development"; Edelman, *Peasants Against Globalization.*

19. See, in particular, John E. Roemer, ed., *Analytical Marxism* (Cambridge: Cambridge University Press, 1986), and his more recent book, *A Future for Socialism* (Cambridge, Mass.: Harvard University Press, 1994). Cf. Alan Carling, "Rational Choice Marxism," *New Left Review* 160 (1986): 24–62.

20. For example, the Latin American left, which produced many of this century's great guerrilla struggles, had largely put this revolutionary past behind it by the early 1990s. See Jorge B. Casteñeda, *Utopia Unarmed: The Latin American Left After the Cold War* (New York: Knopf, 1993); Barry Carr and Steven Ellner, eds., *The Latin American Left: From the Fall of Allende to Perestroika* (Boulder: Westview, 1993).

21. For a good presentation of the neoinstitutionalist position, see Kiren Aziz Chaudhury, "Economic Liberalization and the Lineages of the Rentier State," *Comparative Politics* 27, no. 1 (October 1994): 1–25.

22. Michael McFaul, "Why Russia's Politics Matter," *Foreign Affairs* 74, no. 1 (February 1995): 87–99.

23. Wim Pelupessy and John Weeks, "Adjustment in Central America," in *Economic Maladjustment in Central America,* edited by Wim Pelupessy and John Weeks (New York: St. Martin's Press, 1993).

24. On these points see Jean-Philippe Platteau, "Behind the Market Stage Where Real Societies Exist," in two parts, *Journal of Development Studies* 30 (1994): 533–577 and 753–817, and the comment by Mick Moore; Avner Greif, "Cultural Beliefs and the Organization of Society: A Historical and Theoretical Reflection on Collectivist and Individualist Societies," *Journal of Political Economy* 102 (1994): 912–950.

25. This remains, essentially, the position of the World Bank in *The East Asian Economic Miracle: Economic Growth and Public Policy* (London: Oxford University Press, 1993). For a critique of this report, see Albert Fishlow et al., *Miracle or Design? Lessons from the East Asian Experience* (Washington, D.C.: Overseas Development Council, 1994).

26. Alice Amsden, *Asia's Next Giant: South Korea and Late Industrialization* (New York: Oxford University Press, 1989).

27. World Bank, *The East Asian Economic Miracle.*

28. See, in particular, Amsden, *Asia's Next Giant;* Robert Wade, *Governing the Market: Economic Theory and the Role of Government in East Asian Industrialization* (Princeton, N.J.: Princeton University Press, 1990); Gordon White, ed., *Developmental States in East Asia* (London: Macmillan, 1988). A good synthesis of the developmental-state school can be found in Adrian Leftwich, "Bringing Politics Back In: Towards a Model of the Developmental State," *Journal of Development Studies* 31, no. 3 (1995): 400–427.

29. Friedrich List, *The National System of Political Economy* (New York: Augustus M. Kelly, 1966).

30. A classic discussion of the way in which the backwardness of "latecoming" countries propels them into development policies that differ from those used by the early developers, and which often rely on a heavy dose of state intervention, is found in Alexander Gerschenkron, *Economic Backwardness in Historical Perspective* (Cambridge, Mass.: Harvard Belknap, 1962). For a summary of his thought see the postscript.

31. Hong Kong, the other of the Little Tigers, presents an interesting case, in that its successful development has arisen under the eye of a minimalist state. However, Hong Kong's unique position as an entrepôt for the immense Chinese economy makes it an exception to this rule.

32. Francis Owusu and Ismail Samatar, "Industrial Strategy and the African State: The Botswana Experience," *Canadian Journal of African Studies* 31, no. 2 (1997): 268–299.

33. See Eva A. Paus, "Economic Growth Through Neoliberal Restructuring? Insights from the Chilean Experience," *Journal of Developing Areas* 28 (1994): 31–56.

34. See Sanjaya Lall, *Building Industrial Competitiveness in Developing Countries* (Paris: OECD Development Centre, 1990), p. 60; Sanjaya Lall, "Promoting Technology Development: The Role of Technology Transfer and Indigenous Effort," *Third World Quarterly* 14, no. 1 (1993): 95–108; Seiji Naya and Pearl Imada, "Development Strategies and Economic Performance of the Dynamic Asian Economies: Some Comparisons with Latin America," *Pacific Review* 3 (1990): 303; Louis Putterman and Dietrich Rueschemeyer, eds., *State and Market in Development: Synergy or Rivalry?* (Boulder and London: Lynne Rienner Publishers, 1992); Ross Garnaut, "The Market and the State in Economic Development: Applications to the International Trading System," *Singapore Economic Review* 36, no. 2 (1991): 15; Tony Killick, "What Can We Learn About Long-Term Development from Experiences with Restructuring?" (Berlin: European Association of Development Research and Training Institutes Conference, 1993).

35. See Rhys Jenkins, "The Political Economy of Industrialization: A Comparison of Latin American and East Asian Newly Industrializing Countries," *Development and Change* 22 (1991): 214–215.

36. John Rapley, *Ivoirien Capitalism* (Boulder and London: Lynne Rienner Publishers, 1993), chapter 4.

37. On Côte d'Ivoire, see Rapley, *Ivoirien Capitalism;* on South Korea, see John Lie, "The State, Industrialization and Agricultural Sufficiency: The Case of South Korea," *Development Policy Review* 9 (1991): 37–51; Larry L. Burmeister, "State, Industrialization and Agricultural Policy in Korea," *Development and Change* 2 (1990): 197–223.

38. See Richard Grabowski, "The Failure of Import Substitution: Reality and Myth," *Journal of Contemporary Asia* 24 (1994): 297–309; "Import Substitution, Export Promotion, and the State in Economic Development," *Journal of Developing Areas* 28 (1994): 535–554. In a lecture given at Queen Elizabeth House, University of Oxford (11 November 1993), Robert Wade reached a similar conclusion when he contrasted South Korea with India.

39. See the debate on the subject in the articles by Nicoli Nattrass, Raphael Kaplinsky, and John Sender, *Journal of Southern African Studies* 20 (1994). Cf. Guy Mhone, "Dependency and Underdevelopment: The Limits of Structural Adjustment Programmes and Towards a Pro-Active State-Led Development Strategy," *African Development Review* 7, no. 2 (December 1995): 51–85.

40. Richard Bernal, "Globalisation and Small Developing Countries: The Imperative for Repositioning," in *Globalisation: A Calculus of Inequality,* edited by Denis Benn and Kenneth Hall (Kingston, Jamaica: Ian Randle Publishers, 2000).

41. For more on the Asian crisis, see Peter G. Warr, *Macroeconomic Origins of the Korean Crisis* (Canberra: Australian National University [ANU] Working Paper in Trade and Development 00/04, 2000); Hal Hill, *Indonesia: The Strange and Sudden Death of a Tiger Economy* (Canberra: ANU Working Paper in Trade and Development 99/5, 1999); Peter G. Warr, *Is Growth Good for the Poor? Thailand's Boom and Bust* (Canberra: ANU Working Paper in Trade and Development 98/11, 1998; Peter G. Warr, *What Happened to Thailand?* (Canberra: ANU Working Paper in Trade and Development 99/3, 1998); Rajiv Kumar and Bibek Debroy, *The Asian Crisis: An Alternate View* (Manila: Asian Development Bank Economic Staff Paper No. 59, 1999); Giancarlo Corsetti, "Interpreting the Asian Financial Crisis: Open Issues in Theory and Policy," *Asian Development Review* 16, no. 2 (1998): 18–63; Daekeun Park and Changyong Rhee, "Currency Crisis in Korea: How Was It Aggravated?" *Asian Development Review* 16, no. 1 (1998): 149–180; Yung Chul Park and Chi-Young Song, "The East Asian Financial Crisis: A Year Later," *IDS Bulletin* 30, no. 1 (January 1999); Laurids S. Lauridsen, "The Financial Crisis in Thailand: Causes, Conduct and Consequences," *World Development* 26, no. 8 (1998): 1575–1591.

42. See Joseph Stiglitz, "Capital Market Liberalization, Economic Growth, and Instability," *World Development* 28, no. 6 (2000): 1075–1086; Corsetti, "Interpreting the Asian Financial Crisis."

43. Stephany Griffith-Jones, *Causes and Lessons of the Mexican Peso Crisis* (Helsinki: World Institute for Development Economics Working Paper No. 132, 1997); Nurhan Yenturk, "Short-Term Capital Inflows and Their Impact on Macroeconomic Structure: Turkey in the 1990s," *The Developing Economies* 37, no. 1 (March 1999): 89–113.

44. See, for instance, Pranab Bardhan, "Economics of Market Socialism and the Issue of Public Enterprise Reform in Developing Countries," *Pakistan Development Review* 30 (1992): 565–579.

45. Peter Nolan, "Economic Reform: China's Success, Russia's Failure" (Economic Development Seminar Series, University of Oxford, 13 May 1993).

46. See, for example, Ronald I. McKinnon, *The Order of Economic Liberalization: Financial Control in the Transition to a Market Economy* (Baltimore: Johns Hopkins University Press, 1991).

47. Some specialists on Russia argue that the communist bureaucracy was so entrenched that it could not possibly have been relied on to implement a gradual reform strategy that undermined its own power. See Juliet Johnson, "Should Russia Adopt the Chinese Model of Economic Reform?" *Communist and Post-Communist Studies* 27 (1994): 59–75; Leonid Gordon, "Russia at the Crossroads," *Government and Opposition* 30, no. 1 (1995): 3–26. Cf. Cynthia Roberts and Thomas Sherlock, "Bringing the Russian State Back In: Explanations of the Derailed Transition to Market Democracy," *Comparative Politics* 31, no. 4 (1999): 477–498.

48. See Paus, "Economic Growth through Neoliberal Restructuring?"

49. Claude Freud and Ellen Hanak Freud, "Les cafés robusta africains peuvent-ils encore être compétitifs?" *Cahiers d'Études Africaines* 136 (1994): 597–611.

6

The Political Economy
of Development

TODAY, IN MANY IF NOT ALL THIRD-WORLD COUNTRIES, NEOCLASSICAL REFORMS have spawned constituencies—small businesspeople, independent professionals—that support such policies. At the same time, these reforms have also created opponents who are increasingly active and organized, though if taken together they remain a rather inchoate movement. While the multifarious opposition to the neoclassical model of globalization has yet to produce a common agenda, many in its ranks still tend to favor some form of statist development model. Many look to a state-led model as an attractive alternative to the neoclassical approach with which they are so disgruntled. But how realistic is this option in much of the third world today?

Not very, it would seem. In the least-developed countries (LDCs), those in which the need for development is most pressing but in which the response to neoclassical reforms has been least promising, and which are found mostly in Africa, it is doubtful that more than a handful of states could presently implement a state-led approach to development. These governments lack an essential feature of developmental states: in the contemporary jargon, strength or hardness. It is commonly believed that third-world states, in having to thrust painful development policies on their people, must be authoritarian or somehow separate from society, because they will have to ignore or repress popular opposition. However, closer examination of developmental states reveals that their strength has arisen less from crude power or remoteness from society, and more from a marriage between a technocratic state and a well-organized indigenous capitalist class. Apart from shortfalls in third-world bureaucracies, the economic and political weaknesses of indigenous capitalists in much of the third world seem to preclude developmental states from emerging in many more countries at this time. Africa, in particular, faces dim prospects.

It is not surprising, therefore, that the African development debate now concerns itself less with building developmental states than with reforming existing states. Yet even when local conditions favor the emergence of developmental states, international conditions make the use of IIM far more difficult than it was for those developmental states that used it earlier in the postwar period. The time may have come for third-world countries to reconsider delinking themselves from global capitalism and creating their own, more benign international economy through such means as intraregional trade. Yet while some of the more marginalized parts of the third world show signs of moving in this direction, as a strategy for the third world as a whole it looks unlikely to come to pass.

I   The Crisis of the State in Africa

If a state is to implement IIM, it must have the authority to impose itself on the private sector. It must have the resources, such as trained personnel and support staff, office and communications equipment, transportation, and information, to govern society as extensively as an interventionist state does. It must have the power to direct and indeed transform society, enforcing law and regulating business and personal transactions. In short, the state must be strong, effective, and able to make its presence felt everywhere in the country. In Africa, skeptics doubt that the developmental state can be anything more than a good idea in countries where the state is in crisis or near collapse.[1] In a few countries plagued by civil war, the government's writ ends at the capital city's limits, and beyond lies a netherworld fought over by competing warlords. Most African bureaucracies are understaffed, with poorly paid and often poorly qualified civil servants working with insufficient resources and outdated equipment. The African state can barely keep up with the demands of the rapidly growing cities for proper sanitation, policing, schools, transportation, electricity, and water supplies. It can do even less for the rural areas that provide it with most of its revenue. In any event, corruption and abuse of power are so widespread that citizens in many African countries regard their state with suspicion at best, hostility at worst. They do what they can to avoid the state by smuggling, not paying taxes, and ignoring the law as much as possible. A state so short of power, so deprived of bureaucratic resources, and so distant from its citizenry can do little to spearhead development. If anything, it may actually hinder growth: extortion rackets and instability dissuade people from entering business, and poor prices and support services discourage farmers.

These problems are not peculiar to Africa. All over the third world, neoclassical reforms have shrunken patronage networks while at the same time worsening income distribution. In effect, the supply of political largesse has dried up at just the moment demand for it has risen. The popular response has been, in part, a turn against the state, evidenced by an increasing incidence of political instability, and also a search for new political networks. This, in turn, has opened a window of opportunity for rising political elites to challenge the position of nationalist ones. Thus, we see more ethnic politics, regionalist movements, or the emergence of ministates connected to the drug trade.

Not all of this political ferment is a bad thing. In some places, the weakening of the state and the growth of a class of entrepreneurs and professionals has undermined authoritarian rule and laid the foundation for a democratic opposition. Such changes arguably helped to consolidate democracy in Latin America and to install it—at times haltingly—in East and Southeast Asia. The jury is still out as to whether neoclassical reforms have brought net political gains to the more developed countries of the third world.

Among the poorer ones, though, the verdict is probably easier to reach. If one accepts the argument made so far in this book—that neoclassical reforms are most effective in societies that have already attained a relatively advanced level of development, and that to reach this level a high degree of state guidance is needed—then it follows that a weakening of the state in the less-developed societies will further restrain their development. Another way to look at it is to say that globalization, which to date has been intertwined with neoclassical reforms (although some leftist critics maintain that this is a blend contrived by policymakers, and that globalization and neoclassical economics need not necessarily go together), demands innovative and aggressive responses by third-world governments if their countries are to insert themselves effectively into the evolving global economy. Yet at the same time, neoclassical reforms have weakened the state and produced social tensions that have then consumed the energy of governing elites.[2] In effect, poor countries are being asked to do more with less. Given the resource scarcities they began with, the task is turning out to be greater than many of them can manage.

So if such problems have arisen all over the third world, in the poorer countries, the prevalence of LDCs in Africa has meant that the crisis there has appeared both acute and continental in scope. In response, many specialists have turned their attention to the new topic of governance. A term coined in the halls of the World Bank, governance refers to the effective practice of government that will enhance a regime's legitimacy and thereby draw people back into the formal political and economic spheres.[3] The Bank's prescription for improving governance includes greater scrutiny and, like its cure for the problems of the marketplace, more efficiency. Dictatorships or one-party regimes enjoy too much latitude to abuse their power. Ministers sometimes exercise discretionary power over their departments' budgets, unencumbered by any formal means of auditing. In such conditions, nobody really knows when a politician or official is depositing money into a Swiss bank account. The agents that provide such scrutiny in the West—the media, elected assemblies, opposition parties, and interest groups—may either not exist or be rigidly controlled by their governments. To impose better discipline on governments the World Bank started advocating the rule of law, respect for human rights, citizen involvement in intermediate associations, and perhaps most important of all, a free press. To reduce corruption and improve state efficacy, the Bank has concentrated on paring back the state and improving aid delivery.[4]

In the early 1990s a democratic tide swept over Africa, part of a democratic "wave" then moving through much of the third world. In the wake of the collapse of the Eastern European regimes in 1989, Africans took to the streets of their capitals and echoed the same demand for change. Reluctant governments were forced to concede their requests. Many observers hoped that democracy would change the way in which African governments operated.[5] As one Ivoirien put it in the midst of his country's prodemocracy demonstrations in 1990, "Now that the politicians are afraid of losing their jobs, they will listen to us."

However, the democratic advance soon suffered setbacks in a number of countries. Even where the gains have not been lost in Africa, many Africanists doubt they will make a difference in the way governments operate. They worry that declining economies will continue to provoke the sort of violent struggles for the spoils of office that the 1990s witnessed, possibly jeopardizing future development.[6] Some point to the apparent contradiction of pushing democracy while pulling the state out of the economy. In poor societies, states need to mobilize popular support for both democracy and state legitimacy, and are handicapped by the lack of resources retrenchment leaves in their hands.[7] In Africa, anticolonial movements lost much of their identity when independence came and their mission was accomplished. To retain the support of the people, they had to replace anticolonial ideology with the economic advantages the modern state could bring. Independence meant not only freedom, but also jobs, schools, and clinics. Now that the state offers people increasingly less security, economic well-being, opportunities for education, or basic health care, it is losing much of its raison d'être. People and communities take these tasks upon themselves, forming their own vigilante squads, creating their own mutual-aid funds, and so forth. In short, they are turning their backs on the state.[8] This further undermines the state's ability to play an effective role in development.

Some who despair of the state in Africa see a silver lining in this. They believe that the nation-state is a European creation left behind by Africa's departing colonists, imposed from above within artificially designed boundaries that seldom bear much relationship to precolonial ethnic borders. The nation-state, it is said, is at odds with Africa's traditions of decentralized democracy and checks on central power.[9] To these theorists, Africans who turn their backs on the state and engage in community self-help may be returning to their roots.

Although it is a minority opinion, this view of the African state nonetheless captures the despondence that has gripped many Africanists over the last decade or so. Whereas there have been cases of good state performance in Africa, such as Botswana and Côte d'Ivoire, there have been many abysmal failures: Zaire (now the Democratic Republic of Congo) under Mobutu Sese Seko, Equatorial Guinea under Macias Nguema, the ill-fated Central African "Empire" of Jean-Bedel Bokassa, and Uganda prior to the rise to power of Yoweri Museveni in 1986. In the latter cases, plunder and political collapse not only inhibited development, but even reversed it. Nor is it clear that policies to improve governance, if they do any good, will make it possible for developmental states to emerge in most of Africa. It is important to improve management practices and institutional arrangements, but there are deep economic and political causes for the crisis of the state in Africa. This raises a question that challenges development theory even more than does the question of the appropriate role of the state in the economy: Why is it that some states have piloted development, whereas others have held it back? What explains such glaring differences?

I State Strength

It helps to go back to the East Asian examples and determine what characterized these successful states. The experiences of developmental states there point to an essential fact. To effectively guide economic development, a state must enjoy the power to direct society and lead it through traumatic changes. According to developmental-state theory, the state needs to be relatively insulated against society, giving a highly skilled technocratic bureaucracy the autonomy it needs to impose discipline on the private sector. The state, as some writers put it, must be strong or hard. Bureaucrats must be able to draft policies that promote national development, not the advancement of private lobbyists. Moreover, governments may have to enact unpopular and even harsh policies in the name of development, and the governors must be in a position to ignore or repress the discontent these policies provoke. If, for example, the government decides to open a protected industry to foreign competition, both the industrialists and the workers in that sector stand to lose some or all of their livelihood. The governors have to be able to put down worker uprisings and ignore the political pressure brought to bear by industrialists. The state must also be able to make people comply with unpopular policies. If a government is going to redistribute land or institute a resettlement scheme, it may even need to send troops into the field to force submission.

Many states, particularly in Africa, lack this strength. Some Africanists cite the "uncaptured peasantry" to illustrate this. Peasants frequently ignore state directives, refuse to sell all their output to marketing boards, smuggle goods across borders, and even resist attempts at coercion. For example, in Tanzania, when the state tried to force farmers into villages that would serve as hubs for large collective farms, many peasants refused to comply, even when force was used.[10] In addition to the uncaptured peasantry, there exists the influence of powerful interests. Jean-François Bayart and Patrick Chabal have argued that many African states are so thoroughly penetrated by interests within their societies that they cannot hope to transform those societies.[11] However, this problem is scarcely peculiar to Africa. In the past, many specialists on India blamed the "Hindu rate of growth" on the power of vested interests to repeatedly thwart difficult but necessary policy changes. Perhaps an industrialist was threatened by the potential arrival of a competitor, and was owed a favor by the minister whose election campaign he funded and who had the power to refuse licenses to new firms. Or perhaps the economic ministry's top bureaucrat owed his job to the personal influence of a friend; this friend owned a factory that used imported inputs, and wanted the official to use his position to keep the currency overvalued. Influence asserts itself in many ways. But it seems obvious that if a state cannot insulate itself against such pressures, and worse, cannot successfully implement its policies, it lacks the strength to engineer development. What, then, must governments do to obtain the strength their states need to engineer development?

Authoritarianism in the Third World

Some find the recipe for development unpalatable, but inescapable: an authoritarian regime that can ignore demands from society and repress the population if it becomes too vociferous. Democracy, it is sometimes said, is a luxury for the rich and must be deferred in the interests of development. When, in the 1960s and 1970s, Latin American governments began facing tough economic choices, the political situation deteriorated and a rash of coups d'etat brought authoritarian regimes to power. This led an Argentinian political scientist, Guillermo O'Donnell, to develop a model that linked this seeming new phase in Latin America's history to its stage of development. The bureaucratic-authoritarian model, as O'Donnell called it, maintained that during their import-substituting phases, Latin American governments had been able to remain democratic because ISI offered substantial benefits to the population. Above all, it created jobs for them, so people were happy with the regime. But once ISI had reached the limits of the national market, industry had to start moving into export markets, which meant competition with foreign producers and hence greater pressure on productivity and efficiency. This lowered employment and squeezed the population to reduce spending and increase investment. Only a hard, cold-hearted state could preserve stability through these difficult times. The spotty record of democracy in the third world should therefore come as no surprise.

There are problems with the bureaucratic-authoritarian model, however, notably that the sequence of events in the rise of military dictatorships did not follow that hypothesized in the model.[12] More important, although authoritarian regimes wield great command through their control of repressive power, it is not clear that they are all that hard or strong in terms of their insulation from society. The authoritarian regime of the Philippines' dictator, Ferdinand Marcos, was famously unable to resist being penetrated by private interests, who took advantage of legal monopolies, quotas, franchises and leases, protective tariffs, tax exemptions, and import licenses to enrich themselves at the expense of the economy. It would seem that state strength has to do with more than the ability to coerce the population; this was something the Philippine state *could* do. In fact, the evidence suggests that authoritarian regimes have not been particularly good at implementing reform or economic-austerity programs.[13] For one thing, authoritarian regimes may have naked power but lack intelligence or enlightenment. After all, there have been monumental cases of mismanagement by authoritarian regimes. Marcos found good company in the inept and damaging administrations of Haiti's Duvaliers and Zaire's Mobutu Sese Seko.[14] Nor are authoritarian regimes necessarily immune to societal pressure. If they resist popular pressure, the result may not be an interest-free state but one in which a single interest monopolizes power.[15] Strength seems to involve not only brute force but also the ability to stand above society and lead, rather than be led by it.

The Overdeveloped State?

To explain what it is that allows some third-world states to isolate themselves from societal pressures, some have turned to the theory of the overdeveloped state. Emerging from the Marxist literature on the state, this school focuses on the colonial legacy. It begins with the European nation-state, arguing that it arose from the development of capitalism and so was intimately connected to the society whence it evolved. Its primary task was to defend and promote the interests of the capitalist class. However, when capitalism spread its tentacles, the states created by imperialism differed from their parents. They bore no relation to the society upon which they were imposed. Indeed, their first task was to subjugate *all* local classes. To this end, they were endowed with an unusually strong bureaucratic and military apparatus. Their legitimacy and power originated in a far-off land.

Thus, according to theorists of this school, at the time of independence the new ruling elites took over a state that was overdeveloped, suspended above society, and separated from it.[16]

Although overdeveloped-state theory has traditionally been restricted in its popularity mainly to students of India,[17] variants of the theory gained popularity among some observers of East and Southeast Asia.[18] For example, some have attributed the autonomy of the Taiwanese state to its origins outside of Chinese society. The state was created and staffed by the nationalists who fled to the island from the victorious communists in mainland China. The members of this ruling class bore little in common with the people they came to govern. Theirs was a different culture and dialect, and they have maintained their separateness ever since. Until recently a small minority controlled virtually all political power.[19]

However, in arguing that the postcolonial state had little to do with local class politics, the theory of the overdeveloped state overlooks what are often very important class conflicts. To contemporary political scientists, a theory that separates the state from society is rather like a medical lecturer who treats the human head and body as distinct. The head may govern the body, but that does not make it independent of the body. In recent decades, research on the state has gone well beyond the "black box"— the interest mediator standing above society—of which political science once spoke. Political scientists now see the state as an entity closely linked to and penetrated by society, as well as itself penetrating society. Some states may be more permeable than others, but what seems to determine state strength is not so much the degree as the character of penetration. The state in Africa may appear weak due to a strong society: private interests riddle the state and use it for corrupt purposes while the peasantry largely ignores state directives and operates outside the formal economy, thus eluding "capture." However, many Africanists reject this portrayal of the African state, and believe the problem to be precisely the opposite: society is not too strong, but too weak. Society lacks the independent organizations, such as interest groups, political parties, and news media, that can both resist state abuses and help the state to communicate with its people.[20] Society therefore draws apart from the state, and people form parochial groups (for example, kinship groups) that have particularistic concerns and often aim to insulate their members from the state. So while a strong society may undermine a strong state, it may equally underpin it. The task at hand is to determine what makes a strong society produce a strong rather than a weak state.

The other interesting point is that states need not be authoritarian or remote from society in order to enact unpopular measures. Democratic or otherwise "weak" regimes have in some cases made difficult reforms and engineered development, at times quite effectively.[21] Popular control does not preclude strong leadership. The key to success, it appears, is for the government to generate a consensus in favor of reform or growth.[22] The ability to garner public support seems to be more important to development and reform than does authoritarianism.[23] Leaders must rally potential winners together, and marginalize or divide the losers. This is no mean feat—as Machiavelli pointed out, today's losers are always a more potent group than tomorrow's winners—yet it can be done. Perhaps one of the best examples in recent history is that of the South African regime and the African National Congress, who together paved the way to democracy in that country by building up the support of the white business and middle classes and dividing the right. Compared to such tactics, violent repression of popular opposition is revealed for what it is: a crude, often ineffectual means of maintaining stability, typically undertaken by a regime that has failed to win popular support for change.

So, if regimes do not need to be authoritarian or remote from society in order to be strong, what is it that underlies state strength?

The Importance of State Capacity

Whether or not the theory of the overdeveloped state applies to Taiwan and other Asian countries is open to debate. However, the Taiwanese example points us in the direction of something that is crucial to state strength, and that does arise from colonial legacies: state capacity. Colonialism endowed such countries as South Korea and Taiwan with capable bureaucracies,[24] whereas countries such as Congo were left with slim pickings.[25] The Japanese invested in training indigenous administrators in their Asian possessions, but the European powers generally reserved the administration of their colonies for their own nationals. Only the French put much effort into educating local administrators, and even they produced but few and low-level officials. Basil Davidson once reckoned that when the Belgians abandoned Congo, which was called Zaire during the presidency of Mobutu Sese Seko, they left behind fewer than twenty Africans with postsecondary education, none of whom had serious administrative experience.[26]

Congo was but the extreme version of the rule in Africa. At independence Botswana and Côte d'Ivoire confronted this dearth of state, or administrative capacity, by continuing to hire foreigners who worked alongside the new African recruits. This gave the latter the time to develop both administrative skills and loyalty to the institutions of government, until they came to see themselves as servants of the state rather than of their village, kinship, or political patrons. This was arguably the cause of these countries' relatively high degrees of state capacity,[27] but few other African regimes made use of this strategy. Few could. A nationalist strategy bent on expelling colonialists could scarcely then turn around and invite the colonialists to stick around for a while. But administrative capacity is essential to state strength: one cannot delegate policymaking authority to skilled bureaucrats, nor implement the policies they make, if one does not have them in sufficient number.

Concentration of Power

However, just because a government has administrative capacity does not mean it will be able to use it for developmental purposes. A large bureaucracy may still be permeable and susceptible to influence. To overcome this obstacle, states with a high degree of administrative capacity seem to become developmental when they concentrate their power in the executive branch, which in turn surrounds itself with a technocratic elite.[28] This arrangement, more than authoritarianism or remoteness from society, seems to provide development planners with the autonomy they need to devise and implement effective national strategies. This minimizes the impact of the interdepartmental squabbling that can slow down policymaking in any regime.

No state is internally united. Priorities among departments differ. When the Brazilian finance minister tried to reduce public spending in 1994 by cutting the minimum wage, he immediately ran up against the powerful labor ministry, which wanted to raise the minimum wage. When such conflicts emerge, they can be resolved if one ministry gains enough influence over the government to make its will prevail. However, another way to resolve such conflicts is for the government to create small superministries, staffed by bureaucrats who get the final say in policymaking matters and whose political autonomy vis-à-vis society is ensured by an executive acting as a buffer against powerful interests.

At critical junctures in their histories, many states have gone through something like what Marx called a Bonapartist moment: a turning point, often a crisis, in which political power was largely granted to, or usurped by, the executive branch or even one leader. In some cases, such as in Côte d'Ivoire and Botswana, this came with independence, when a strong party helped to cement a new government's hold on power.[29] In the case of South Korea, it arose from a coup in which the military, allied to the bureaucracy, broke the political networks that had sustained ISI.[30] In other cases economic crisis prompts strong action, leading sometimes to a military intervention.[31] In all cases, the common feature is not an authoritarian regime, but one with concentrated executive power that delegates policymaking to technocrats.

This made it possible for regimes to break free from or at least weaken the hold of the scourge of many third-world, and especially African, states: patrimonialism. Patrimonialism, a concept originated by Max Weber and elucidated in Richard Sandbrook's work on Africa,[32] severely erodes a state's autonomy. Politics in a patrimonial state is highly personal: individuals, not parties or interest groups, build up networks of supporters. Whereas in other states individuals must find means outside the state to do this (for example, political parties), leaders of patrimonial regimes use the state itself. They attract supporters with offers of plum government jobs, contracts, and opportunities for corruption. For this reason, directorships on marketing boards or senior positions in customs offices are eagerly pursued rewards for political loyalty, because they allow officials to directly skim money off the economy. Because of the way appointments are made, a patrimonial state enjoys little autonomy from the political networks on which it is based; corruption is widespread and the bureaucracy is riddled with political appointees who owe favors to those who arranged their appointments. In other words, it is hardly a skilled, technocratic, autonomous bureaucracy. Civil servants direct their loyalty to the leader rather than to the state.

Meanwhile, the networks excluded from power are completely denied the spoils of office. Politics tends to become an all-or-none affair, given that political office is not a means to an end, but the end itself. Struggles for this "cash cow" can cause severe political instability; in Africa, networks organized along ethnic lines compete for power in sometimes vicious battles. Such political instability frightens away investors, and it does not help when successful ventures find themselves prey to police officers or fire departments who demand their cut lest fires break out, a practice that became endemic in Mobutu's Zaire. This is the grand version of what happens in any African city whenever somebody parks a car on a public street. Young boys appear before the engine has even been turned off, offering, for a small fee, to guard the vehicle against vandals or thieves. The drivers always pay, less for the service the boys render than for the assurance that they will not ruin the car themselves.

If a state is to become developmental, it is essential for the government to reduce patrimonial politics so as to insulate decisionmakers from the excessive influence of societal interests. But what are the political forces that are likely to drive the assault on patrimonialism? It takes more than a committed military and bureaucracy or a strong party to make a state developmental. If some strong societies produce weak states, while others produce strong states, then what is the missing element in the former case? Given the existence of a state with a high degree of administrative capacity and concentrated decisionmaking, it appears that the final ingredient that cements the rise of the developmental state is a domestic capitalist class.

Class Politics in the Third World

At the heart of much political struggle is the conflict over access to economic resources, whether it be jobs, government spending in a given region or on a particular program, or favorable tax legislation. Money may not be the crux of all political struggles; anybody involved in the abortion debate will point out that some of the most intense political struggles are not over money. But a good many political struggles ultimately revolve around who gets what share of the pie. Furthermore, economic strength is usually an essential component of political strength: although rich parties are not guaranteed electoral victory, parties with no economic resources and no prospects of finding them are almost always assured obscurity.

One of the major achievements of modern capitalism is that it removes much of the political struggle from the state. Not only political leaders can proffer plum jobs; so too can rich industrialists. The state is no longer the sole means of gaining control over resource allocation; private economic power plays at least as important a role in this process as does public office. Capitalist power therefore seems to undermine patrimonial politics. It renders it less necessary, since the spoils of power can be had in the private sector. Indeed, capitalism and patrimonialism may have a difficult time co-existing. Patrimonial government preys upon private entrepreneurs, and it is in the collective interest of these entrepreneurs to limit predatory behavior by the state and maintain political stability. Capitalists share an interest in expanding the size of the private sphere and creating clear separations between private and public power to defend their accumulated gains. Rolling back the frontiers of the state may equally benefit the state by clearly defining its role and capacities while protecting it somewhat against excessive private penetration.

Of course, capitalists may not recognize their common interests. The crony capitalism of the Philippines saw capitalists taking advantage of, rather than resisting, patrimonial politics. Individual businesspeople fought to get preferential access to scarce resources ahead of their rivals. Organization is therefore essential if the capitalist class is to act as a bulwark against patrimonialism. Entrepreneurs must agree upon a common set of rules to which they all will submit. They must, through interest groups and chambers of commerce, develop a common program. If they are linked in this way, they are less likely to "break ranks" and seek political gains at the expense of their rivals, leaving their differences to be settled in the marketplace. Organization may also be essential to make up for the capitalist class's political weaknesses. In a first-world country, most of the state's revenue, whether from taxes or borrowing, flows directly from the capitalist economy. Capitalism thus forms the very lifeblood of the modern state. In third-world countries, by contrast, the modern capitalist sector still accounts for a comparatively small share of economic output, very small in the case of the least-developed economies; a capitalist class must make up for its deficit in economic strength by means of political organization.

Finally, in addition to organization, capitalists must make up for their shortcomings in economic power by linking their organizations (and sometimes individuals) to entry points in the state. This permits a two-way information flow: capitalists can express their concerns to policymakers, and policymakers can at the same time communicate more effectively with chief players in the economy. Where capitalists fail to establish such linkages, they risk becoming politically marginalized, and worse, preyed upon, as happened to some emerging African bourgeoisies at the time of independence.[33]

Such linkage has come to be referred to as "embedded autonomy," after the work of the developmental-state theorist Clive Hamilton. Of course, organization and linkage might prove so effective that the state becomes a mere tool of the capitalist class. However, if the state is strong, and has concentrated decisionmaking in the executive power that is surrounded by a technocratic elite, the capitalist class will be able to communicate but not to dominate. The bureaucracy will retain sufficient autonomy from the capitalists to withstand their pressures when need be.[34] This brings to mind the Marxist debate of the 1970s that generally concluded that the most effective capitalist regimes were those that were able to overlook and even repress the demands of certain fractions of capital in order to govern in the interest of the whole class.[35]

In line with Hamilton's reasoning, it appears that not just any group of capitalists can provide the coalition to underpin a developmental state. It probably needs to be a capitalist class rooted in production, and not merely trade or services. Businesspeople invested in trade can satisfy themselves with access to state licenses,[36] and if they make the move to production under an ISI policy they may go no further than taking cover under state protection and making profits from final assembly of finished goods.[37] Moreover, such capitalists worry less about political stability, because profits in trade rise when stability deteriorates, whereas they fall for those invested in production. Instability drives traders out of the market, which makes commodities scarce and increases their price and hence revenue to the seller. By contrast, in unstable situations, factory owners may have to invest more heavily in security, or purchase expensive power generators to make up for power cuts, and in other such ways raise their costs of production, which eats into their profits. States linked to traders, therefore, seem more likely to come under pressure to slide into patrimonial behavior. This may not altogether preclude the eventual rise of an industrial bourgeoisie, which may later come into conflict with the "old" class; recent years have seen the development of such conflicts between "old" and "new" entrepreneurs in several countries. However, as history has shown, patrimonial politics slows industrial development.

Equally important, a developmental state depends not only on a productive bourgeoisie, but on a *local* one. Foreign capitalists may provide the investment and technology needed for development, but they are less likely to "deepen" their presence and create backward linkages in the economy, as they tend to repatriate their profits rather than reinvest them locally.[38] More important is the fact that foreign capitalists tend to exert political pressure on the host government by acting through the embassies of their home governments, and thus tend to avoid domestic politics. However, if it is assumed that any development policy that will cause a major restructuring of the economy will create losers as well as winners, a regime needs to mobilize political support for itself. A well-organized local class that articulates a developmental ideology, propagates these ideas through the media, and supports the political candidates of a developmental party can help neutralize the challenges of losers, be they landed oligarchies or urban petty bourgeoisies and working classes. No other class is likely to perform this task. Although peasantries should ordinarily benefit from a developmental state, especially in those cases in which the regime has spearheaded land reform, as a class they are usually too atomized and disorganized to provide a political foundation for the state (which is not to say they cannot be organized by another class, namely a bourgeoisie).[39]

History appears to show that it is difficult, if not impossible, for a state to build an industrial bourgeoisie from scratch. It may be equally difficult to build one out of a merchant bourgeoisie. Latin America's early statist experiments, though appearing to have created an industrial class, in fact were taking advantage of the presence of nascent industrial classes that had begun to emerge in the late nineteenth century. Similarly, once the Chinese and Vietnamese states decided to change their development strategies and opened up to the world economy, they were able to exploit the resources and talents of large expatriate business communities in developing new industries. The absence of a productive bourgeoisie may not be an insurmountable obstacle to development, but it does make the emergence of a developmental state a good deal less likely.

In each state said to be developmental, domestic productive capitalists have been closely linked to the bureaucracy.[40] Writers on the East Asian NICs cite this as a key factor in their economic success.[41] In the cases of India and Zimbabwe, the shift to reform is said to have been motivated by the rise of new, dynamic fractions of the bourgeoisie.[42] In Egypt, the success of reform has been credited to the political strength of the bourgeoisie and the concomitant weakness of the rival classes threatened by reform;[43] this experience parallels Colombia's shift toward reform and export orientation since the late 1960s.[44] In Côte d'Ivoire, the indigenous bourgeoisie led the independence movement and captured the postcolonial state, turning it to developmental ends.[45] It is also alleged that the small protobourgeoisie led Botswana to independence, with similar consequences.[46] In South Africa, theorists have attributed both the construction and the abolition of apartheid to shifts in the relative power of fractions of capital,[47] with popular support or struggles tipping the balance in each case. Jonathan Barker's thesis that any reform in Africa will be motivated by a triple alliance among international financial capital (the World Bank and the IMF), private capital (foreign and domestic), and "progressive" small farmers[48] has also been affirmed in the case of Mozambique's reform experience.[49]

One hastens to add that Barker is not optimistic that such an alliance will emerge in many of Africa's countries. His pessimism points to a phenomenon that may lie at the heart of Africa's disappointing postcolonial development record. At the time of independence, indigenous bourgeoisies in much of sub-Saharan Africa were politically weak. Seldom did they play a prominent role in independence struggles. Urban petty bourgeoisies consequently took center stage and led the independence movements. These new ruling elites, unconstrained by bourgeois civil societies, were left with surprising latitude to use—and abuse—the state.

| Africa Against the Tide

It is thus not surprising to find that whereas development theorists elsewhere are concerned with devising policy blends that demand state action, Africanists are moving in the opposite direction. Whereas developmental-state theory implies a maintenance or even increase of the state's role in the economy, Africanists are increasingly calling for state retreat. In the form of decentralization or devolution, this is seen as a way to improve the delivery of services and mobilize people in support of development efforts.[50] The hope is that by shortening the distance between administrators and administered, scrutiny will increase. Public officials will be forced to account to the people whose lives they affect—not only to other state officials or political allies, but to ordinary folk as well. Their actions will be more closely monitored and, because of their close contact with the grassroots, they will be more attuned to the needs and abilities of the people for whom they are designing programs. In turn, because the people's influence on policymaking will increase, they will be more likely to become involved in development programs and thereby make these programs more effective.

Nobody considers decentralization an ideal solution, but merely the best of a set of undesirable options. Whether or not it will improve governance is difficult to say. The evidence is mixed,[51] and it may prove effective only if done gradually,[52] allowing local bureaucratic capacity to be developed over time. After all, if there is a shortage of skilled bureaucrats in a centralized state, one can expect the situation at the local level to be at least as bad. The most optimistic prognosis might be that any change that makes government more responsive will increase its legitimacy, thereby leading to its long-term strengthening.[53] However, the states that emerge will not be strong in the East Asian mold; these were highly centralized rather than decentralized.

The glum assessment of the state and the prospects of bourgeois power in much of Africa dampens hopes of developmental states emerging in all but a few countries. It is not that capitalist development will not occur. It may be difficult for indigenous capitalists to emerge on a large scale in small economies,[54] especially if those economies are dominated by producers and distributors from a neighboring economy, as is the case in much of southern Africa, but elsewhere capitalists are prospering. Even in Mobutu's Zaire, by reputation the predatory, antidevelopmental state par excellence, entrepreneurs continued their activities.[55] But these activities will remain inchoate—linkage into an emerging capitalist economy being minimized—and concentrated disproportionately in those sectors that offer fast returns and are most easily concealed from the public eye, in particular trade. Certainly, entrepreneurs in hostile or unpredictable policy environments will hesitate to move into manufacturing.[56] Thus, the much-needed structural transformation will not likely come. In the absence of state direction, whether minimalist or maximalist, coordinated national development is unlikely to occur. One of the Marxist canons may be correct after all: a bourgeois revolution, in some form, may have to precede national capitalist development.

❙ International Obstacles to Developmental States

Even where domestic conditions favor the emergence of developmental states, it appears that the time for third-world countries to make use of IIM may have passed. This is because the international conditions so favorable to this strategy thirty or forty years ago have now turned against it.

Any country making use of IIM must engage in what first-world trade negotiators call unfair trading practices. They must shelter their own markets from competition with the industrialists of first-world trading partners, yet at the same time try to maintain relatively easy access to those same markets. This annoys their trading partners. Countries may try using moral arguments to justify this unbalanced trading arrangement. This, in effect, was what third-world governments tried in the 1970s and 1980s when they propounded the idea of a new international economic order (NIEO), which would have altered the rules governing such things as international trade and aid to make them more favorable to the third world. However, the cool response of first-world governments to NIEO proposals seems to show that moral suasion has yet to succeed in extracting many concessions from these governments.

For a time, however, Cold War geopolitics did succeed in this. During the Cold War the United States and its North Atlantic Treaty Organization

(NATO) partners were eager to build up a network of allies in their stand-off with the Soviet bloc. This led them to provide aid to client states, and to turn a blind eye to unfair trading practices in such countries as Japan and South Korea, because the economic prosperity of these countries was drawing them more squarely into the capitalist camp. Moreover, given the healthy world economy of the postwar period, the strategy proved relatively painless: U.S. producers may not have had the same access to Japan as Japanese producers had to the United States, but Japan's booming economy was still causing increases in demand for U.S. goods.

The world economy slowed down, however, and competition for market access became more fierce. The United States lost its desire to do its trading partners any favors. First-world governments under pressure from their electorates to trim budget deficits and create jobs have slashed aid budgets and thrown up trade barriers in the name of keeping jobs at home. Barriers are now removed only if trading partners make similar concessions; this negates the possibility of using unfair trading practices as a development policy. With the collapse of the Soviet Union, the need to attract and keep third-world allies has all but disappeared. In the 1990s many first-world governments quickly reoriented their African aid budgets to the newly opened economies of Eastern Europe, where the future returns were seen to be higher.

Today, first-world governments drive hard bargains. If third-world governments want access to their markets, first-world governments demand something in return. On the day the IMF reported its renewed optimism for the prospects of growth in the global economy in the late twentieth century, Ecuador took the United States to task over its growing protection of its market.[57] So, while South Korean success stemmed from the actions of a developmental state, it ultimately relied on a propitious opening at the low end of the U.S. car market—a window that in 2002 seems to be narrowing, if not closing.[58] Similarly, Taiwan enacted adjustment policies during a growth phase in the world economy and opened gradually to world trade; present-day adjusters confront a more slowly growing and increasingly protectionist world economy.[59] Even those who advocate outward orientation in the face of today's increasing protectionism acknowledge that the best that developing countries can hope to do under such circumstances is to poach from the market shares of rival developing countries.[60] This strategy is possibly logical for individual countries, but it cannot work for the third world as a whole.[61]

The Balance of Power in the Global Political Economy

For the foreseeable future it is not likely that third-world governments will be able to extract significant concessions or favors, such as unequal market access, from the first world.[62] Many third-world countries are weaker today than they were a half-century ago. Whereas Latin American governments emerged from the Depression in a cloud of trade pessimism, owing to the new problems in the global economy, third-world governments emerged from the Cold War in a similar cloud of pessimism due to their new problems in the global *political* economy.

The growth of national debt has emerged as a key weakness of many third-world countries. The need for governments to obtain credit simply to meet existing loan obligations places many developing countries in a particularly vulnerable position vis-à-vis developed-country lending agencies, including the World Bank and the IMF. This weakness is compounded by the strength that creditor agencies have obtained by the use of a form of cartelization, through such measures as cross-default provisions, whereby a default on a loan to one bank is treated as a default by all banks. This means that individual third-world countries face a united front of creditor countries: even if David can beat Goliath, a whole army of Goliaths will take more than a slingshot to fell. Some developing countries, such as South Korea, avoided falling into this trap of vulnerability by exercising restraint and borrowing little during the lending booms of the 1980s. Others, such as Brazil, remain powerful because their economy and debt are so immense that they cannot be easily isolated for severe punitive action—as was Peru when, under President Alan Garcia, it tried unsuccessfully to impose a ceiling on debt repayments. Countries such as Brazil illustrate Keynes's adage that if you owe the bank $100 and cannot pay, you have a problem, but if you owe the bank $1,000,000 and cannot pay, the bank has a problem. But many more countries are quite weak, some to the point of virtual dependence on the IMF and/or the World Bank.

Assuming that third-world governments cannot turn trade relationships to their advantage, the value of their continuing to trade with the first world comes into doubt. The world market, in its present form, sometimes acts against the interests of the third world. The international market has dispersed sellers but comparatively concentrated buyers. For example, although several third-world countries export cocoa, only a few large companies in the developed world buy it. Specialists on West Africa are quick to point out that Nestlé, the chief purchaser of cocoa in the region, is richer than all the governments of the region combined. Such concentrated purchasing power opens up possibilities for such things as collusion in price setting, which weakens individual developing countries vis-à-vis their developed counterparts. Although poor countries might not always get the best prices on the goods they sell, they often end up paying a premium on the manufactured goods they import, especially if their markets are considered marginal.[63]

It is not automatic that developing countries will be weak on the world market; it depends on the commodity being traded. If, for example, a country enjoys the enviable position of being the concentrated seller of a strategic commodity, its political power increases considerably. During the Cold War, for instance, South Africa was the only reliable source of affordable strategic metals upon which the U.S. defense industry relied. This gave the country a degree of political leverage over the United States it might not otherwise have enjoyed, and helps to explain the soft stance the United States took against the apartheid regime. On the whole, however, third-world countries suffer from a deficit of market power.[64] More often than not they are weak, sometimes severely so, competing with numerous other countries in the sale of a small range of goods for which demand is relatively elastic, and for which the market is dominated by one or a few big purchasers.[65] In the face of such a concentration of market power in the hands of the so-called Seven Sisters, the world's biggest oil companies, the Persian Gulf countries created their own oil companies to gain some leverage over the market. They also successfully used OPEC to coordinate supply to the world market, thereby gaining a great deal of power during the 1970s.

At the time of the first oil shock, many in the third world judged that the time had finally come for the third world to break the first world's alleged domination of the world's markets. It was said that commodity power would enable the rise of the developing countries. In the event, OPEC's power proved to be relatively short-lived. In part this arose from the normal workings of the market—price rises led to the search for substitutes and improvements in energy efficiency—and in part from the efforts of developed-country governments to circumvent and rein in OPEC. In the end, OPEC proved to be a disappointment. Although at times it provoked dramatic leaps in oil prices, over the long run it has failed to secure long-term price increases much above what an unregulated market would have granted.[66] At the same time, the oil shocks wrought debilitating effects on much of the third world, raising their energy costs while reducing demand for their exports due to the recessions that followed. Moreover, the effects of the so-called Dutch disease [67] made such oil exporters as Mexico and Nigeria even more dependent on oil for their revenue, with terrible consequences when the inevitable price crashes finally came. On the whole, cartelization, which can only be applied to a few commodities in any case, will apparently do little to rectify any imbalance that exists in the world economy.

The IMF and the World Bank are currently able to wring substantial concessions from weak third-world governments,[68] yet few or none from first-world governments. The result is that at a time of increasing protectionism in the first world, third-world countries are being forced to throw open their economies to a competition that can be grossly unfair. This can severely damage these economies. In the early 1990s, for example, the European Community was dumping its heavily subsidized beef in West Africa, driving the Sahelian beef industry to the brink of extinction. The irony was that the European Community was at the same time funding the development of the Sahelian beef industry as part of its aid program.

If the global political economy does not permit the use of IIM in the third world, and trade with the first world presently puts third-world countries in an unequal relationship from which they do not always benefit, where are third-world governments to turn?

I   A New Beginning for the Third World?

In April 1995, Zambia's president, Frederick Chiluba, gave a speech to a gathering at the University of the West Indies in Jamaica in which he played upon historic ties between Africa and the Caribbean. He called for third-world countries to join together in trading blocs that would foster trade among third-world countries (or South-South trade, as it is sometimes called)[69] and depend less on trade with the first world. Zambia had been buffeted by harsh economic winds in the previous couple of decades, and structural adjustment left it battered. Chiluba echoed the sentiment of many intellectuals, particularly those in the third world, that it was time for the third world to break off from the world economy and find its own way forward.

South-South trade offers several benefits. First, it allows producers to take advantage of complementarities. Some cotton-producing countries could specialize in textiles production, metal-producing countries could specialize in metal industries, and so forth. Second, it reduces strains on foreign exchange. Trade on the world market is generally carried on in a small number of first-world currencies, notably the U.S. dollar. The more imports one seeks, the more U.S. dollars one needs, and the more primary goods one must therefore export to obtain these. This investment in primary production absorbs an increasing amount of a country's resources, inhibiting the development of an industrial sector. However, if instead a group of third-world countries could agree to use their own medium of exchange, the need for foreign exchange would decline, and resources could be concentrated in the development of secondary industry. Third, such trade can lead to the production of goods that are more appropriate to third-world countries. Because, for example, African soap producers compete with soap companies from the first world, they must match their products in terms of promotion, packaging, and a number of other features that raise the price of soap. If, however, a regional soap market were closed off to first-world imports, and only local producers were allowed to sell, it would enable them to develop a product that might be more suited to local needs. This sort of protectionism is not the same as import substitution; it is more akin to the structure of the European Community or the North American Free Trade Agreement (NAFTA), whereby intraregional trade coexists with insulation against much of the world economy. Finally, South-South trade can help countries to build new comparative advantages, because they can concentrate on developing their manufacturing industries rather than rely on traditional primary exports: although South-South trade accounts for only about 5 percent of all world trade, 60 percent of the goods traded are manufactured goods.[70]

On paper, therefore, South-South trade can look like a panacea. Unfortunately, the idea may remain on paper. When President Chiluba threw Zambia's doors open to textiles imports from South Africa, Zambia's own textiles industry promptly disappeared.[71] Such an effect would be repeated anywhere that free-trade agreements among third-world countries were enacted. Effective intraregional trade would almost certainly require the participation of dominant, even overbearing, regional powers. For example, southern African countries could not create much of a free-trade area without South Africa, because they would have been trading many of the same commodities.[72] Once South Africa—which wants those countries' primary goods and can offer them finished goods—was brought in, the same thing that happened in Zambia became inevitable elsewhere. After all, South Africa's economy is three times greater than the combined weight of the region's economies.[73]

Anywhere intraregional trade was tried, this pattern would repeat itself. Nigeria, Côte d'Ivoire, or Kenya would replace South Africa.[74] Although the net gains to the region would be significant, it is likely that these gains would be concentrated in a few countries.[75] The effect would be the strengthening of regional hegemons at the expense of minor powers, a prospect that many African elites find unpalatable.[76] It is no surprise, therefore, that intra-African trade has elicited a good deal more talk than action. Moreover, many of the powerful third-world economies that might lead South-South trade are at present more interested in expanding than reducing their ties to the first world. Although in the past Latin American governments tried to create regional trade blocs, many are today looking north to eventual integration into NAFTA.

Yet as its governments fail to impose themselves on their societies, Africa may be transforming itself quietly. In the franc zone of West Africa, African entrepreneurs who are aware that reliance on developed-country markets may be risky have been expanding their exports to and increasing their links with businesspeople in neighboring countries.[77] Nigerian businesspeople have also shown a keen interest in cross-border activities.[78] In fact, intra-African trade may be rising more rapidly than official figures suggest, given that so much of it is concealed.[79] Moreover, the opening up to Western trade of Eastern Europe, and the concomitant reduction of interest and investment in Africa by the Western countries, not to mention the current trend toward regionalization of trade into sheltered blocs such as the European Community and NAFTA, may compel a greater South-South self-reliance.[80] Once apartheid was abolished in South Africa, the integration of the region became almost a historical inevitability. However, this may be a trade among those left behind, not a true South-South trade, because many in the third world are keen to leave it.

The third world has polarized, both economically and politically. Some countries, such as the East Asian NICs, have become strong. Others, particularly in sub-Saharan Africa, are in an economic mess at a time of severe internal and external political weakness. By the end of the twentieth century, in the forty-eight least-developed countries, of which thirty-three were in Africa, conditions had become even worse than they had been in the 1980s, the "lost decade." Their share of world exports had declined, food production per capita had decreased, their infrastructure had deteriorated, and most of them were even more dependent on agricultural-commodity exports than they had been when they started out.[81] In short, those countries that most desperately need assertive government action to develop their economies are those least likely to produce it.

▌ Conclusion

One conclusion seems inescapable. Some states, regardless of the economic potential of their countries, simply may not be able to engineer development in their current form. The heartening success stories of East Asia may find few imitators.

In fact, it is not only in Africa that the emerging practice of development is running in a direction contrary to that of the theory. The crisis of the state, which sees fiscal constraints forcing public authorities to renounce many of their functions, is international in its scope. Few of the world's states are currently building up their capacities. Most are going the opposite way, abandoning some functions or giving them off to agents in the private sector. Faced with a combination of slowed economic growth, stiffer competition from low-cost East Asian producers, and rising fiscal deficits and debt burdens, governments in most countries have been forced to pare back their public sectors in order to lower their economies' production costs and/or restore current-account balances. Structural adjustment has then added to this process in much of the third world.

In first-world countries, retrenchment is giving way to political struggles over the state's diminishing resource base, and to debates over how to redefine the state's role in society. In the third world, retrenchment is giving way to a sometimes anarchic development process, in which nonstate actors such as nongovernmental organizations (NGOs) and private companies increasingly play the leading roles. Indeed, it is sometimes noted that in the poorest countries, NGOs—whose agendas and interests sometimes run at cross-purposes to one another—sometimes play an even stronger role than states in directing development. Meanwhile, private companies are taking on formerly public tasks, especially where public utilities have been privatized. In countries in which governments have been unable to maintain infrastructure or security, private firms or networks have taken on these tasks for their own benefit.

The time for hard questions is approaching. If the experience of the East Asian NICs was exceptional, if conditions have changed for the worse in the world economy and the international political economy, if the political and economic prospects for some countries are growing bleaker all the time, a serious reconsideration of what development is and should entail may be in order. The time for another paradigm shift may be drawing near.

I Notes

1. For general discussions on the condition of the African state, see Donald Rothchild and Naomi Chazan, eds., *The Precarious Balance: State and Society in Africa* (Boulder and London: Westview Press, 1988); Ann Seidman, "Towards a New Vision of Sustainable Development in Africa: Presidential Address to 1990 Annual Meeting of the African Studies Association," *African Studies Review* 35, no. 1 (1992): 10.

2. Jessica Byron, "The Impact of Globalisation on the Caribbean," in *Globalisation: A Calculus of Inequality,* edited by Denis Benn and Kenneth Hall (Kingston, Jamaica: Ian Randle Publishers, 2000).

3. Goran Hyden defines governance specifically as "the conscious management of regime structures with a view to enhancing the legitimacy of the public realm" in "Governance and the Structure of Politics," in *Governance and Politics in Africa,* edited by Goran Hyden and Michael Bratton (Boulder and London: Lynne Rienner Publishers, 1992), p. 7. The World Bank uses the more narrow definition of "the exercise of political power to manage a nation's affairs" according to Michael Bratton and Donald Rothchild, "The Institutional Bases of Governance in Africa," in *Governance and Politics in Africa,* edited by Goran Hyden and Michael Bratton (Boulder and London: Lynne Rienner Publishers, 1992), p. 265.

4. Bratton and Rothchild, "The Institutional Bases of Governance."

5. See, for example, Thandika Mkandawire, "The Political Economy of Development with a Democratic Face," in *Africa's Recovery in the 1990s: From Stagnation and Adjustment to Human Development,* edited by Giovanni Andrea Cornia, Ralph van der Hoeven, and Thandika Mkandawire (New York: St. Martin's Press, and London: Macmillan, for UNICEF, 1992); J.-F. Médard, "L'état patrimonialisé," *Politique Africaine* 39 (1990): 25–36.

6. See, for example, Timothy M. Shaw, *Reformism and Revisionism in Africa's Political Economy in the 1990s* (New York: St. Martin's Press, and London: Macmillan, 1993), chapter 5; Christopher Clapham, "Democratisation in Africa: Obstacles and Prospects" (African Studies Association Conference, Stirling, September 1992); Michael Bratton and Nicolas van de Walle, "Popular Demands and State Responses," in *Governance and Politics in Africa,* edited by Goran Hyden and Michael Bratton (Boulder and London: Lynne Rienner Publishers, 1992); Richard Jeffries,

"The State, Structural Adjustment and Good Government in Africa," *Journal of Commonwealth and Comparative Politics* 31 (1993): 20–35.

7. Clapham, "Democratisation in Africa"; Kigane Mengisteab and Bernard I. Logan, "Africa's Debt Crisis: Are Structural Adjustment Programs Relevant?" *Africa Development* 16, no. 1 (1991): 95–113.

8. For an example of this, see Lars Rudebeck, "The Effects of Structural Adjustment in Kandjadja, Guinea-Bissau," *Review of African Political Economy* 49 (1990): 34–51. Tom Forrest has also come across vigilante squads that do policing in Nigeria (personal communication, July 1995).

9. Basil Davidson, *The Black Man's Burden* (London: James Currey, 1992), and D. Darbon, "L'état prédateur," *Politique Africaine* 39 (1990): 37–45.

10. See Goran Hyden, *Beyond Ujamaa in Tanzania* (Berkeley: University of California Press, 1980).

11. Jean-François Bayart, *The State in Africa* (London: Longman, 1993); Patrick Chabal, "Some Reflections on the Post-Colonial State in Portuguese-Speaking Africa," *Africa Insight* 23 (1993): 129–135.

12. José Serra, "Three Mistaken Theses Regarding the Connection Between Industrialization and Authoritarian Regimes," in *The New Authoritarianism in Latin America,* edited by David Collier (Princeton, N.J.: Princeton University Press, 1979).

13. Karen L. Remmer, "The Politics of Economic Stabilization: IMF Standby Programs in Latin America, 1954–1984," *Comparative Politics* 19, no. 1 (1986): 1–24; Stephan Haggard and Robert F. Kaufman, eds., *The Politics of Economic Adjustment* (Princeton, N.J.: Princeton University Press, 1992), pp. 32–34; John Healey and Mark Robinson, *Democracy, Governance and Economic Policy: Sub-Saharan Africa in Comparative Perspective* (London: Overseas Development Institute, 1992), p. 122; Robert H. Bates and Anne O. Krueger, *Political and Economic Interactions in Economic Policy Reform* (Oxford: Basil Blackwell, 1993), p. 459; Mick Moore, "Economic Liberalization Versus Political Pluralism in Sri Lanka," *Modern Asian Studies* 24 (1990): 341–383; Richard Ball and Gordon C. Rausser, *Governance Structures and the Durability of Economic Reforms: Evidence from Inflation Stabilizations* (Berkeley: University of California at Berkeley Department of Agriculture and Resource Economics, California Agricultural Experiment Station, Working Paper No. 648, 1993).

14. Stephan Haggard and Steven B. Webb, "What Do We Know About the Political Economy of Economic Policy Reform?" *World Bank Research Observer* 8 (1993): 146.

15. John Toye, "Interest Group Politics and the Implementation of Adjustment Policies in Sub-Saharan Africa," *Journal of International Development* 4 (1992): 193.

16. Hamza Alavi, "The State in Post-Colonial Societies," *New Left Review* 74 (1972): 59–81; John S. Saul, "The State in Post-Colonial Societies: Tanzania," in John S. Saul, *The State and Revolution in Eastern Africa* (New York and London: Monthly Review Press, 1979).

17. Jorgen Dige Pedersen suggests that the popularity of the model among some Indianists is unwarranted. He argues that it overstates the power of the bureaucracy, and overlooks the rise to prominence of the agrarian bourgeoisie and the modern "high-tech oriented fractions" of the industrial bourgeoisie in the 1980s. See "State, Bureaucracy and Change in India," *Journal of Development Studies* 28 (1992): 616–639.

18. See, for example, Alice Amsden, *Asia's Next Giant: South Korea and Late Industrialization* (New York: Oxford University Press, 1989); Larry L. Burmeister,

"State, Industrialization and Agricultural Policy in Korea," *Development and Change* 21 (1990): 197–223; Fatimah Halim, "The Transformation of the Malaysian State," *Journal of Contemporary Asia* 20, no. 1 (1990): 64–88.

19. Robert Wade, *Governing the Market: Economic Theory and the Role of Government in East Asian Industrialization* (Princeton, N.J.: Princeton University Press, 1990).

20. Dwayne Woods, "Civil Society in Europe and Africa: Limiting State Power Through a Public Sphere," *African Studies Review* 35, no. 2 (1992): 77–100; Clapham, "Democratisation in Africa," pp. 13–15; Healey and Robinson, *Democracy, Governance and Economic Policy,* pp. 89–91. See also John W. Harbeson et al., eds., *Civil Society and the State in Africa* (Boulder and London: Lynne Rienner Publishers, 1994), and John Lucas, "The State, Civil Society and Regional Elites: A Study of Three Associations in Kano, Nigeria," *African Affairs* 93 (1994): 21–38.

21. India may provide a case in point. See Vijay Joshi, "Democracy and Development in India," *The Round Table* 333 (1995): 73–79; Jagdish Bhagwati, *India in Transition: Freeing the Economy* (Oxford: Clarendon Press, 1993), pp. 82–83; E. Sridharan, "Economic Liberalisation and India's Political Economy: Toward a Paradigm Synthesis," *Journal of Commonwealth and Comparative Politics* 31, no. 3 (1999): 13–19. Cf. Steven Radelet, "Reform Without Revolt: The Political Economy of Economic Reform in the Gambia," *World Development* 20 (1992): 1087–1099.

22. Gustav Ranis, "East and South-East Asia: Comparative Development Experience," *Bangladesh Development Studies* 20, nos. 2–3 (1992): 69–88; Ball and Rausser, *Governance Structures;* Bates and Krueger, *Political and Economic Interactions,* pp. 457–458; Haggard and Kaufman, *The Politics of Economic Adjustment,* p. 30.

23. Healey and Robinson, *Democracy, Governance and Economic Policy,* p. 91; Iyanatul Islam, "Political Economy and East Asian Economic Development," *Asian-Pacific Economic Literature* 6, no. 2 (1992): 69–101.

24. Amsden, *Asia's Next Giant,* p. 32; Kristen Nordhaug, "Late Industrialization and Democracy: The Case of Taiwan," in *Development Theory: Recent Trends. Proceedings of the NFU Annual Conference 1992* (Bergen: Report of the Chr. Michelsen Institute, 1993).

25. Deborah A. Bräutigam, "What Can Africa Learn from Taiwan? Political Economy, Industrialization Policy, and Adjustment," *Journal of Modern African Studies* 32 (1994): 111–138.

26. Basil Davidson, *Africa in History* (New York: Collier Books, 1974), p. 288.

27. Richard Crook pioneered this controversial theory. See "State Capacity and Economic Development: The Case of Côte d'Ivoire," *IDS Bulletin* 19, no. 4 (1988): 19–25.

28. Even those outside the developmental-state school seem to accept this. See, for instance, Anne O. Krueger, *Political Economy of Policy Reform in Developing Countries* (Cambridge, Mass., and London: MIT Press, 1993), chapter 7; Bates and Krueger, *Political and Economic Interactions,* p. 462.

29. Strong parties are an element in state strength emphasized by Haggard and Webb, "What Do We Know," pp. 150–151.

30. Stephan Haggard, Byung-Kook Kim, and Chung-In Moon, "The Transition to Export-Led Growth in South Korea, 1954–1966," *Journal of Asian Studies* 50 (1991): 850–873.

31. See, for example, Ziya Öniş, "Redemocratization and Economic Liberalization in Turkey: The Limits of State Autonomy," *Studies in Comparative International Development* 27, no. 2 (1992): 3–23.

32. Richard Sandbrook, *The Politics of Africa's Economic Stagnation* (Cambridge: Cambridge University Press, 1985), and *The Politics of Africa's Economic Recovery* (Cambridge: Cambridge University Press, 1993).

33. For a couple of examples, see Susanne Mueller, "Retarded Capitalism in Tanzania," *Socialist Register* (1980): 203–226, and "The Historical Origins of Tanzania's Ruling Class," *Canadian Journal of African Studies* 15 (1981): 459–497; Andrew Coulson, *Tanzania: A Political Economy* (Oxford: Clarendon Press, 1982), on Tanzania; Patrick Manning, "L'Affaire Adjovi: La bourgeoisie foncière naissante au Dahomey, face à l'administration," in *Entreprises et Entrepreneurs en Afrique,* vol. 2, edited by Catherine Coquery-Vidrovitch and Alain Forest (Paris: Éditions l'Harmattan, 1983), on Dahomey (Benin). Of the eight territories in French West Africa, apart from Côte d'Ivoire only Senegal had a strong core of people who could loosely be called capitalists in the pre-independence Territorial Assembly. For details, see Ruth Schachter Morgenthau, *Political Parties in French-Speaking West Africa* (Oxford: Clarendon Press, 1964), appendix VIII, pp. 400–401. Cf. E. A. Brett, "State Power and Economic Inefficiency: Explaining Political Failure in Africa" (Manchester, England: Political Science Association Conference 1985).

34. Georg Sorensen, "Democracy, Authoritarianism and State Strength," *European Journal of Development Research* 5, no. 1 (1993); see also Amsden, *Asia's Next Giant,* p. 35.

35. See, for example, Nicos Poulantzas, *L'état, le pouvoir, le socialisme* (Paris: Presses Universitaires de France, 1978); Claus Offe and V. Ronge, "Theses on the Theory of the State," *New German Critique* 6 (1975): 137–147.

36. Thus, in Nigeria, the businesspeople who acceded to political power at the time of independence were traders who sought state power for the commercial opportunities and fast returns it offered; see Gavin Williams, *The Origins of the Nigerian Civil War* (Milton Keynes, England: Open University Press, 1983), pp. 33–34.

37. For some examples of this sort of behavior, see Mete Pamir, *Determinants of Late Development: A Study of Turkey's Late Industrialisation Attempt Until 1946* (Bergen: Chr. Michelsen Institute Report, 1993).

38. My research in Côte d'Ivoire in February 1994 confirmed this.

39. For an example of this kind of class politics in practice, see John Rapley, *Ivoirien Capitalism* (Boulder: Lynne Rienner Publishers, 1993), chapters 3 and 6.

40. See the conclusion to Louis Putterman and Dietrich Rueschemeyer, *State and Market in Development: Synergy or Rivalry?* (Boulder and London: Lynne Rienner Publishers, 1992).

41. Seiji Naya and Pearl Imada, "Development Strategies and Economic Performance of the Dynamic Asian Economies: Some Comparisons with Latin America," *Pacific Review* 3 (1990): 301; Islam, "Political Economy and East Asian Economic Development," p. 77; Ezra F. Vogel, *The Four Little Dragons: The Spread of Industrialization in East Asia* (Cambridge, Mass.: Harvard University Press, 1991); Haggard, Kim, and Moon, "The Transition to Export-Led Growth," p. 869.

42. Tor Skålnes, "The State, Interest Groups and Structural Adjustment in Zimbabwe," *Journal of Development Studies* 29 (1993): 401–428; Pedersen, "State, Bureaucracy and Change in India," and "Explaining Economic Liberalization in India: State and Society Perspectives," *World Development* 28, no. 2 (2000): 265–282.

43. Raymond A. Hinnebusch, "The Politics of Economic Reform in Egypt," *Third World Quarterly* 14, no. 1 (1993): 159–171.

44. Carlos E. Juárez, "Trade and Development Policies in Colombia: Export Promotion and Outward Orientation, 1967–1992," *Studies in Comparative International Development* 28, no. 3 (fall 1993): 67–97.

45. Rapley, *Ivoirien Capitalism,* chapter 3.

46. J. Stephen Morrison, "Botswana's Formative Late Colonial Experience," in *Botswana: The Political Economy of Democratic Development*, edited by Stephen John Stedman (Boulder and London: Lynne Rienner Publishers, 1993); Balefi Tsie, "The Political Context of Botswana's Development Performance," *Southern Africa Political and Economic Monthly* 6, no. 12 (September 1993): 35–39; Abdi Ismail Samatar, *An African Miracle: State and Class Leadership and Colonial Legacy in Botswana Development* (Portsmouth, N.H.: Heinemann, 1999). However, there is disagreement over the support base of the contemporary Botswana state. See Roger Charlton, "Bureaucrats and Politicians in Botswana's Policymaking Process: A Re-interpretation," *Journal of Commonwealth and Comparative Politics* 29 (1991): 265–282; D. R. Gasper, "Development Planning and Decentralization in Botswana," in *Decentralizing for Participatory Planning?* edited by P. de Valk and K. H. Wekwete (Aldershot, England: Gower, 1990). Writers on Botswana often stress its exceptionality. Among other things, while it has exhibited state strength and spearheaded growth very effectively, it has not behaved like a developmental state in that it has not intervened extensively to promote industrialization. Roy Love has asserted that the Botswana state has been assisting its "cattle capitalists" to make the transition to urban capitalism, much as happened in Côte d'Ivoire, though the data is still sketchy and the scale more modest than in Côte d'Ivoire, let alone the more famous developmental states. See "Drought, Dutch Disease and Controlled Transition in Botswana Agriculture," *Journal of Southern African Studies* 20 (1994): 71–83, and cf. Samatar, *An African Miracle*.

47. Dan O'Meara, *Volkskapitalisme: Class, Capital and Ideology in the Development of Afrikaner Nationalism, 1934–1948* (Cambridge: Cambridge University Press, 1983); Merle Lipton, *Capitalism and Apartheid* (Aldershot, England: Wildwood House, 1986).

48. Jonathan Barker, *Rural Communities Under Stress* (Cambridge: Cambridge University Press, 1989).

49. Merle L. Bowen, "Beyond Reform: Adjustment and Political Power in Contemporary Mozambique," *Journal of Modern African Studies* 30 (1992): 255–279.

50. James S. Wunsch and Dele Olowu, *The Failure of the Centralized State: Institutions and Self-Governance in Africa* (Oxford: Westview Press, 1990); Robert Klitgaard, *Adjusting to Reality: Beyond "State Versus Market" in Economic Development* (San Francisco: ICS Press, 1991); Giovanni Andrea Cornia, Ralph van der Hoeven, and Thandika Mkandawire, *Africa's Recovery in the 1990s: From Stagnation and Adjustment to Human Development* (New York: St. Martin's Press, and London: Macmillan, for UNICEF, 1992); Goran Hyden, "Responses from Below: A Tale of Two Tanzanian Villages," *Food Policy* 15 (1990): 299–305; Akin L. Mabogunje, "Mobilizing Nigeria's Grassroots for Increased Food Production: Reaching Out from the Centre," *Food Policy* 15 (1990): 306–312; Alain de Janvry, Elisabeth Sadoulet, and Erik Thorbecke, "Introduction to Special Section on State, Market and Civil Organisations," *World Development* 21 (1993): 573; Frances Stewart, "Contribution to EADI Session on Governance, Adjustment and Reform" (Berlin: European Association of Development Research and Training Institutes Conference, 1993). Cf. the World Bank's current stance, which is that central governments should continue to finance services, while leaving service delivery in the hands of private sectors and nongovernmental associations; see Robert Hecht and Philip Musgrove, "Rethinking the Government's Role in Health," *Finance & Development* (September 1993): 6–9.

51. For a survey of findings, see *Public Administration and Development* 12 (1992): 1–122. Ingham and Kalam have identified a shift in the decentralization literature away from cautious optimism toward a view that decentralization is not self-evidently good. See Barbara Ingham and A. K. M. Kalam, "Decentralization and

Development: Theory and Evidence from Bangladesh," *Public Administration and Development* 12 (1992): 377.

52. William Tordoff, "Decentralisation, Comparative Experience in Commonwealth Africa," *Journal of Modern African Studies* 32 (1994): 555–580.

53. Bratton and Rothchild, "The Institutional Bases of Governance," pp. 269, 284.

54. Bayart, *The State in Africa,* pp. 91–92.

55. Janet MacGaffey, *Entrepreneurs and Parasites: The Struggle for Indigenous Capitalism in Zaire* (Cambridge: Cambridge University Press, 1987).

56. Tom Forrest, *The Advance of African Capital: Studies in the Growth of Nigerian Private Enterprise* (Edinburgh: Edinburgh University Press, for the International African Institute, 1994), chapter 9.

57. BBC World Service, 28 September 1994.

58. Andrew E. Green, "South Korea's Automobile Industry: Development and Prospects," *Asian Survey* 32 (1992): 411–428.

59. Deborah A. Bräutigam, "What Can Africa Learn from Taiwan? Political Economy, Industrialization Policy, and Adjustment," *Journal of Modern African Studies* 32 (1994): 111–138.

60. Naya and Imada, "Development Strategies and Economic Performance," p. 311.

61. Richard Grabowski, "Import Substitution, Export Promotion, and the State in Economic Development," *Journal of Developing Areas* 28 (1994): 540. See also Syed Nawab Haider Naqvi, "Development Economics: The Winds of Change," *Pakistan Development Review* 31 (1992): 352.

62. For a general discussion, see Diana Tussie and David Glover, "Developing Countries in World Trade: Implications for Bargaining," in *The Developing Countries in World Trade: Policies and Bargaining Strategies,* edited by Tussie and Glover (Boulder: Lynne Rienner Publishers, and Ottawa: International Development Research Centre, 1993), p. 226.

63. Dragoslav Avramovic, *Developing Countries in the International Economic System: Their Problems and Prospects in the Markets for Finance, Commodities, Manufactures and Services* (New York: Human Development Report Office Occasional Paper No. 3, 1992); Alexander J. Yeats, "Do African Countries Pay More for Imports? Yes," *World Bank Economic Review* 4 (1990): 1–20.

64. For details, see Luc Soete, "Technological Dependency: A Critical View," in *Dependency Theory: A Critical Reassessment,* edited by Dudley Seers (London: Frances Pinter, 1981).

65. See Soete, "Technological Dependency," for a detailed examination of the conditions of market strength and weakness.

66. See M. A. Adelman, "Oil Fallacies," *Foreign Policy* 82 (1991): 3–16.

67. Dutch disease refers to a situation in which one export industry produces a large influx of foreign currency into an economy. This influx leads to currency overvaluation, because the value of the local currency is bid up by all the foreign exchange flowing into the economy seeking conversion. This raises the cost of money, and hence investment, causing investment to fall in all industries save for the export industry in question. At the same time, currency overvaluation makes other exports less competitive on the world market. When the price for the main export commodity comes back down, the economy will have few other sectors to fall back on for export revenue, because they will have been discouraged during the boom days.

68. However, one must avoid overstating the degree of this dependence. See Haggard and Webb, "What Do We Know," p. 157; Miles Kahler, "External Influence,

Conditionality, and the Politics of Adjustment," in *The Politics of Economic Adjustment,* edited by Stephan Haggard and Robert R. Kaufman (Princeton, N.J.: Princeton University Press, 1992). An appropriate view of the relationship between third-world governments and the IMF and the World Bank is to see the former not as tools of the latter, but rather weak clients.

69. The third world is sometimes referred to as the South, because so many of the world's poorest countries lie in the Southern Hemisphere, whereas most of the developed countries lie in the Northern Hemisphere.

70. Frances Stewart, in a review in *The World Economy* 17, no. 4 (July 1994): 623–624.

71. *The Economist,* 1 July 1995.

72. Austin B. A. Ngwira, "Southern Africa: Regional Integration Without National Integration" (Maseru: Congress of the Southern African Development Research Association, organized by the Institute of Southern African Studies, National University of Lesotho, 1993).

73. BBC World Service, 29 August 1995.

74. Even proponents of South-South trade acknowledge that it would close down a lot of factories. See, for example, Cornia, van der Hoeven, and Mkandawire, *Africa's Recovery in the 1990s,* chapter 7.

75. For example, Dickson Yeboah contends that this would result from a shift to intra-African trade in food goods. See "Intra-African Food Trade: An Empirical Investigation," *The Developing Economies* 31, no. 1 (1993): 54–101.

76. At the 1993 Congress of the Southern African Development Research Association, for instance, scholars from outside South Africa were very anxious that their countries' dependence on their powerful neighbor should be reduced, regardless of the advent of black majority rule in South Africa.

77. Rapley, *Ivoirien Capitalism,* p. 123.

78. Forrest, *The Advance of African Capital,* chapters 8 and 9.

79. Jean-Pierre Barbier, "Des marchés protégés aux marchés libres," *Afrique Contemporaine* 164 (1992): 99–108. See also Brenda Chalfin, "Border Zone Trade and the Economic Boundaries of the State in North-East Ghana," *Africa* 71, no. 2 (2001): 202–224.

80. Sandro Sideri, "Restructuring the Post–Cold War World Economy: Perspectives and a Prognosis," *Development and Change* 24 (1993): 7–27; see also Edmond J. Keller, "Towards a New African Order? Presidential Address to the 1992 Annual Meeting of the African Studies Association," *African Studies Review* 36, no. 2 (1993): 1–10.

81. *Financial Times* (London), 4 July 1995, p. 27, reporting on a UN Conference on Trade and Development report.

7

Conclusion

As we enter the twenty-first century, the world looks very different from what it was like at the dawn of the twentieth century. Then, a few European countries controlled most of the globe's land mass. If Europe, and especially Britain, were beginning to wane in power, it was only to pass the torch to another Western power, the United States. In spite of colonialism, the world was a big place. The vast majority of the planet's inhabitants passed their lives in their small corner of the globe, foreign travel being accessible only to a privileged few, for whom it was a long and cumbersome process. Cargo ships traversed the seas, but national economies remained largely self-sufficient, providing many of their own energy and food supplies, and markets for their products. Communications technology, though far ahead of where it had been a century earlier, was only beginning to breach the great distances separating parts of the world. Far-off lands were still shrouded in romance and mystery, and the dream of Shangri-La, of a hidden idyll in some uncharted corner of the globe, remained faintly realistic. Although the first inklings of pessimism began to appear in philosophical and artistic circles in the late nineteenth century, in the main human faith in progress remained relatively unlimited. Modernism, with its belief in the evident superiority of the present, reigned supreme in architecture, and the art world still gave rise to movements, such as futurism, that venerated technology. The "white man's burden," which Europeans cited to justify the civilizing task of empire, was, despite its paternalism, a mentality that saw the world as moving forward and getting better. Nobody gave much thought to the idea that the planet's resources or carrying capacity might be limited, because those limits were not evident. There was little worry about a population explosion because there was plenty of unoccupied land on the planet.

Today, colonialism is a thing of the past in all but a few corners of the globe. And while the Western powers, led by the United States, continue to dominate the globe, many argue that the Western Age has entered its final act, and soon the curtain will open on the Pacific Age. In this century China will resume its historic place as the world's largest economy, and will be joined by several burgeoning economies in East and Southeast Asia. Still, in per capita terms China will remain poor for the foreseeable future, and its military dominance will not spread beyond a few of its immediate neighbors (such as Tibet), whereas technologically and militarily the West will continue to lead. The twenty-first century will thus see more than one pole in the world economy, to which will gravitate several countries, as a number of third-world countries enter the ranks of the middle-income and developed nations. Meanwhile, many countries, especially in sub-Saharan Africa, will become ever more firmly rooted in the third world.

Yet despite the growing gap between rich and poor and the end of colonialism, the world is a much smaller place. Computer and telecommunications technology links far corners of the globe within seconds, and the low cost of air travel makes the whole world accessible to Western travelers. There remain virtually no undiscovered or isolated corners of the earth. However, information tends to flow in one direction: satellite dishes in West Africa import U.S. sitcoms but export little African news, while there are few Nepalese backpackers who spend a year hiking through Europe after graduation. Faith in progress has come into question. Environmental consciousness and the fear of a population time bomb have in the last generation led many in the first world to call for a slowing of the planet's growth and to adopt a more skeptical attitude to technology. After a century in which science made possible the Holocaust and nuclear annihilation, modernism has ceded to postmodernism. This intellectual current calls into question the very concept of progress, and looks favorably on Nietzsche's idea of eternal recurrence, in which good and evil are constants that only alter their appearance from generation to generation and place to place.

New Age visionaries enthuse about the prospects of the future, in which a communications revolution remakes human consciousness and solves many of the world's problems. Through the use of new information technologies, third-world activists are starting to forge links with their peers in the first world, and thereby beginning to raise the consciousness of first-world populations. At the same time, just as highways in Africa run side by side with footpaths along which women carry bundles of firewood and babies strapped to their backs, the information highway surges ahead at a time when many African governments are struggling not to lose the battle against the most basic of ailments, such as diarrhea, that take millions of children's lives every year. So far, the agenda the first-world nations are drawing up for themselves still excludes much of the world. The third world will have to draw its own agenda, including its plans for development.

The tools used in the past, however, may no longer do the job. The extent of global interconnectedness, which allows goods, information, and capital to flow freely around the world and integrate most of the world's countries, has made autarky a thing of the past. A century or so ago it was feasible for a government to talk of charting its own autonomous route into the future. Today such a strategy, or even a development model that simply sought to reduce the degree of an economy's inclusion in the world economy, would probably be unworkable. One reason for this is that human capital is mobile today. Third-world middle classes, whose intellectual and managerial contribution to development is essential, have developed first-world tastes and attitudes. A government that sought to reduce their access to Hollywood videos and Parisian fashions in order to turn resources to investment might well watch them leave the country. The costs of cutting trade are onerous, and trying to protect one's producers will almost certainly entail losses of access to foreign markets.

On the other hand, the alternative to policies of increased national self-sufficiency, namely a warm embrace of the world economy, has been discredited by practice, as Chapter 4 has shown. The possibility that there might be an altogether different way to develop an economy, as the bold socialist experiment attempted to prove, has apparently been refuted as well. Where does this leave those countries that remain squarely in the third world? Is it true, as some have argued, that development has failed and the age of progress has reached its endpoint?

Let us draw together the strands of this book. In the postwar period, the ascendancy of Keynesian and structuralist economics provided the theoretical justification for state interventions in market economies, especially those in the third world. Radical thought pushed the state's role further and, in some cases, made it all-encompassing. However, once applied, these state-led strategies fell short of expectations, and by the 1970s they seemed to have outlived their usefulness. Neoclassical theory then resurfaced and made policy prescriptions that generally pointed in one direction: reducing the role of the state, and expanding the freedom of the market. These policy changes bore some fruit, but they too fell short of expectations, or yielded undesirable consequences. In response, a new statism has arisen in development thought. Unfortunately, this statism is probably not feasible in many third-world countries today. It is as if the development debate has reached a dead end, or at least a major obstacle. It may be time to begin looking for a new paradigm.

I The Search for a New Paradigm

In the philosophy of science, a paradigm is the general convention of thought that governs a discipline. For long stretches of time a given paradigm dominates the field and sets the debate within that discipline. Over time, however, bits and pieces of evidence begin to accumulate that do not fit the paradigm. But because science is conservative, its practitioners disregard these anomalies for as long as possible. Eventually the weight of evidence becomes too great, the old paradigm collapses, and a period of ferment follows in which the search for a new paradigm begins and all is thrown open to question. This period lasts until a new paradigm emerges that gains broad acceptance within the community of its discipline.

Development studies may now have entered a revolutionary phase. Neoclassical theory, though still dominant, is finding a lot of anomalies it cannot easily accommodate. Alternative paradigms, in particular socialist thought, have fallen as well. Although the academic left feels reinvigorated by the fall of these orthodoxies, it is having to renounce its twentieth-century faith in the state as an agent of social transformation. The search for a new paradigm has begun. Whereas it is possible to say that development thought has reached a crisis point, it is likely to overcome that crisis eventually. But what shape development thought will take in the coming years is open to debate. In the meantime, a number of questions will have to be considered in the attempt to put together a new paradigm, a new approach to development.

Can Development Models Be Universalized?

At the heart of this question lies an even more fundamental question: Are humans fundamentally alike? Neoclassical thought, for example, assumes that all humans are rational utility maximizers, and so the correct economic and political model will work anywhere. The Victorian belief in the white man's burden, which some suggest lives on in the activities of many development NGOs, premised itself on the similar view that the West discovered these universal laws of behavior a little earlier than everyone else, and was able to teach others how to use them to their advantage.

In the twentieth century, such assumptions faced no small amount of criticism, however. Anthropologists researched peoples so different from those in the Western world that they questioned whether or not there was anything, beyond the most basic level, that united human beings. In recent years postmodernism has rejected outright the idea of fundamental human characteristics. Everything, suggest the postmodernists, is relevant only to its context, and contexts differ markedly from place to place, and even within the same place from time to time. From this they infer that only people from a given context can possibly understand it and theorize about it. For example, only an African can develop a development model that can be applied with any success to Africa.

This ties into the ongoing debate surrounding culture and development. Culture refers to a people's intellectual, spiritual, and moral endowment.

The relationship between a person and his or her culture has sometimes been likened to that between a fish and water: he or she swims in it, lives in it, breathes it, and depends on it, but is unaware of its presence and, like a fish out of water, becomes aware of its importance only when taken out of it.[1] Some argue that cultures produce people to a greater degree than people produce cultures, and that therefore what emerges from or functions in one culture cannot be transposed to another. Along this line of reasoning, it is suggested that capitalism itself can emerge only out of certain cultures, and thus cannot be expected to develop elsewhere, at least not in a form recognizable to those in the heartland of capitalism in the West.

The paradigmatic treatise on this subject may be Max Weber's *The Protestant Ethic and the Spirit of Capitalism*. Weber argued that Calvinist and nonconformist Protestant societies placed a high value on thrift, hard work, and the production of wealth as a means to glorify God and do his work. By contrast, Catholic cultures were said to place lower values on such practices, or indeed to be suspicious of them, especially the production of wealth. Thus, it followed that the Protestant societies of Northern Europe led the way into the Industrial Revolution while the Catholic societies in the south always lagged behind. In a similar vein it has been argued that individualist cultures tolerate innovation but collectivist ones rein it in and thereby slow development.[2] Weber's thesis has met an uneven reception over the decades, but the concept of the Protestant work ethic has fixed itself a place in popular consciousness. A similar variant has emerged in recent years to explain East Asian success. Nationalists in East and Southeast Asia credit their economic success to their cultural superiority not only to other Asians, but indeed to the rest of the world.

Both neoclassical economists and leftist theorists are uneasy with this subject. For the former, discussions of culture throw up a number of assertions that defy quantification and cannot be integrated into mathematical models. For the latter, the problem stems from intellectual ancestry. Even non-Marxists among the left have tended to adopt Marx's fundamental premise that consciousness is a product of material conditions, and thus culture responds to rather than motivates economic change. Added to this attitude is a suspicion that once one injects the variable of culture into an equation, one makes possible all sorts of racist claims regarding higher and lower peoples.

The hypothesis that some cultures are prone to develop while others are prone to lag behind may be questionable: although some have argued that, for example, Indian and African cultures are ill-suited to development,[3] in fact they have yielded some impressive success stories. After all, in the latter decades of the twentieth century, Botswana and not one of the East Asian NICs was the world's fastest-growing economy. However, unless one accepts that the laws of economics codified in Western textbooks are universal, it does not stand to reason that profoundly different cultures will automatically yield identical economies. Some argue that the market produces its own culture,[4] or that capitalist development will everywhere yield capitalist institutions and values such as liberal democracy and respect for individual rights.[5] Others suggest that whereas different cultures can produce capitalist economies, the way these economies operate will differ somewhat.[6] Thus, Japanese managerial techniques, based on a paternalistic relationship between employer and employee, have often run into opposition when applied in the United States, where workers are more accustomed to seeking equality with their employers through unionization and collective bargaining.

Development theorists would probably do best to at least remain sensitive to culture. At the same time, those who insist that culture predetermines or in some cases precludes development need to provide empirical justification for their claims. Merely alleging, for instance, that the reason for the differences in development experiences between India and Japan is simply cultural will not convince a skeptic. The pioneering research of such neoclassical theorists as P. T. Bauer (discussed in Chapter 3), who found similar responses to price incentives in people from profoundly different cultures, cannot be ignored. Such findings do not refute the importance of culture but may establish that humans are essentially the same.

What Role Will Environmental Issues Play in Development Theory?

More perplexing to development theory than culture is the issue of the environment. In the 1960s and 1970s there arose a concern with environmental issues in the study of development. However, discussion was largely confined to the periphery of the field. Then, in 1987 the World Commission on Environment and Development, usually referred to as the Brundtland Commission, spawned an explosion of literature on a concept it popularized in its report: sustainable development, the principle that any development should be sustainable over the long term. Deforestation, for example, must be accompanied by reforestation, and pollution should only be released in amounts the atmosphere can absorb.

There are some who doubt that sustainable development is an operational concept. They do not think it is possible to construct adequate measures of environmental degradation for evaluating development policies, given that some environmental effects manifest themselves only over the long term or in a widely dispersed manner. For example, pollutants released into the atmosphere often cross international boundaries. How does one locate the polluter and determine the costs it should bear? At what point does development become unsustainable? Who determines what is and is not sustainable?

In addition, many people now wonder whether rapid development can be sustained at all. In recent years people have gained an acute awareness that an apparently limitless human demand for resources faces a planet endowed with limited supplies and/or carrying capacity for pollutants. In particular, global warming leapt to the top of the agenda in the 1990s, giving rise to the 1997 Kyoto Accord, with its plan to cap planetary greenhouse-gas emissions. That the planet was warming seemed incontestable. That greenhouse gases—the emissions that result from the burning of fossil fuels—were behind this warming was, for a time, the topic of lively debate. However, when in 2001 an international panel of scientists—the Intergovernmental Panel on Climate Control (IPCC)—released a report endorsing the thesis that warming resulted from greenhouse-gas emissions and was perhaps worse than feared,[7] the debate, at least among academics, appeared close to resolved. Many environmentalists have raised the alarm that the planet will choke from the demands being placed on it, and many people fear that that day is not far off. At the leftist margins of development studies, one response to the environmental challenge has been a wholesale repudiation of development. The so-called new economics school maintains that development has been a complete failure, and it calls for a radical rethinking of the concept of development and what it entails.[8]

However, ending development may create more problems than it solves. Leaders of third-world countries point out that the voices against development tend to emanate from the first world, which has already reaped its harvest. To many in the third world, in calling for an end to development the first world can appear hypocritical, rather like someone who emigrates to a prosperous land and then turns around and calls for a halt to immigration. Nor may a moratorium on development be needed before environmental problems can be addressed. Although in principle it is true that the planet has a fixed limit to many resources (minerals, for example), in practice technological development allows the approach of these limits to be postponed to the distant future. Meanwhile, many other resources are renewable (land and water, for example); in regard to "carrying capacity," or the population a region's resources can support, it is clear that much of the third world, in particular Africa, retains considerable unused capacity for development.[9]

Globally, though, the planet's ability to absorb pollution may be nearing a dangerous threshold, if it has not already passed it. The IPCC report noted that while rich countries accounted for most greenhouse-gas emissions, it was poor countries in tropical regions that were suffering most acutely from their effects. Sustainability is thus now a pressing concern. Whether or not sustainable development is an operational concept is still moot; the environmental assessment of development projects is a field that remains in its infancy. Yet there are grounds for cautious optimism. Improved means of measuring the environmental impact of development, such as factoring resource depletion or environmental degradation into national accounts, seem to be emerging.[10] What does seem clear, though, is that factoring the environment into development policies will require further intervention by the government. Although a few theorists maintain that the free market can rectify all environmental problems,[11] theirs are dissident voices. In truth, the existing research suggests that the free market, via structural-adjustment programs, has not improved environmental conditions and may actually have worsened them.[12]

Even if market incentives are relied upon to encourage the adoption of "green" technology, government activism is required to establish an incentive structure. Take, for example, pollution rights, a means proposed to reduce industrial pollution by relying on market incentives. The idea is that firms will be issued with rights to release only so much pollution into the atmosphere. Firms that exceed their limit will have to buy the excess pollution rights from cleaner firms that have come in under the limit. If there are many heavy polluters, they will bid up the price of these rights, making it a profitable activity for firms to adopt cleaner technology so that they can recoup their investment by selling pollution rights. Thus, no government coercion will be necessary; the market will take care of it all. Yet the government will need to determine the acceptable limits on pollution and issue rights, much as it does with the money supply, and to enforce penalties on those who exceed their rights. The state may be able to minimize its new role in environmental management, but it will not be able to withdraw from the task altogether.

One change in the environmental debate in development studies is especially promising. Not long ago, the political right dismissed environmentalists as granola-crunching Luddites in bulky sweaters. Today, virtually everyone agrees that the environment question must be taken into account by economic theory. They may not be sure how to approach the issue, or how to bring it into their discipline, but development theorists are becoming environmentally conscious. Even the IMF has indicated its receptiveness to the concept of sustainable development.[13]

Nevertheless, optimism must be tempered with caution. As with other dimensions of theory, what is found to be possible in principle may yet prove difficult in practice. Several theorists agree that although sustainable development is probably economically feasible, the unavoidable costs it will entail may yet prove politically insurmountable.[14] Sustainable development will require people to do more than buy "green" products or stuff paper into recycling bins. Its success may very well depend on first-world populations moving away from their "consumption-oriented lifestyles and expectations."[15]

Indeed, many environmentalists lament what they see as the cynical behavior of political leaders in co-opting environmental issues in order to serve their own political ends, often at a disservice to the environment. During the 2000 U.S. election campaign, Green Party presidential candidate

Ralph Nader called Bill Clinton the great anaesthetizer, suggesting the then-president had succeeded in disarming the environmental movement with soothing words while his government worsened matters with its policies. There may be some truth to this, though the Clinton administration was probably not exceptional, typifying as it did what might be called liberal environmentalism.

In particular, the Clinton administration took as fact the so-called environmental Kuznets curve. This enabled the U.S. government to tell its people that there would be no trade-off between growth and the environment, as many if not most environmentalists allege. In effect, they were told that they could have their cake and eat it too, a claim that obviously has enormous political appeal. It is, however, highly suspect.

The basic idea behind the environmental Kuznets curve is that as an economy grows, it shifts toward more capital- and knowledge-intensive forms of production. It thus becomes more efficient or, in the popular jargon, "lighter." As, for example, an economy progresses from manufacturing to service production, it consumes fewer natural resources per unit of output, and thus produces fewer pollutants. A bank or Internet firm may produce as much economic output as a factory, but without a smokestack. So, following this logic, as an economy grows its pollution output increases, but it then crosses a threshold into leaner production, and its pollution output comes down. The solution, therefore, is simple: grow your way out of an environmental crisis, and the faster the growth, the quicker the solution would come. Thus, a combination of progrowth policies, combined with liberalization policies that would accelerate the globalization of capitalism, thereby bringing growth to the third world, was the proposed recipe for the environmental problem.

Both the evidence in support of and the theory underlying the environmental Kuznets curve are weak, though.[16] Empirically, although it now appears to be a reasonable rule that as growth proceeds, eventually a threshold is crossed after which resource unit–input per unit of output declines, any gains are more than offset by the greater rate of output. For example, cars may become more energy-efficient, but people buy a lot more cars. Thus, what evidence we have so far is that input consumption and pollution output have proceeded apace in the first-world countries, and most certainly in the United States. The image popularized by the Clinton administration and its sympathizers in the media was of the computer chip, embodying as much value-added as a car, but weighing far less and consuming a relatively minute share of natural resources in its production. This image might be correct if consumption stopped at the point the chip was made. But the image of a weightless Internet economy must be set against the fact that hand-held Internet devices reportedly have the electrical capacity of a refrigerator. Because their users keep them connected to the Internet twenty-four hours a day, whole warehouses filled with servers and cooled by air conditioners are required to operate as well. Indeed, the vision of a hyper-efficient Internet economy was belied in the summer of 2000 when the state of California, the Internet heartland, began to suffer rolling blackouts due to the excessive energy demands of the burgeoning "new" economy.

Nevertheless, some optimists maintain that future technological developments, or even the widespread application of existing technologies, will resolve any future problems. Julian Simon makes much of the past failures by environmentalists to make future predictions because they fail to anticipate future developments, and makes a convincing argument for extrapolating future developments from past trends.[17] But if we apply that principle, we see the sort of problems that lie ahead. Let us assume, for instance, that a combination of convergence and efficiency improvements applies. That is, first-world economic growth spills over into the third world, and brings with it efficiency gains that ultimately lead to the market solving, on a global scale, the very environmental problems it has caused. By the end of this century, it was postulated, the world would be uniformly rich, clean, and healthy. Does this vision stand to reason? We can do a simple test. If we assume that the economies of the first world will continue to grow at a 3 percent annual growth rate over the next century; that the global population will stabilize at around 10 billion by 2050, with the increase coming in the third world; and that the third-world countries will grow at rates that enable them to more or less converge with the first world by the end of the century, the global economy will then end up roughly 140 times greater than it is today. Now let us extrapolate from past trends in efficiency gains. The efficiency of the car, thanks to improvements in engine efficiency and a lightening of the body, generally improved by roughly a factor of four in the second half of the twentieth century, measured by fuel consumption. Evidently, past trends in efficiency gains will clearly be outstripped—as they have been so far—by output increases.

Conservative politicians in the first world try to shift the focus of blame by saying that the bulk of *future* pollution output will take place in the third world. Therefore, the costs of future environmental regulation should be borne at least equally by poor countries, not solely by the rich ones as is the usual demand of third-world governments. Barring some future technological revolution that results in hyper-efficient production, what this amounts to—though obviously nobody wants to say it too openly—is a call for third-world countries to content themselves with lower levels of per capita output than their first-world counterparts. This argument is weak. Aside from its dubious moral underpinnings—it can look a bit like locking the environmental gate after the polluting horses of the industrial countries have already bolted—it is almost certainly impractical. Convergence is not just a moral imperative, it is also a political and environmental one. If the first world remains rich and the third world remains poor, the world is likely to become more unstable, as was discussed in Chapter 4, with debilitating effects on the economy and society. But the environmental crisis is certain to worsen, as poverty tends to encourage inefficient and environmentally unsound consumption practices.[18] In that sense, growth in the third world *will* lead to more environmentally sound practices, but if the world as a whole is currently living just within or even beyond its means, third-world growth may well have to be offset by either a stabilization or even a retreat from current output levels in the first world.[19] At a minimum, first-world countries will have to provide the third world with generous financial assistance to enable investments in efficient technologies, as the current output of much of the third world does not provide sufficient capital for such.[20]

To date, only the most radical voices in the first world have been willing to call publicly for the rich countries to draw down their existing output to resolve the growing environmental problem. Most others have either evaded the issue or placed their faith in the future growth of the third world providing the resources needed to improve efficiency. But as we have seen, this is a questionable proposition. Some optimists nevertheless cling to the possibilities of endless growth with the conviction that the future will see technological innovations we can scarcely imagine now, but that will eventually cause efficiency to improve at exponential rates, in place of the steady gains we have seen in the past. That may be so, but now it would be the technological optimists—some call them utopians or cornucopians—not the environmentalists, who are violating Simon's rule to rely on past trends rather than purely speculative future ones. But even if we concede the faith in the future of the technological optimists, their prediction is governed by flawed theoretical assumptions.

In the absence of government regulation to direct how future efficiency improvements will be used, there is no reason to suppose that they will translate into reduced output of pollutants, or reduced consumption of inputs; the evidence to date suggests the contrary.[21] The optimists assume that efficiency gains will, in effect, free up resources that can be put to the service of the environment: cars powered by hyper-efficient engines will thus leave oil in the ground or keep pollutants from filling the air. However, left to the market, efficiency gains will merely translate into price reductions: reduced fuel use will not only save consumers money, but will also reduce the demand for fuel. Reduced demand in the context of fixed supply will thereby lower price, leading to even more cost savings. But these savings will flow into the pockets of consumers, creating demand for additional products. Indeed, continued growth is premised on the creation of new technologies, which create unanticipated new environmental problems whose effects are, on balance, permanent.[22] In other words, efficiency gains would simply accelerate consumption. This has been the historical pattern. In the absence of government policies that redirect the resources saved by efficiency toward environmental preservation—taxes that discourage consumption, for instance—there is no reason to expect it to be any different in the future.

There is no free lunch, Margaret Thatcher once declared. In that respect conservative politicians in the West are perhaps being more honest than their liberal counterparts when they say there will have to be a trade-off between growth and the environment. The only manner in which environmentalists differ from conservatives is simply in maintaining that the price is one worth paying. But the claim that we can grow our way out of environmental problems is one that deserves to be treated with a healthy dose of suspicion. In the 1990s, despite its government's rhetorical commitment to the Kyoto Protocol's call for reductions in carbon emissions, the U.S. economy's output of greenhouse gases increased year upon year. The emperor of the new economy turned out to have no clothes.

It seems fair to say that a genuine commitment to solving the environmental problem will entail costs, and it is not at all obvious that prosperous people in the first world, let alone poor people in the third world, are yet willing to bear those costs. For most, environmentalism has so far been a cuddly, user-friendly concept. The challenges it poses to development theory are likely surmountable. We can only hope that it will prove the same to political leaders and ordinary people. Though it may seem harsh, it may also be fair to say that to date, the major political leaders of the first world have fallen far short of the caliber needed to tackle the growing environmental problem. The world will thus have to wait for a new generation of leaders who possess both vision and courage, qualities that were in short supply during the pragmatic 1990s.

Is There a Population Time Bomb, and How Will It Affect the Third World?

Related to the question of the environment is that of population growth. In the 1970s a series of studies raised fears that the world was approaching an environmental Armageddon.[23] The planet's population was growing far faster than it had ever done before. These studies revived the prediction Thomas Malthus made in the late eighteenth century that population growth would soon outstrip food production. Although technological change, in particular more productive agricultural technologies, discredited Malthus's earlier prediction, it seemed now to regain its relevance. While population growth had slowed almost to a halt in the first world, it was charging ahead in the third world. It was predicted that before long there would be so many people on the planet that there would not be enough resources, in particular food and water, to go around. Ever since these apocalyptic predictions were made, the West has maintained a morbid fascination with the fear of population growth, and every so often someone produces a book or an article that claims to have discovered early signs of an impending crisis. In February 1994, for instance, Robert Kaplan wrote a much-discussed article, "The Coming Anarchy," in the *Atlantic Monthly* in which he suggested that crumbling states and civil wars in West Africa, allegedly fought over a declining resource base, presaged a violent and anarchic future that would eventually engulf most of the planet.

Though popular and compelling, such pessimism does not win as many converts in academic circles as it does in society at large. Journalists eager to uncover omens of Armageddon sometimes find evidence of overpopulation where none exists. Kaplan's article, for example, neglected to mention that Africa is, for the most part, not a densely populated continent, especially when compared to the more developed parts of the world in Europe and East Asia. Moreover, the economic decline and civil wars he cited as evidence of people fighting over a diminishing share of the pie simplified problems that had other causes. The economic decline bottomed out within the year and growth resumed, and one of the two civil wars he discussed showed signs of attenuating shortly afterwards. Besides, as was mentioned in the discussion on the environment, it has long been known that the planet could, if universally brought under the influence of modern technology, support many times over its current population.[24]

Many development theorists, especially those from the third world, reject outright the suggestion that population growth is a problem. They sometimes add that first-world observers emphasize population growth to detract attention from the real issue plaguing the third world: poverty. Most specialists now agree that the main cause of hunger, for example, is not overpopulation but poverty. After all, while African children starve or go hungry, the planet currently produces more than enough food to nourish humanity. Much of it, however, goes to waste in European and North American storehouses. One could add that environmentally unsustainable practices, such as slash-and-burn farming or the collection of firewood for fuel, often arise because people cannot afford the more convenient but expensive alternatives such as farming with chemical fertilizers or cooking with electricity. Even in third-world countries where population density is straining the environment, the adoption of modern agricultural technology would make it possible to support a growing population.[25] It is popular in the first world to advocate family-planning clinics as a solution to the third world's rapidly growing population, but it is not clear that increasing the availability of contraceptive technology will necessarily increase its use.[26] In many third-world settings, parents who limit their family size will equally limit their household labor force and the pool of people who will look after them when they get old.[27] Not surprisingly, this debate over how to deal with third-world population growth provoked some serious differences between first-world and third-world delegates at the UN's 1994 Conference on Population.

Nevertheless, many if not most development specialists maintain that even if population growth does not plunge us into environmental catastrophe in the near future, it remains a problem. They assert that unless the world's population growth rate slows, sometime in the twenty-first century it will place strains on the planet. In the meantime, growing populations are putting pressure on government budgets, as the latter struggle to keep pace with the health, housing, and education needs of new generations. This diverts resources from development and may slow growth, though one should avoid overstating this effect; the evidence that high population growth slows economic growth is not strong.[28]

Whatever remedies they propose for the short term, most specialists agree that in the long run successful development offers the best means to reduce fertility, especially if women are drawn into the development process and are among its chief beneficiaries.[29] In the meantime, an emerging school of thought argues that if left alone, the population problem will eventually take care of itself. There is evidence that as population density increases, people adopt more intensive and environmentally sustainable agricultural practices, which can in turn prompt development and thereby reduce fertility.[30] Along these lines it is worth noting that Africa's population-growth rate, which has often prompted fears of massive overpopulation in the twenty-first century, has recently showed signs of slowing.[31] It is too early to make very much of these findings, but time may show that the late-twentieth-century Western world's fear of the population explosion, like early-nineteenth-century Malthusian fears, was exaggerated. Indeed, by the turn of the century, the balance of scholarly opinion was shifting toward saying that population growth was no longer a critical problem in the third world.

What Will the New Balance Between State and Society Be?

Whatever one makes of them, neoclassical reforms have profoundly and permanently altered the societies of the third world. Neoclassical theorists have in recent years placed much emphasis on the connection between democracy and capitalism, arguing either that the spread of free-market capitalism has helped spread democracy, or conversely that democracy has facilitated the growth of capitalism.[32] These arguments are not novel. From at least the time of Barrington Moore's classic study of democracy and dictatorship,[33] there has been an understanding among political scientists that capitalism, by creating constituencies with autonomous economic interests that they seek to protect from the state, has helped provide the foundation for the growth of democracy. Nevertheless, the path forward is not necessarily a straight one. As Moore himself argued, early capitalist development can veer off into authoritarianism, and the recent evidence in support of the capitalism-democracy nexus is ambiguous.

Nonetheless, over the longer term, it appears clear that the advance of capitalism puts limits on the powers of government. This may help consolidate democracy, though it may also lead to more fragmentation and political instability. Thus, authoritarian governments have, on the one hand, been weakened by rising middle classes in Latin America. On the other hand, a new generation of populists—typified by Venezuela's Hugo Chavez, Peru's Alberto Fujimori, and the Philippines' Joseph Estrada, whose own commitment to democratic principles has been suspect—has been able to exploit the resultant political vacuum to play upon the growing anxieties of the poor.

Many political scientists, particularly those influenced by neoclassical thought, have put their faith in the emergent civil societies to restore balance and stability to third-world countries. Our understanding of civil society owes much to Robert Putnam's work on both Italian and U.S. democracy,[34] and the gist of his reasoning is that organizations that forge collective identities and mobilize people for inclusion in democratic society are a key element in the consolidation of democracy. As applied to the third world, the concept of civil society has been assigned the additional advantage of connecting citizens with the state, and thereby making it possible to mobilize support for public policies. Related to this type of thinking has been the equally popular concept of social capital, which originated in sociology[35] but has both imported economic reasoning and been exported into the economics discipline. The basic idea here is that certain social values—most importantly, trust—reduce transaction costs in the economy and thereby facilitate growth and development. There is some debate as to whether social capital can be built up by public policies, but the thinking behind it resembles that behind civil society: both are attempts to "build up" society in order to make up for the evident deficiencies that have emerged in many countries in the wake of the downsizing of the state.

Now in widespread circulation in the social sciences, both the concepts of civil society and social capital are dismissed by some theorists as neoclassical fads, an effort by neoclassical economics to colonize all the other social sciences.[36] This economistic thrust, which arguably began with rational choice theory, and showed up in the quantitative approach that originated in economics and is now becoming more widespread in the other social science disciplines, appears to be most advanced in U.S. universities. While resisted elsewhere, the prestige of the empirical approach, not to mention of the social-scientific press in the United States, has ensured a rapid spread for these ideas. The question is, Apart from their theoretical merits, what practical solutions do these concepts offer third-world societies? The research we have suggests that the faith that emergent civil societies could take up the slack left by retreating states has perhaps been unjustified. At one time there was much hope that nongovernmental organizations could assume resource-allocating functions, rein in corruption, and help build civil society. In fact, results in the field have been less encouraging.[37] It appears there is no automatic shift toward stronger societies as states weaken.

Yet in some places, this has happened. One way to assess how the neoclassical age altered the world is to draw up balance sheets of winners and losers to determine if, on balance, structural adjustment improved life in the third world. A theme pervading this book has been that structural adjustment has done the most good to economies that were most advanced, and the most harm in the less-developed countries. It simply came too early to the poorest countries. Much the same conclusion seems reasonable when stacking winners against losers (an approach that has obvious ethical limitations, but has generally had to govern the thinking of development theorists, who in the nature of their discipline must deal with aggregates rather than individuals). As a rule, neoclassical reforms freed middle classes from both political and economic constraints, but left the poor—and particularly the urban poor in the formal sector—more vulnerable. The rising middle classes of the third world have thus led the campaigns against authoritarianism and corruption that we have seen in recent years. Equally, in a paradoxical sort of way, while neoclassical reforms cannot be held responsible for causing many of the ethnic and regional tensions that beset several third-world countries—structural adjustment did not create the poor conditions in which many Latin American indigenous people live, for instance, though in some cases it aggravated them—the weakening of the state they brought with them created a window of opportunity for activists to express their grievances. Similarly, India's Dalits see opportunities today to forge cross-national links that will help emancipate them from the domination of nationalist elites, so they are less likely than other Indians to see the erosion of sovereignty as all bad.[38]

Yet where such liberating movements appear to have been most effective has been in those societies where the middle class, which provides the leadership for such movements, is densest. Politically, therefore, it may be possible to say that in more-developed third-world societies with relatively large middle classes, the gains of structural adjustment may outweigh the losses—though it is impossible to reach a definite conclusion and, moreover, it would be wrong to ignore the losses. But in societies with small middle classes, the pain wrought by structural adjustment has arguably created windows for more-radical manifestations, such as ethnic politicians or populist authoritarians. Both politically and economically, therefore, neoclassical reforms may have done more harm than good in poor societies, including the least-developed countries. Without a large constituency to sustain them, they appear unsustainable, in addition to being undesirable.

The emergent political economies of the twenty-first century will thus probably see a continued shift away from the state and toward society, but this process will be neither continuous nor even. Retreating states have left nascent democracies in some countries, but anarchy and resurgent authoritarianism in others. The common criticism made of the neoclassical approach, that it is a one-size-fits-all method, appears to be as true of politics as it is of economics. The world's poorest countries still require activist states not only to develop their economies, but to also thereby build up the social classes—those associated with the growth of industry—that will be able to one day assume the challenge of retreating states. Yet for many of the world's countries, that day has not yet arrived.

I Drawing Together the Strands

We can start to see the elements of what the next generation of development thinking will probably look like. On the one hand, the state needs to be brought back into development. In the more-developed third-world societies, this would take the form more of reorientation than expansion. But in the poorer societies, an expanded role for the state, beyond the confines permitted by neoclassical theory, appears necessary. And yet, the resources necessary for this currently lie beyond the reach of these societies. They have neither the fiscal base to support strengthened bureaucracies, let alone to invest on a greatly expanded scale in human-capital formation, nor the administrative capacity to assume many more tasks than they currently perform. Moreover, if the lessons of the past teach us anything, it is that poor countries will develop when they are given access to first-world markets without having to reciprocate; that is, when they are allowed to protect their emergent industries while exporting to rich markets. What emerges from these findings is a recognition that if the world's poorest countries, where most of the planet's people still live, are to develop, they will need resources that are currently beyond their reach. The only obvious source for this capital is the first-world countries.

Imposing much of the burden of development on the first world is a conclusion that also arises from consideration of the planet's growing environmental problem, and in particular the challenge of global warming. Whether by providing the capital needed to invest in environmentally sound technologies, or by providing the capital needed to spur the long-term growth that will in turn create demand in the third world for these new technologies—an approach that is perhaps more expensive but also, probably, more sustainable—first-world countries will probably have to bear the expense of environmental adjustment. If they do not, then poor countries will continue to exploit the advantages of cheap but polluting technologies, with deleterious effects on the global environment.

However, as the discussion in the section on the environment high-lighted, capital exported from the first world for such purposes probably cannot be generated by additional growth in the rich countries. Equally, rapid growth in the third world may compound global environmental prob-lems, and it may have to fall to the first-world countries to accept the bur-den of this, in the form of slowed—some say even reversed—growth. The rich countries therefore find themselves between a rock and a hard place: either bear the economic cost of third-world development, or bear the po-litical—greater instability—and environmental costs of third-world under-development. The choice is not easy, but it probably has to be made.

The last chapter argued that third-world countries can no longer uni-laterally impose the costs of development on their first-world counterparts, and that in multilateral negotiations, first-world governments currently evince little willingness to accept the burden. Therefore, if such a willing-ness is to arise, it will need to be mobilized at a popular level. We can thus conclude that the era of national solutions is probably at an end. Poor coun-tries cannot develop on their own, and rich countries will leave them to re-main poor at a great cost to themselves. And if the era of endless growth were to come to an end, what cultural challenge could possibly provoke what would surely be a huge paradigm-shift—what first-world politician today can win an election on a platform of making voters poorer? At the margins of development thought, but increasingly prevalent on the streets of the world's political and financial capitals at international gatherings, are those voices calling for a rethinking of what development has come to mean. One third-world critique has been that while it is materially wealthy, the first world is spiritually poor. Although spirituality has been, as one the-orist puts it, a development taboo,[39] it is surfacing in development thought, in particular via some environmentalist work.[40] Moreover, one by-product of globalization and deepening integration has been the growth of a global civil society, as activists in the first and third worlds forge links with one an-other. Along these vectors, a cultural critique of development appears al-ready to be growing. In time, this may help cause the intellectual and cul-tural shift that will prod first-world elites to broach what remains, for now, unthinkable. Therefore, in a curious sort of way, while many politicians and journalists dismiss these voices of protest for being opposed to development, time may reveal that the demands they made were actually functional to it.

Depending on how one looks at them, the solutions appear both sim-ple and difficult. Simple, in that the requirements of a new big push of in-vestment, funded by the first world from its already ample capital stock, seem fairly straightforward. What the poor countries need desperately is a rapid expansion in human capital (schools), administrative capacity (which again requires education expenditure), and privileged access to the markets of the rich countries during a build-up period. But engineering this will be exceedingly complex. Given its past record, aid alone does not seem a solution; building the educational infrastructure in countries lacking the administrative capacity to manage such is particularly troublesome; and trade agreements create problems of coordination best addressed by international agreements, but we know how difficult these are to reach. More daunting yet is the task of mobilizing support in first-world countries for such an agenda.

Nevertheless, one thing seems clear. Globalization is making the world even smaller. Increasingly, the problems of the third world are becoming those of the first world. This means that rich countries no longer have the luxury of leaving the problems of development to their poor partners. In this century, it may well be that the world will rise or fall as one. Development theorists are only just starting to broach the challenges this entails. Political leaders, who will have to effect the changes, have yet to even entertain the questions. Yet whether in the barrios and ghettos of the third world, where rising instability is causing problems for political leaders, or on the tidy streets of first-world ski resorts, where a new generation of young militants are creating headaches for their leaders, the challenge is being issued. Time will tell if it is accepted.

I Notes

1. The metaphor was given to me by Bruce Berman.

2. Avner Greif, "Cultural Beliefs and the Organisation of Society: A Historical and Theoretical Reflection on Collectivist and Individualist Societies," *Journal of Political Economy* 102, no. 5 (1994): 912–950.

3. See Arunaday Saha, "Traditional Indian Concept of Time and Its Economic Consequences," *Project Appraisal* 5 (1990): 113–120, on India; Daniel Etounga Manguelle, *L'Afrique a-t-elle besoin d'un programme d'ajustement culturel?* (Paris: Éditions Nouvelles du Sud, 1991), on Africa. At first sight Saha seems to make a good point: it may be that the Indian concept of time leads to a slackened work pace and lax enforcement of deadlines. However, in a labor-surplus economy, this may not be as debilitating as it would be in a high-cost labor economy. It is arguable that, consciously or otherwise, lost labor time is factored into the low wage rates paid to workers in a labor-surplus economy such as India's. Jean-Philippe Platteau argues that the generalized norms of morality that "allow a society to reduce enforcement costs and the mistakes unavoidable (given asymmetric information) in any process of (central) law implementation" are unlikely to emerge in present-day sub-Saharan Africa. See Jean-Philippe Platteau, "Behind the Market Stage Where Real Societies Exist," in two parts, *Journal of Development Studies* 30 (1994): 533–577 and 753–817.

4. See, for example, Mick Moore's response to Jean-Philippe Platteau, which follows "Behind the Market Stage."

5. This may be one of the few points on which modernization theorists and orthodox Marxists agree. Francis Fukuyama's theory that capitalism's spread across the globe drags in its wake liberal democracy differs from Marx's predictions only in its view of liberal democracy as the ultimate, rather than the penultimate stage

of history. See Francis Fukuyama, *The End of History and the Last Man* (London: Hamish Hamilton, 1992).

6. See, for example, Charles Hampden-Turner and Fons Trompenaars, *The Seven Cultures of Capitalism: Value Systems for Creating Wealth in the United States, Britain, Japan, Germany, France, Sweden and the Netherlands* (London: Piatkus, 1994), which looks at the different managerial techniques used in different cultures.

7. United Nations, *IPCC Special Report on the Regional Impacts of Climate Change: An Assessment of Vulnerability* (New York: United Nations, 2001).

8. Wolfgang Sachs, ed., *The Development Dictionary* (London: Zed Books, 1992).

9. See David W. Pearce and Jeremy J. Warford, *World Without End: Economics, Environment, and Sustainable Development* (New York: Oxford University Press, for the World Bank, 1993), pp. 155–159; David Grigg, *The World Food Problem* (Oxford: Basil Blackwell, 1985), chapter 6; John Cole, *Development and Underdevelopment* (London: Routledge, 1987), pp. 30–33.

10. Raymond F. Mikesell, *Economic Development and the Environment: A Comparison of Sustainable Development with Conventional Development Economics* (London and New York: Mansell, 1992), p. 140.

11. Walter Block, ed., *Economics and the Environment: A Reconciliation* (Vancouver: Fraser Institute, 1990).

12. David Kaimowitz et al., "The Effects of Structural Adjustment on Deforestation in Lowland Bolivia," *World Development* 27, no. 3 (1999): 505–520; Rachel A. Schurman, "Snails, Southern Hake and Sustainability: Neoliberalism and Natural Resource Exports in Chile," *World Development* 24, no. 11 (1996): 1695–1709. See also Veena Jha, *Reconciling Trade and the Environment: Lessons from Case Studies in Developing Countries* (Cheltenham, England: Edward Elgar, for the United Nations Conference on Trade and Development, 1999).

13. See, for example, the *IMF Survey* of 14 June 1993.

14. Edward Barbier, *Environmental Management and Development in the South: Prerequisites for Sustainable Development* (London: London Environmental Economics Centre Discussion Paper DP 91-07, 1991), p. 26; Mikesell, *Economic Development and the Environment*, p. 144.

15. See Merle Jacob, "Toward a Methodological Critique of Sustainable Development," *Journal of Developing Areas* 28 (1994): 237–252.

16. For details, see David Wallace, *Sustainable Industrialization* (London: Royal Institute of International Affairs, 1996), chapter 3; Kenneth Arrow et al., "Economic Growth, Carrying Capacity, and the Environment," *Environment and Development Economics* 1 (1996): 104–110; Hemamala Hettige et al., "Industrial Pollution in Economic Development: The Environmental Kuznets Curve Revisited," *Journal of Development Economics* 62 (2000): 445–476.

17. Julian L. Simon, ed., *The State of Humanity* (Oxford: Blackwell, 1995).

18. See P. K. Rao, *Sustainable Development: Economics and Policy* (Oxford: Blackwell, 2000).

19. Cf. David I. Stern et al., "Economic Growth and Environmental Degradation: The Environmental Kuznets Curve and Sustainable Development," *World Development* 24, no. 7 (1996): 1151–1160.

20. Xiaoli Han and Lata Chatterjee, "Impacts of Growth and Structural Change on CO_2 Emissions of Developing Countries," *World Development* 25, no. 3 (1997): 395–407.

21. See, for example, Mozaffar Qizilbash, "Sustainable Development: Concepts and Rankings," *Journal of Development Studies* 37, no. 3 (February 2001): 134–161.

22. Douglas E. Booth, *The Environmental Consequences of Growth: Steady-State Economics as an Alternative to Ecological Decline* (London and New York: Routledge, 1998).

23. Donella H. Meadows et al., *The Limits to Growth* (London: Earth Island Ltd., for the Club of Rome, 1972); Lester Brown, *The Twenty-Ninth Day* (New York: Norton, for the Worldwatch Institute, 1978); David and Marcia Pimmentel, *Food, Energy and Society* (London: Edward Arnold, 1979); Dennis L. Meadows et al., *Dynamics of Growth in a Finite World* (Cambridge, Mass.: Wright-Allen Press Inc., 1974).

24. As early as 1958, Colin Clark made the point that Africa could, in theory, feed many times its current population. Colin Clark, "Population Growth and Living Standards," in *The Economics of Underdevelopment,* edited by A. N. Agarwala and S. P. Singh (Oxford: Oxford University Press), p. 42.

25. See, for example, Ezekiel Kalipeni, "Population Growth and Environmental Degradation in Malawi," *Africa Insight* 22, no. 4 (1992): 273–282.

26. For various perspectives on this question, see Naushin Mahmood, "The Desire for Additional Children Among Pakistani Women: The Determinants," and "Motivation and Fertility Control Behaviour in Pakistan," *Pakistan Development Review* 31 (1992): 1–30, 119–144; George J. Mergos, "The Economic Contribution of Children in Peasant Agriculture and the Effect of Education: Evidence from the Philippines," *Pakistan Development Review* 31 (1992): 189–201; Christian O. E. Enoh, "Women's Attitudes to Contraceptive Technology—Some Pointers from West Africa: A Study in Akwa Ibom State, Nigeria," *Science, Technology and Development* 10 (1992): 375–383; T. K. Sundari Ravindarn, "Users' Perspectives on Fertility Regulation Methods," *Economic and Political Weekly* 28, nos. 46–47 (1993): 2508–2512; Nicole Bella, "La fécondité au Cameroun," *Population,* 50th year, 1 (January-February 1995).

27. On this subject, see, for example, John Hoddinott, "Rotten Kids or Manipulative Parents: Are Children Old Age Security in Western Kenya?" *Economic Development and Cultural Change* 40 (1992): 545–565; Mergos, "The Economic Contribution of Children in Peasant Agriculture."

28. On this point, see Vibha Kapuria-Foreman, "Population and Growth Causality in Developing Countries," *Journal of Developing Areas* 29 (1995): 531–540.

29. Sudhin K. Mukhopadhyay, "Adapting Household Behaviour to Agricultural Technology in West Bengal, India: Wage Labor, Fertility, and Child Schooling Determinants," *Economic Development and Cultural Change* 43 (1994): 91–115. This case study found that if incomes rose but flowed into male hands, fertility would rise in response to development, whereas if incomes rose but flowed into women's hands, fertility would decline in response to development. The reason offered was that because women predominate in childbearing and child rearing, increasing women's income would increase the opportunity cost of bearing children. See also Simeen Mahmud, "Explaining the Relationship Between Women's Work and Fertility: The Bangladesh Context," *Bangladesh Development Studies* 16, no. 4 (December 1988): 99–113.

30. See Mary Tiffen, "Population Density, Economic Growth and Societies in Transition: Boserup Reconsidered in a Kenyan Case-Study," *Development and Change* 26, no. 1 (1995): 31–65; Mary Tiffen, Michael Mortimore, and Francis Gichuki, *More People, Less Erosion: Environmental Recovery in Kenya* (London: John Wiley, 1994).

31. See the special issue on demographic transition in Africa of the *Journal of International Development* 7, no. 1 (January-February 1995). Fertility among black

South Africans has also dropped recently, according to a study at Johannesburg's Centre for Development and Enterprise (SAPA, 12 September 1995).

32. See, for example, Mancur Olson, "Dictatorship, Democracy, and Development," *American Political Science Review* 87, no. 3 (1993): 567–576; David A. Leblang, "Property Rights, Democracy and Economic Growth," *Political Research Quarterly* 49, no. 1 (March 1996): 5–26; David A. Leblang, "Political Democracy and Economic Growth: Pooled Cross-Sectional and Time-Series Evidence," *British Journal of Political Science* 27 (1997): 453–472.

33. Barrington Moore Jr., *Social Origins of Dictatorship and Democracy* (London: Penguin, 1966).

34. Robert Putnam, "Bowling Alone: America's Declining Social Capital," *Journal of Democracy* (January 1995): 64–78; Robert Putnam, *Making Democracy Work: Civic Traditions in Modern Italy* (Princeton, N.J.: Princeton University Press, 1994).

35. James Coleman "Social Capital in the Creation of Human Capital," *American Journal of Sociology* 94 (1988) supplement: S95-S120.

36. Ben Fine, "The Developmental State Is Dead—Long Live Social Capital?" *Development and Change* 30 (1999): 1–19.

37. See, for example, Andrew Kiondo, "When the State Withdraws: Local Development, Politics and Liberalisation in Tanzania," in *Liberalised Development in Tanzania: Studies on Accumulation Processes and Local Institutions*, edited by P. Gibbon (Uppsala, Sweden: Nordiska Afrikainstitutet, 1995); Rob Jenkins and Ann-Marie Goetz, "Contsraints on Civil Society's Capacity to Curb Corruption: Lessons from the Indian Experience," *IDS Bulletin* 30, no. 4 (1999): 39–49; Susan Dicklitch, *The Elusive Promise of NGOs in Africa: Lessons from Uganda* (New York: St. Martin's Press, 1998). See also Jennifer Widner with Alexander Mundt, "Researching Social Capital in Africa," *Africa* 68, no. 1 (1998): 1–24.

38. P. Devanesan, *The Dynamics of Exclusion and Cultural Mediation: The Case of the Dalits of India in the Context of Globalization* (Washington, D.C.: unpublished report, Woodstock Theological Center, Georgetown University, 2001).

39. Kurt Alan Ver Beek, "Spirituality: A Development Taboo," *Development in Practice* 10, no. 1 (February 2000): 31–43.

40. See, for instance, John B. Cobb Jr., *The Earthist Challenge to Economism: A Theological Critique of the World Bank* (London: Macmillan, 1999).

SUGGESTED READINGS

I Structuralism

Bleaney, Michael, and David Greenaway. "Long-Run Trends in the Relative Price of Primary Commodities and in the Terms of Trade of Developing Countries." *Oxford Economic Papers* 45 (1993): 349–363.

Cuddington, John T. "Long-Run Trends in 26 Primary Commodity Prices: A Disaggregated Look at the Prebisch-Singer Hypothesis." *Journal of Development Economics* 39 (1992): 207–227.

Gerschenkron, Alexander. *Economic Backwardness in Historical Perspective.* Cambridge, Mass.: Harvard Belknap, 1962.

Lewis, W. A. "Economic Development with Unlimited Supply of Labour." *Manchester School of Social and Economic Studies* 22, no. 2 (1954).

Myrdal, Gunnar. *Asian Drama.* New York: Pantheon Books, 1968.

Nurkse, Ragnar. "Balanced and Unbalanced Growth." In *Equilibrium and Growth in the World Economy,* edited by Gottfried Haberler and Robert M. Stern. Cambridge, Mass.: Harvard University Press, 1961.

Prebisch, R. *The Economic Development of Latin America and Its Principal Problems.* New York: United Nations, 1950.

Rosenstein-Rodan, P. N. "Problems of Industrialization of Eastern and South-Eastern Europe." *Economic Journal* 53, (June-September 1943).

Scandizzo, Pasquale L., and Dimitris Diakosavvas. "Trends in the Terms of Trade of Primary Commodities, 1900–1982: The Controversy and Its Origins." *Economic Development and Cultural Change* 39 (1991): 231–264.

Seers, Dudley. "The Limitations of the Special Case." *Bulletin of the Oxford Institute of Economics and Statistics* 25, no. 2 (1963).

Singer, H. W. "The Distribution of Gains Between Investing and Borrowing Countries." *American Economic Review* 2 (1950).

I Modernization Theory

Almond, G. A., and G. B. Powell. *Comparative Politics: A Developmental Approach.* Boston: Little, Brown, 1965.

Apter, David E. *The Politics of Modernization*. Chicago: University of Chicago Press, 1965.
Fukuyama, Francis. *The End of History and the Last Man*. London: Hamish Hamilton, 1992.
Rostow, W. W. *The Stages of Economic Growth*. Cambridge: Cambridge University Press, 1966.
Weiner, Myron, ed. *Modernization: The Dynamics of Growth*. New York: Basic Books, 1966.

I Dependency Theory

Amin, Samir. *Le développement du capitalisme en Côte d'Ivoire*. Paris: Editions de Minuit, 1967.
———. *Unequal Development*. New York: Monthly Review Press, 1976.
Bagchi, A. K. *The Political Economy of Underdevelopment*. New York: Cambridge University Press, 1982.
Baran, Paul. *The Political Economy of Growth*. New York: Monthly Review Press, 1957.
Blomström, Magnus, and Björn Hettne. *Development Theory in Transition*. London: Zed Books, 1984.
Cardoso, F. H., and E. Faletto. *Dependency and Development in Latin America*. Berkeley: University of California Press, 1979.
Dos Santos, T. "The Crisis of Development Theory and the Problem of Dependence in Latin America." In *Underdevelopment and Development,* edited by Henry Bernstein. Harmondsworth, England: Penguin, 1973.
Evans, Peter. *Dependent Development: The Alliance of Multinational, State, and Local Capital in Brazil*. Princeton, N.J.: Princeton University Press, 1979.
Frank, André Gunder. *Capitalism and Underdevelopment in Latin America*. New York: Monthly Review Press, 1967.
Kaplinsky, Rafael. "Capitalist Accumulation in the Periphery: The Kenya Case Re-Examined." In "Debates," *Review of African Political Economy* 17 (1980): 83–113.
Kay, G. B. *Development and Underdevelopment: A Marxist Analysis*. London: Macmillan, 1975.
Laclau, Ernesto. "Feudalism and Capitalism in Latin America." In *Politics and Ideology in Marxist Theory*. London: New Left Books, 1977.
Langdon, Steven. "Multinational Corporations and the State in Africa." In *Transnational Capitalism and National Development,* edited by J. J. Villamil. Sussex: Harvester Press, 1979.
Leys, Colin. *Underdevelopment in Kenya*. London: Heinemann, 1975.
———. "Development and Dependency: Critical Notes." *Journal of Contemporary Asia* 7 (1977): 92–107.
Rodney, Walter. *How Europe Underdeveloped Africa*. Dar es Salaam: Tanzania Publishing House, 1972.
Soete, Luc. "Technological Dependency: A Critical View." In *Dependency Theory: A Critical Reassessment,* edited by Dudley Seers. London: Frances Pinter, 1981.
Warren, Bill. *Imperialism: Pioneer of Capitalism*. London: New Left Books, 1980.

I   Neoclassical Theory

Balassa, Bela, et al. *The Structure of Protection in Developing Countries*. Baltimore: Johns Hopkins University Press, for the World Bank and Inter-American Development Bank, 1971.

Bates, Robert H. *Markets and States in Tropical Africa*. Berkeley: University of California Press, 1981.

Bates, Robert H., and Anne O. Krueger. *Political and Economic Interactions in Economic Policy Reform*. Oxford: Basil Blackwell, 1993.

Bauer, P. T. *Equality, the Third World and Economic Delusion*. Cambridge, Mass.: Harvard University Press, 1981.

———. "Remembrance of Studies Past: Retracing the First Steps." In *Pioneers in Development*, edited by Gerald M. Meier and Dudley Seers. New York: Oxford University Press, for the World Bank, 1984.

Bhagwati, Jagdish. "Directly Unproductive, Profit-Seeking (DUP) Activities." *Journal of Political Economy* 90 (1982): 988–1002.

Friedman, Milton. "The Role of Monetary Policy." *American Economic Review* 58 (1968): 1–17.

Hayek, F. A. *The Constitution of Liberty*. London: Routledge, 1990.

———. *The Fatal Conceit: The Errors of Socialism*. London: Routledge, 1988.

Johnson, Harry G. *Money, Trade and Economic Growth*. London: George Allen and Unwin, 1964.

Killick, Tony. *A Reaction Too Far: Economic Theory and the Role of the State in Developing Countries*. London: Overseas Development Institute, 1989.

Krueger, Anne O. "The Political Economy of the Rent-Seeking Society." *American Economic Review* 64 (June 1974): 291–303.

———. "Trade Strategies and Employment in Developing Countries." *Finance and Development* 21, no. 4 (June 1984): 23–26.

Krueger, Anne O., et al. *Trade and Employment in Developing Countries*. Chicago: University of Chicago Press for the National Bureau of Economic Research, 1983.

Krugman, Paul, and Lance Taylor. "Contractionary Effects of Devaluation." *Journal of International Economics* 8 (1978): 445–456.

Lal, Deepak. *The Poverty of 'Development Economics*. London: Institute of Economic Affairs, 1983.

Little, Ian M. D. *Economic Development: Theory, Policy, and International Relations*. New York: Basic Books, 1982.

Monroe, Kristen Renwick, ed. *The Economic Approach to Politics: A Critical Reassessment of the Theory of Rational Action*. New York: HarperCollins, 1991.

Myint, Hla. "Economic Theory and the Underdeveloped Countries." *Journal of Political Economy* 73 (1965): 477–491.

———. "The Neo-Classical Resurgence in Development Economics: Its Strengths and Limitations." In *Pioneers in Development*, second series, edited by Gerald M. Meier. New York: Oxford University Press, for the World Bank, 1987.

Nozick, Robert. *Anarchy, State, and Utopia*. New York: Basic Books, 1974.

Olson, Mancur. *The Logic of Collective Action*. Cambridge: Cambridge University Press, 1965.

Schultz, T. W. *Transforming Traditional Agriculture*. Chicago and London: University of Chicago Press, 1964.

Stewart, Frances. "The Fragile Foundations of the Neoclassical Approach to Development." *Journal of Development Studies* 21 (1985): 282–292.

Taylor, Lance. "Polonius Lectures Again: The World Development Report, the Washington Consensus, and How Neoliberal Sermons Won't Solve the Economic Problems of the Developing World." *Bangladesh Development Studies* 20, nos. 2–3 (1992): 23–53.

———. "The Rocky Road to Reform: Trade, Industrial, Financial, and Agricultural Strategies." *World Development* 21 (1993): 577–590.

———, ed. *The Rocky Road to Reform: Adjustment, Income Distribution, and Growth in the Developing World.* Cambridge, Mass., and London: MIT Press, 1993.

Toye, John. *Dilemmas of Development.* Oxford: Basil Blackwell, 1987.

I   Development Experiences

I   Latin America

Baer, Werner. *Industrialization and Economic Development in Brazil.* Homewood, Ill.: Richard D. Irwin, 1965.

Furtado, Celso. *Economic Development of Latin America.* Cambridge: Cambridge University Press, 1970.

Hofman, André A. *The Economic Development of Latin America in the Twentieth Century.* Cheltenham, England: Edward Elgar, 2000.

Jenkins, Rhys. "The Political Economy of Industrialization: A Comparison of Latin American and East Asian Newly Industrializing Countries." *Development and Change* 22 (1991): 197–231.

Juárez, Carlos E. "Trade and Development Policies in Colombia: Export Promotion and Outward Orientation, 1967–1992." *Studies in Comparative International Development* 28, no. 3 (fall 1993): 67–97.

Lustig, Nora. *Mexico: The Remaking of an Economy.* Washington, D.C.: Brookings Institution, 1992.

Mamalakis, Markos J. *The Growth and Structure of the Chilean Economy.* New Haven and London: Yale University Press, 1976.

Naya, Seiji, and Pearl Imada. "Development Strategies and Economic Performance of the Dynamic Asian Economies: Some Comparisons with Latin America." *Pacific Review* 3 (1990): 296–313.

Roberts, Bryan. *Cities of Peasants.* London: E. Arnold, 1978.

Thorp, Rosemary. *Progress, Poverty and Exclusion: An Economic History of Latin America in the Twentieth Century.* Washington, D.C.: Inter-American Development Bank, 1998.

Thorp, Rosemary, and Geoffrey Bertram. *Peru 1890–1977: Growth and Policy in an Open Economy.* London: Macmillan, 1978.

I   Africa

Bowman, Larry W. *Mauritius: Democracy and Development in the Indian Ocean.* Boulder and San Francisco: Westview Press, 1991.

Forrest, Tom. *Politics and Economic Development in Nigeria.* Boulder and Oxford: Westview Press, 1993.

Himbara, David. *Kenyan Capitalists, the State, and Development.* Boulder and London: Lynne Rienner Publishers, 1994.

Leys, Colin. "Confronting the African Tragedy." *New Left Review* 204 (1994).

MacGaffey, Janet. *Entrepreneurs and Parasites: The Struggle for Indigenous Capitalism in Zaire.* Cambridge: Cambridge University Press, 1987.

Mubarak, Jamil Abdalla. *From Bad Policy to Chaos in Somalia: How an Economy Fell Apart.* Westport, Conn.: Praeger, 1996.

O'Meara, Dan. *Volkskapitalisme: Class, Capital and Ideology in the Development of Afrikaner Nationalism, 1934–1948.* Cambridge: Cambridge University Press, 1983.

Rapley, John. *Ivoirien Capitalism: African Entrepreneurs in Côte d'Ivoire.* Boulder and London: Lynne Rienner Publishers, 1993.

Riddell, Roger C. *Manufacturing Africa: Performance and Prospects of Seven Countries in Sub-Saharan Africa.* London: James Currey; Portsmouth, N.H.: Heinemann, 1990.

Rimmer, Douglas. *Staying Poor: Ghana's Political Economy, 1950–1990.* Oxford: Pergamon Press, 1992.

Samatar, Ismail. *An African Miracle: State and Class Leadership and Colonial Legacy in Botswana Development.* Portsmouth, N.H.: Heinemann, 1999.

Sandbrook, Richard. *The Politics of Africa's Economic Recovery.* Cambridge: Cambridge University Press, 1993.

Williams, Gavin. "Why Structural Adjustment Is Necessary and Why It Doesn't Work." *Review of African Political Economy* 60 (June 1994): 214–225.

Young, Crawford. *Ideology and Development in Africa.* New Haven: Yale University Press, 1982.

Asia

Bardhan, Pranab. *The Political Economy of Development in India,* expanded ed. Delhi: Oxford University Press, 1998.

Bhagwati, Jagdish. *India in Transition: Freeing the Economy.* Oxford: Clarendon Press, 1993.

Boltho, Andrea. "Was Japanese Growth Export-Led?" *Oxford Economic Papers* 48 (1996): 415–432.

Booth, Anne. *The Indonesian Economy in the Nineteenth and Twentieth Centuries: A History of Missed Opportunities.* London: Macmillan, 1998.

Bräutigam, Deborah A. "What Can Africa Learn from Taiwan? Political Economy, Industrialization Policy, and Adjustment." *Journal of Modern African Studies* 32 (1994): 111–138.

Burmeister, Larry L. "State, Industrialization and Agricultural Policy in Korea." *Development and Change* 21 (1990): 197–223.

Fforde, Adam, and Stefan de Vylder. *From Plan to Market: The Economic Transition in Vietnam.* Boulder: Westview, 1996.

Francks, Penelope. *Japanese Economic Development.* London: Routledge, 1991.

Garnaut, Ross. "The Market and the State in Economic Development: Applications to the International Trading System." *Singapore Economic Review* 36, no. 2 (1991): 13–26.

Gomez, Terence, and Jomo K.S. *Malaysia's Political Economy: Politics, Patronage and Profits.* Cambridge: Cambridge University Press, 1997.

Green, Andrew E. "South Korea's Automobile Industry: Development and Prospects." *Asian Survey* 32 (1992): 411–428.

Haggard, Stephan, Byung-Kook Kim, and Chung-In Moon. "The Transition to Export-Led Growth in South Korea, 1954–1966." *Journal of Asian Studies* 50 (1991): 850–873.

Husain, Ishrat. *Pakistan: The Economy of an Elitist State*. Karachi: Oxford University Press, 1999.

Islam, Nurul. *Development Planning in Bangladesh*. New York: St. Martin's Press, 1977.

Owen, Roger, and Şevket Pamuk. *A History of the Middle East Economies in the Twentieth Century*. London: I. B. Tauris, 1998.

Ranis, Gustav. "East and South-East Asia: Comparative Development Experience." *Bangladesh Development Studies* 20, nos. 2–3 (1992): 69–88.

Rodan, Garry. *The Political Economy of Singapore's Industrialisation: National State and International Capital*. London: Macmillan, 1989.

Steinberg, David I. *Burma's Road Toward Development*. Boulder: Westview Press, 1981.

Vogel, Ezra F. *The Four Little Dragons: The Spread of Industrialisation in East Asia*. Cambridge, Mass., and London: Harvard University Press, 1992.

Walder, Andrew G. "China's Transitional Economy: Interpreting Its Significance." *China Quarterly* 144 (1995): 963–979.

Woronoff, Jon. *Korea's Economy: Man-Made Miracle*. Oregon: Pace International Research, 1983.

I   Rural Development

Bryceson, Deborah Fahy, and Vali Jamal, eds. *Farewell to Farms: Deagrarianisation and Employment in Africa*. Aldershot, England: Ashgate, 1997.

Freebairn, Donald K. "Did the Green Revolution Concentrate Incomes? A Quantitative Study of Research Reports." *World Development* 23 (1995): 265–279.

Grabowski, Richard. *Pathways to Economic Development*. Cheltenham, England: Edward Elgar, 1999.

Hart, Keith. *The Political Economy of West African Agriculture*. New York: Cambridge University Press, 1982.

Lipton, Michael. *Why Poor People Stay Poor*. London: Temple Smith, 1977.

Schumacher, E. F. *Small Is Beautiful: A Study of Economics as If People Mattered*. London: Abacus, 1974.

Scott, James C. *The Moral Economy of the Peasant*. New Haven: Yale University Press, 1976.

I   Socialism in the Third World

Bernstein, Henry. "Notes on State and Peasantry: The Tanzanian Case." *Review of African Political Economy* 21 (1981): 44–62.

Coulson, Andrew. *African Socialism in Practice*. Nottingham: Spokesman, 1979.

———. *Tanzania: A Political Economy*. Oxford: Clarendon Press, 1982.

Horowitz, Irving L. *Cuban Communism,* 7th revised edition. New Brunswick, N.J.: Transaction Publishers, 1991.

Hyden, Goran. *Beyond Ujamaa in Tanzania*. Berkeley: University of California Press, 1980.

White, Gordon. *Riding the Tiger: The Politics of Economic Reform in Post-Mao China*. Stanford, Calif.: Stanford University Press, 1993.

White, G., R. Murray, and C. White, eds. *Revolutionary Socialist Development in the Third World*. Lexington: University Press of Kentucky, 1983.

Wubneh, Mulatu, and Yohannis Abate. *Ethiopia: Transition and Development in the Horn of Africa*. Boulder: Westview; London: Avebury, 1988.

I Structural Adjustment

I *General*

Adhikari, R., C. Kirkpatrick, and J. Weiss, eds. *Industrial and Trade Policy Reform in Developing Countries*. Manchester and New York: Manchester University Press, 1992.

Doroodian, Khosrow. "Macroeconomic Performance and Adjustment Under Policies Commonly Supported by the International Monetary Fund." *Economic Development and Cultural Change* 41 (1993): 849–864.

Dunham, David, and Saman Kelegama. "Stabilization and Adjustment: A Second Look at the Sri Lankan Experience, 1977–1993." *The Developing Economies* 35, no. 2 (June 1997): 166–184.

Frenkel, Jacob A., and Mohsin S. Khan. "Adjustment Policies of the International Monetary Fund and Long-Run Economic Development." *Bangladesh Development Studies* 20, nos. 2–3 (1992): 1–22.

Greenaway, David, et al. "Trade Liberalization and Growth in Developing Countries: Some New Evidence." *World Development* 25, no. 11 (1997): 1885–1892.

Harrison, Ann, and Gordon Hanson. "Who Gains from Trade Reform? Some Remaining Puzzles." *Journal of Development Economics* 59 (1999): 125–154.

Kawai, Hiroki. "International Comparative Analysis of Economic Growth: Trade Liberalization and Productivity." *The Developing Economies* 32 (1994): 373–397.

Loxley, John. "Structural Adjustment in Africa: Reflections on Ghana and Zambia." *Review of African Political Economy* 47 (1990): 8–27.

Mengisteab, Kigane. "Export-Import Responses to Devaluation in Sub-Saharan Africa." *Africa Development* 16, nos. 3–4 (1991): 27–43.

Paus, Eva A. "Economic Growth Through Neoliberal Restructuring? Insights from the Chilean Experience." *Journal of Developing Areas* 28 (1994): 31–56.

Perkins, Dwight H., and Michael Roemer, eds. *Reforming Economic Systems in Developing Countries*. Cambridge, Mass.: Harvard Institute for International Development, 1991.

Rahman, Sultan Hafeez. "Structural Adjustment and Macroeconomic Performance in Bangladesh in the 1980s." *Bangladesh Development Studies* 20, nos. 2–3 (1992): 89–125.

Ramirez, Miguel D. "Stabilization and Trade Reform in Mexico, 1983–1989." *Journal of Developing Areas* 27 (1993): 173–190.

Rhodd, Rupert G. "The Effect of Real Exchange Rate Changes on Output: Jamaica's Devaluation Experience." *Journal of International Development* 5, no. 3 (1993): 291–303.

Rodriguez, Francisco, and Dani Rodrik. *Trade Policy and Economic Growth: A Skeptic's Guide to the Cross-National Evidence*. Cambridge, Mass.: National Bureau of Economic Research Working Paper No. 7081, 1999.

Rothchild, Donald, ed. *Ghana: The Political Economy of Recovery.* Boulder and London: Lynne Rienner Publishers, 1991.

Sridharan, E. "Economic Liberalisation and India's Political Economy: Towards a Paradigm Synthesis." *Journal of Commonwealth and Comparative Politics* 31, no. 3 (1993): 1–31.

Yaghmaian, Behzad. "An Empirical Investigation of Exports, Development, and Growth in Developing Countries: Challenging the Neoclassical Theory of Export-Led Growth." *World Development* 22 (1994): 1977–1995.

Structural Adjustment and Industry

Akinlo, Anthony Enisan. "The Impact of Adjustment Programmes on Manufacturing Industries in Nigeria, 1986–1991: A Sample Study." *African Development Review* 8, no. 1 (June 1996): 61–96.

Guhathakurta, Subhrajit. "Electronics Policy and the Television Manufacturing Industry: Lessons from India's Liberalization Efforts." *Economic Development and Cultural Change* 42 (1994): 845–868.

Haggblade, Steve, Carl Liedholm, and Donald C. Mead. "The Effect of Policy Reforms on Non-Agricultural Enterprises and Employment in Developing Countries: A Review of Past Experiences." In *The Other Policy,* edited by Frances Stewart, Henk Thomas, and Ton de Wilde. London and Washington, D.C.: Intermediate Technology Publications, in association with Appropriate Technology International, 1990.

Hay, Donald. "The Post-1990 Brazilian Trade Liberalisation and the Performance of Large Manufacturing Firms: Productivity, Market Share and Profits." *Economic Journal* 111 (2001): 620–641.

Jenkins, Rhys. "Trade Liberalization and Export Performance in Bolivia." *Development and Change* 27 (1996): 693–716.

Mellor, Patricio. "Review of the Chilean Trade Liberalization and Export Expansion Process." *Bangladesh Development Studies* 20, nos. 2–3 (1992): 155–184.

Noorkabash, Farhad, and Alberto Paloni. "Structural Adjustment Programs and Industry in Sub-Saharan Africa: Restructuring or De-industrialization?" *Journal of Developing Areas* 33 (summer 1999): 549–580.

Sahota, Gian S. "An Assessment of the Impact of Industrial Policies in Bangladesh." *Bangladesh Development Studies* 19, nos. 1–2 (1991): 157–199.

Sharma, Kishor, et al. "Liberalization and Productivity Growth: The Case of Manufacturing Industry in Nepal." *Oxford Development Studies* 28, no. 2 (2000): 205–221.

Weiss, John. "Trade Policy Reform and Performance in Manufacturing: Mexico 1975–88." *Journal of Development Studies* 29 (1992): 1–23.

Structural Adjustment and Agriculture

Abdulai, Awudu, and Wallace Huffman. "Structural Adjustment and Economic Efficiency of Rice Farmers in Northern Ghana." *Economic Development and Cultural Change* 48, no. 3 (April 2000): 503–520.

Azam, Jean-Paul. "The Agricultural Minimum Wage and Wheat Production in Morocco (1971–89)." *Journal of African Economies* 1 (1992): 171–191.

Bivings, E. Leigh. "The Seasonal and Spatial Dimensions of Sorghum Market Liberalization in Mexico." *American Journal of Agricultural Economics* 79 (May 1997): 17–34.

Commander, Simon, ed. *Structural Adjustment and Agriculture*. London: Overseas Development Institute; Portsmouth, N.H.: Heinemann, 1989.

Diakosavvas, Dimitris, and Colin Kirkpatrick. "Exchange-Rate Policy and Agricultural Exports Performance in Sub-Saharan Africa." *Development Policy Review* 8 (1990): 29–42.

Diaz, Polo, and Tanya Korovkin. "Neo-Liberalism in Agriculture: Capitalist Modernization in the Chilean Countryside During the Pinochet Years." *Canadian Journal of Latin American and Caribbean Studies* 15, no. 30 (1990): 197–219.

Gunawardana, P. J., and E. A. Oczkowski. "Government Policies and Agricultural Supply Response: Paddy in Sri Lanka." *Journal of Agricultural Economics* 43 (1992): 231–242.

Harriss, Barbara, and Ben Crow. "Twentieth Century Free Trade Reform: Food Market Deregulation in Sub-Saharan Africa and South Asia." In *Development Policy and Public Action*, edited by Marc Wuyts, Maureen Mackintosh, and Tom Hewitt. Oxford: Oxford University Press, in association with The Open University, 1992.

Mamingi, Nlandu. "The Impact of Prices and Macroeconomic Policies on Agricultural Supply: A Synthesis of Available Results." *Agricultural Economics* 16 (1997): 17–34.

Morales, Juan Antonio. "Structural Adjustment and Peasant Agriculture in Bolivia." *Food Policy* 16 (1991): 58–66.

Sahn, David E., and Jehan Arulpragasam. "The Stagnation of Smallholder Agriculture in Malawi: A Decade of Structural Adjustment." *Food Policy* 16 (1991): 219–234.

Selvaraj, K. N. "Impact of Government Expenditure on Agriculture and Performance of Agricultural Sector in India." *Bangladesh Journal of Agricultural Economics* 16, no. 2 (December 1993): 37–49.

Seshamani, V. "The Impact of Market Liberalization on Food Security in Zambia." *Food Policy* 23, no. 6 (1998): 539–551.

Staal, Steven J., and Barry I. Shapiro. "The Effects of Recent Price Liberalization on Kenyan Peri-Urban Dairy." *Food Policy* 19 (1994): 533–549.

| Social Aspects

Adekanye, J. 'Bayo. "Structural Adjustment, Democratization and Rising Ethnic Tensions in Africa." *Development and Change* 26 (1995): 355–374.

Baer, Werner, and William Maloney. "Neoliberalism and Income Distribution in Latin America." *World Development* 25, no. 3 (1997): 311–327.

Berg, Elliott, et al. *Poverty and Structural Adjustment in the 1980s: Trends in Welfare Indicators in Latin America and Africa*. Washington, D.C.: Development Alternatives, 1994.

Beyer, Harald, et al. "Trade Liberalization and Wage Inequality." *Journal of Development Economics* 59 (1999): 103–123.

Davies, Rob, and David Sanders. "Economic Strategies, Adjustment and Health Policy: Issues in Sub-Saharan Africa for the 1990s." *Transformation* 21 (1993): 78–93.

Diagana, Bocar, et al. "Effects of the CFA Franc Devaluation on Urban Food Comsumption in West Africa: Overview and Cross-Country Comparisons." *Food Policy* 24 (1999): 465–478.

Hecht, Robert, and Philip Musgrove. "Rethinking the Government's Role in Health." *Finance & Development* (September 1993): 6–9.

Kelly, Thomas J. *The Effects of Economic Adjustment on Poverty in Mexico*. Aldershot, England: Ashgate, 1999.

Killick, Tony. "Structural Adjustment and Poverty Alleviation: An Interpretive Survey." *Development and Change* 26 (1995): 305–331.

Mhone, Guy C. Z. "The Social Dimensions of Adjustment (SDA) Programme in Zimbabwe: A Critical Review and Assessment." *European Journal of Development Research* 7, no. 1 (1995): 101–123.

Nelson, Joan M. "Poverty, Equity, and the Politics of Adjustment." In *The Politics of Economic Adjustment,* edited by Stephan Haggard and Robert R. Kaufman. Princeton, N.J.: Princeton University Press, 1992.

Osmani, S. R. "Is There a Conflict Between Growth and Welfarism? The Significance of the Sri Lanka Debate." *Development and Change* 25 (1994): 387–421.

Vivian, Jessica. "How Safe Are 'Social Safety Nets'? Adjustment and Social Sector Restructuring in Developing Countries." *European Journal of Development Research* 7, no. 1 (1995): 1–25.

I   Political Aspects

Brysk, Alison, and Carol Wise. "Liberalization and Ethnic Conflict in Latin America." *Studies in Comparative International Development* 32, no. 2 (1997): 76–104.

Byron, Jessica. "The Impact of Globalisation on the Caribbean." In *Globalisation: A Calculus of Inequality*, edited by Denis Benn and Kenneth Hall. Kingston, Jamaica: Ian Randle Publishers, 2000.

Gamarra, Eduardo A. "Market-Oriented Reforms and Democratization in Latin America: Changes of the 1990s." In *Latin American Political Economy in the Age of Neoliberal Reform,* edited by William C. Smith, Carlos H. Acuña, and Eduardo A. Gamarra. New Brunswick, N.J., and London: Transaction Publishers, 1994.

Haggard, Stephan, and Robert R. Kaufman, eds. *The Politics of Economic Adjustment.* Princeton, N.J.: Princeton University Press, 1992.

Haggard, Stephan, and Steven B. Webb. "What Do We Know About the Political Economy of Economic Policy Reform?" *World Bank Research Observer* 8 (1993): 143–168.

Jeffries, Richard. "The State, Structural Adjustment and Good Government in Africa." *Journal of Commonwealth and Comparative Politics* 31 (1993): 20–35.

I   The State in the Third World

Alavi, Hamza. "The State in Post-Colonial Societies." *New Left Review* 74 (1972): 59–81.

Ayittey, George B. N. *Africa in Chaos*. London: Macmillan, 1998.

Bayart, Jean-François. *The State in Africa*. London: Longman, 1993.

Brett, E. A. "Rebuilding Organization Capacity in Uganda Under the National Resistance Movement." *Journal of Modern African Studies* 32, no. 1 (1994): 53–80.

Chabal, Patrick, and Jean-Pacal Daloz. *Africa Works: Disorder as Political Instrument*. Oxford: James Currey, and Bloomington: Indiana University Press, 1999.

Charlton, Roger. "Bureaucrats and Politicians in Botswana's Policy-Making Process: A Re-interpretation." *Journal of Commonwealth and Comparative Politics* 29 (1991): 265–282.

Collier, David, ed. *The New Authoritarianism in Latin America*. Princeton, N.J.: Princeton University Press.

Crook, Richard C. "State Capacity and Economic Development: The Case of Côte d'Ivoire." *IDS Bulletin* 19, no. 4 (1988): 19–25.

Darbon, D. "L'état prédateur." *Politique Africaine* 39 (1990): 37–45.

Davidson, Basil. *The Black Man's Burden: Africa and the Curse of the Nation-State*. London: James Currey, 1992.

Frimpong-Ansah, Jonathan H. *The Vampire State in Africa: The Political Economy of Decline in Ghana*. Trenton, N.J.: Africa World Press, 1992.

Halim, Fatimah. "The Transformation of the Malaysian State." *Journal of Contemporary Asia* 20, no. 1 (1990): 64–88.

Harbeson, John W., et al., eds. *Civil Society and the State in Africa*. Boulder and London: Lynne Rienner Publishers, 1994.

Islam, Iyanatul. "Political Economy and East Asian Economic Development." *Asian-Pacific Economic Literature* 6, no. 2 (1992): 69–101.

List, Friedrich. *The National System of Political Economy*. New York: Augustus M. Kelly, 1966.

Lucas, John. "The State, Civil Society and Regional Elites: A Study of Three Associations in Kano, Nigeria." *African Affairs* 93 (1994): 21–38.

Moore, Mick. "Economic Liberalization Versus Political Pluralism in Sri Lanka." *Modern Asian Studies* 24 (1990): 341–383.

Nayar, Baldev Raj. "The Politics of Economic Restructuring in India: The Paradox of State Strength and Policy Weakness." *Journal of Commonwealth and Comparative Politics* 30 (1992): 145–171.

Önis, Ziya. "Redemocratization and Economic Liberalization in Turkey: The Limits of State Autonomy." *Studies in Comparative International Development* 27, no. 2 (1992): 3–23.

Pedersen, Jorgen Dige. "State, Bureaucracy and Change in India." *Journal of Development Studies* 28 (1992): 616–639.

Remmer, Karen L. "The Politics of Economic Stabilization: IMF Standby Programs in Latin America, 1954–1984." *Comparative Politics* 19, no. 1 (1986): 1–24.

Rivera, Temario C. "The State, Civil Society, and Foreign Actors: The Politics of Philippine Industrialization." *Contemporary Southeast Asia* 16 (1994): 157–177.

Saul, John S. "The State in Post-Colonial Societies: Tanzania." In *The State and Revolution in Eastern Africa*, John S. Saul. New York and London: Monthly Review Press, 1979.

Skålnes, Tor. "The State, Interest Groups and Structural Adjustment in Zimbabwe." *Journal of Development Studies* 29 (1993): 401–428.

Sorensen, Georg. "Democracy, Authoritarianism and State Strength." *European Journal of Development Research* 5, no. 1 (1993): 6–34.

Villacorta, Wilfrido V. "The Curse of the Weak State: Leadership Imperatives for the Ramos Government." *Contemporary Southeast Asia* 16 (1994): 67–92.

Woods, Dwayne. "Civil Society in Europe and Africa: Limiting State Power Through a Public Sphere." *African Studies Review* 35, no. 2 (1992): 77–100.

Governance and Decentralization

Crook, Richard C., and James Manor. "Democratic Decentralisation and Institutional Performance: Four Asian and African Experiences Compared." *Journal of Commonwealth and Comparative Politics* 33 (1995): 309–334.

Healey, John, and Mark Robinson. *Democracy, Governance and Economic Policy: Sub-Saharan Africa in Comparative Perspective*. London: Overseas Development Institute, 1992.

Hyden, Goran, and Michael Bratton, eds. *Governance and Politics in Africa*. Boulder and London: Lynne Rienner Publishers, 1992.

Ingham, Barbara, and A. K. M. Kalam. "Decentralization and Development: Theory and Evidence from Bangladesh." *Public Administration and Development* 12 (1992): 373–385.

Tordoff, William. "Decentralisation, Comparative Experience in Commonwealth Africa." *Journal of Modern African Studies* 32 (1994): 555–580.

Wunsch, James S., and Dele Olowu. *The Failure of the Centralized State: Institutions and Self-Governance in Africa*. Oxford: Westview Press, 1990.

| State Enterprises

Bavon, Al. "Does Ownership Matter? Comparing the Performance of Public and Private Enterprises in Ghana." *Journal of Developing Areas* 33 (1998): 53–72.

Cook, Paul. "Privatization and Public Enterprise Performance in Developing Countries." *Development Policy Review* 10 (1992): 403–408.

Crane, George T. "State-Owned Enterprises and the Oil Shocks in Taiwan: The Political Dynamics of Economic Adjustment." *Studies in Comparative International Development* 24, no. 4 (1989–1990): 3–23.

Ellis, Frank. "Private Trade and Public Role in Staple Food Marketing: The Case of Rice in Indonesia." *Food Policy* 18 (1993): 428–438.

Ganesh, G. *Privatisation Experience Around the World*. New Delhi: Mittal Publications, 1998.

Grosh, Barbara, and Rwekaza S. Mukandala, eds. *State-Owned Enterprises in Africa*. Boulder and London: Lynne Rienner Publishers, 1994.

Kannapiran, Chinna A. "Commodity Price Stabilisation: Macroeconomic Impacts and Policy Options." *Agricultural Economics* 23 (2000): 17–30.

Naqvi, Syed, Nawab Haider, and A. R. Kemal. "The Privatization of the Public Industrial Enterprise in Pakistan." *Pakistan Development Review* 30 (1991): 105–144.

Narayana, D. "Coffee Trade in India: Is There a Case for Privatisation?" *Economic and Political Weekly* 28 (1993): 1853–1856.

Ram, Rati. "Productivity of Public and Private Investment in Developing Countries: A Broad International Perspective." *World Development* 24, no. 8 (1996): 1373–1378.

Roland, Gérard. "On the Speed and Sequencing of Privatisation and Restructuring." *Economic Journal* 104 (1994): 1158–1168.

Tangri, Roger. *The Politics of Patronage in Africa: Parastatals, Privatization and Private Enterprise*. London: James Currey, 1999.

Yoder, Richard A., Philip L. Borkholder, and Brian D. Friesen. "Privatization and Development: The Empirical Evidence." *Journal of Developing Areas* 25 (1991): 425–434.

| The Developmental State

Amsden, Alice. *Asia's Next Giant: South Korea and Late Industrialization*. New York: Oxford University Press, 1989.

Johnson, Chalmers. *MITI and the Japanese Miracle*. Stanford, Calif.: Stanford University Press, 1982.

Leftwich, Adrian. "Bringing Politics Back In: Towards a Model of the Developmental State." *Journal of Development Studies* 31, no. 3 (1995): 400–427.

Wade, Robert. *Governing the Market: Economic Theory and the Role of Government in East Asian Industrialization*. Princeton, N.J.: Princeton University Press, 1990.

White, Gordon, ed. *Developmental States in East Asia*. London: Macmillan, 1988.

I Contemporary Leftist Thought

Bardhan, Pranab. "Economics of Market Socialism and the Issue of Public Enterprise Reform in Developing Countries." *Pakistan Development Review* 30 (1992): 565–579.

Brass, Tom. "Old Conservatism in 'New' Clothes." *Journal of Peasant Studies* 22 (1995): 516–540.

Carling, Alan. "Rational Choice Marxism." *New Left Review* 160 (1986): 24–62.

Corbridge, Stuart. "Post-Marxism and Development Studies: Beyond the Impasse." *World Development* 18 (1990): 623–639.

Escobar, Arturo. *Encountering Development: The Making and Unmaking of the Third World*. Princeton, N.J.: Princeton University Press, 1995.

Kiely, Ray. "The Last Refuge of the Noble Savage? A Critical Assessment of Post-Development Theory." *European Journal of Development Research* 11, no. 1 (June 1999): 30–55.

Pieterse, Jan Nederveen. "After Post-development." *Third World Quarterly* 21, no. 2 (2000): 175–191.

Rist, Gilbert. *The History of Development: From Western Origins to Global Faith*. London and New York: Zed Books, 1997.

Roemer, John E. *A Future for Socialism*. Cambridge, Mass.: Harvard University Press, 1994.

I The Environment

Arrow, Kenneth, et al. "Economic Growth, Carrying Capacity, and the Environment." *Environment and Development Economics* 1 (1996): 104–110.

Fearnside, Philip M. "Forests or Fields? A Response to the Theory that Tropical Forest Conservation Poses a Threat to the Poor." *Land Use Policy* 10 (1993): 108–121.

Jacob, Merle. "Toward a Methodological Critique of Sustainable Development." *Journal of Developing Areas* 28 (1994): 237–252.

Mikesell, Raymond F. *Economic Development and the Environment: A Comparison of Sustainable Development with Conventional Development Economics*. London and New York: Mansell, 1992.

Pearce, David W., and Jeremy J. Warford. *World Without End: Economics, Environment, and Sustainable Development*. New York: Oxford University Press, for the World Bank, 1993.

Rao, P. K. *Sustainable Development: Economics and Policy*. Oxford: Blackwell, 2000.

United Nations, Intergovernmental Report on Climate Change. *IPCC Special Report on the Regional Impacts of Climate Change: An Assessment of Vulnerability*. 2001.

Wallace, David. *Sustainable Industrialization*. London: Royal Institute of International Affairs, 1996.
World Commission on Environment and Development. *Our Common Future*. Oxford and New York: Oxford University Press, 1987.
World Development 24, no. 2, issue on sustainable development (February 1996).

I Culture and Development

Glegg, Steward R., et al., eds. *Capitalism in Contrasting Cultures*. Berlin: Walter de Gruyter, 1990.
Greif, Avner. "Cultural Beliefs and the Organization of Society: A Historical and Theoretical Reflection on Collectivist and Individualist Societies." *Journal of Political Economy* 102, no. 5 (1994): 912–950.
Hampden-Turner, Charles, and Fons Trompenaars. *The Seven Cultures of Capitalism: Value Systems for Creating Wealth in the United States, Britain, Japan, Germany, France, Sweden and the Netherlands*. London: Piatkus, 1994.
Platteau, Jean-Philippe. "Behind the Market Stage Where Real Societies Exist," two parts. *Journal of Development Studies* 30 (1994): 533–577 and 753–817.
Weber, Max. *The Protestant Ethic and the Spirit of Capitalism*, translated by Talcott Parsons. New York: Charles Scribner's Sons, 1958.

I Population

Boserup, Ester. *The Condition of Agricultural Growth*. London: Earthscan, 1993.
Clark, Colin. "Population Growth and Living Standards." In *The Economics of Underdevelopment*, edited by A. N. Agarwala and S. P. Singh. Oxford: Oxford University Press, 1958.
Kamuzora, C. L. "Refining the Issues for Realistic Population-Development Policies in Africa." *African Review* 18, nos. 1–2 (1991): 71–88.
Mahmud, Simeen. "Explaining the Relationship Between Women's Work and Fertility: The Bangladesh Context." *Bangladesh Development Studies* 16, no. 4 (1988): 99–113.
Mamdani, M. *The Myth of Population Control*. New York: Monthly Review Press, 1973.
Mukhopadhyay, Sudhin K. "Adapting Household Behaviour to Agricultural Technology in West Bengal, India: Wage Labor, Fertility, and Child Schooling Determinants." *Economic Development and Cultural Change* 43 (1994): 91–115.
Simon, J. *The Ultimate Resource*. Princeton, N.J.: Princeton University Press, 1981.
Tiffen, Mary. "Population Density, Economic Growth and Societies in Transition: Boserup Reconsidered in a Kenyan Case-Study." *Development and Change* 26, no. 1 (1995): 31–65.
Tiffen, Mary, Michael Mortimore, and Francis Gichuki. *More People, Less Erosion: Environmental Recovery in Kenya*. London: John Wiley, 1994.

INDEX

ABOUT THE BOOK

THOROUGHLY UPDATED TO REFLECT THE MOST RECENT TRENDS IN WORLD AFFAIRS, as well as in the scholarly literature, this lucidly written book provides both an assessment of the current state of development theory and an extensive survey of structural adjustment's results throughout the developing world.

Rapley traces the evolution of development theory from its strong statist orientation in the early postwar period, through the neoclassical phase, to the middle-of-the-road position of the present day, drawing attention to the inadequacy of existing models. Using a wide range of examples, he shows where, how, and why various approaches to development have worked, or failed. He concludes with a look at one of the most disturbing subjects theorists and practitioners alike must tackle: why development appears to be so far out of reach for so many poor countries.

John Rapley is senior lecturer in the Department of Government, University of the West Indies (Mona). His publications include *Ivoirien Capitalism: African Entrepreneurs in Côte d'Ivoire.*